Reading Families

READING FAMILIES

WOMEN'S LITERATE PRACTICE IN LATE MEDIEVAL ENGLAND

Rebecca Krug

Cornell University Press

Ithaca and London

First published 2002 by Cornell University Press

Printed in the United States of America

Library of Congress Cataloging-in-Publication Data

Krug, Rebecca.
Reading families : women's literate practice in late medieval England / Rebecca Krug.
p. cm.
Includes bibliographical references and index.
ISBN 0-8014-3924-8 (cloth : alk. paper)
1. English literature—Middle English, 1100–1500—History and criticism. 2. English literature—Women authors—History and criticism. 3. Women—Books and reading—England—History—To 1500. 4. Women and literature—England—History—To 1500. I. Title.
PR275.W6 K78 2002
820.9'9287'0902—dc21

2002004076

Cornell University Press strives to use environmentally responsible suppliers and materials to the fullest extent possible in the publishing of its books. Such materials include vegetable-based, low-VOC inks and acid-free papers that are recycled, totally chlorine-free, or partly composed of nonwood fibers. For further information, visit our website at www.cornellpress.cornell.edu.

Cloth printing 10 9 8 7 6 5 4 3 2 1

Contents

Preface

This book is about women's engagement with the written word in late medieval England. Although at the end of the Middle Ages an unprecedented number of Englishwomen came to employ written texts in their daily lives, this development does not imply that all or even the majority of women could read and write; what it does mean is that material conditions, linguistic modes, and imaginative habits were becoming aligned in ways that made it seem natural for women to think of writing as a part of everyday life. Michael Clanchy has shown that in contrast with the earlier Middle Ages, when literate skills were primarily the preserve of clerics, beginning in the thirteenth century writing and the production of documents came increasingly to be associated with the courts and their maintenance of legal and financial affairs. A number of interesting and important books have been written that enlarge upon Clanchy's thesis, most recently, Steven Justice's *Writing and Rebellion: England in 1381* and Richard Firth Green's *Crisis of Truth: Literature and Law in Ricardian England.* However, although recent scholarship has described the impact of literacy and text-based knowledge across social divides, less attention has been paid to the manner in which men's and women's literate practices differed. Seeking to consider the difference, in this book I look specifically at the literate practice of two women, Margaret Paston and Margaret Beaufort, and at that of two communities in which women were centrally important, the Norwich Lollards and the Bridgettines at Syon. My claim is that in the later Middle Ages, people defined themselves in terms of family relationships but came to see their social circumstances increasingly as produced by writing. As English culture became more dependent on written texts, even women, whose participation in literate activities continued to be discounted, began unsystematically and unofficially to acquire text-based skills and knowledge to satisfy the demands of their lives.

Recent studies of medieval women and writing often assume that women's participation in literate culture is evidence that women rejected medieval misogyny. In these discussions, writing and reading are described as acts of resistance against dominant social configurations. I insist, in contrast, that for most medieval women, acquisition of literate skills and text-based knowledge was a practical response to social changes and not a revolutionary act. This does not mean that women were unable to use their literate capabilities or textual knowledge in ways that challenged and reimagined social possibilities; rather, my point is that women's participation in literate culture will be poorly understood if we continue to think about it in terms of a dichotomy between resistance and submission. Complex, familial dynamics and social configurations encouraged individual women and communities of women to engage in text-based activities; in this book I consider how women's literate practice served and reshaped and resisted cultural directives that revolved around ideas about the medieval family.

Many people helped me as I wrote this book. I am especially grateful to my former colleagues at Harvard University, Larry Benson, Dan Donoghue, Joe Harris, and Derek Pearsall, and my colleagues at the University of Minnesota, Lianna Farber and Michael Lower, for their advice, intelligence, and friendship. Students at Harvard and Minnesota have also contributed a great deal to this project: Molly Hennessey, Katharine Horsley, Karolyn Kinane, Ziva Mann, Susie Phillips, Jason Puskar, Gustavo Secchi, and Jane Tolmie have my most sincere gratitude for their encouragement and interest. Participants in the Harvard Medieval Doctoral Conference offered responses to some of this material at our Thursday meetings, and I thank Mary-Jo Arn, David Benson, Wendy Larson, and Rick Emmerson in particular for their insights. At the book's earliest stages, I had the good fortune to work at Indiana University with Sheila Lindenbaum, Judith Anderson, Alfred David, and Paul Strohm. I am grateful to them and to Rob Fulk and Larry Clopper for their guidance.

Several scholars have read and commented on parts of this project. I thank David Benson and Andrew Galloway for reading the entire manuscript with care and understanding, Dan Donoghue for advice on the introduction, Katherine French for encouragement and a historian's view of chapter 1, Stephen Greenblatt for suggestions about chapter 3, and Nicholas Watson for a thoughtful response to an early version of chapter 4. Conversations with Theresa Kemp, Cynthea Masson, Sarah McNamer, Christine Petto, Susie Phillips, and Claire Waters allowed me to rethink key points in my argument; I am grateful for their ideas and enthusiasm. As I wrote this book, scholars, colleagues, and friends provided me with excellent, professional advice, often about the book but more often about academic life generally. I thank Pam and David Benson, Marshall and Jane Brown, Linda and Al David, Leo Damrosch, Shirley Nelson Garner, Christoph Irmscher, Ken and Ilinca Johnston, Cal Kendall, Barbara Lewalski, Patricia Powell, Paul Strohm, and Nicholas Watson for their kindness and good sense. Bernie Kendler was just the editor I needed. He has my thanks and admiration. Thanks also to the manuscript editor, Karen Hwa, and copy editor, Kathryn Gohl.

My parents, Bill and Mary Krug; my sister, Heather; my parents-in-law, Janet and Bob Stamm, and Rachel Singer and Michael Goldberg; my sister-in-law Jessica; and my oldest friend, Christine Evert Thompson, contributed to this book in numerous ways. I appreciate their love and support. I am grateful to Jon Diamond for his unflagging enthusiasm, hospitality, and friendship. Finally, my greatest debt is to Brian Goldberg—my first, best, and most brilliant reader.

Abbreviations

EETS	Early English Text Society
e.s.	extra series
o.s.	old series
s.s	supplementary series
KM	Michael Jones and Malcolm Underwood. *The King's Mother: Lady Margaret Beaufort, Countess of Richmond and Derby.* Cambridge: Cambridge University Press, 1992.
STC	*Short-Title Catalogue of Books Printed in England, Scotland, and Ireland, and English Books Printed Abroad, 1475–1640. First Compiled by A. W. Pollard and G. R. Redgrave.* 2d ed. Edited by Katherine F. Pantzer. London: Bibliographical Society, 1976.
T	*Heresy Trials in the Diocese of Norwich, 1428–1431.* Edited by Norman P. Tanner. Camden Society, ser. 4, vol. 20. London: Office of the Royal Historical Society, 1977.

Reading Families

INTRODUCTION

From Law to Practice:
Women, Resistance, and Writing

Who painted the leon, tel me who?
By God, if wommen hadden writen stories,
As clerkes han within hir oratories
They wolde han writen of men more wikkednesse
Than al the merk of Adam may redresse.

GEOFFREY CHAUCER, *The Wife of Bath's Prologue*

In recent years medievalists have shown a steadily increasing interest in the ways that marginalized groups have, despite their disadvantaged status, been able to confront and resist dominant social forces. For feminist critics, this interest has culminated in the pervasive search for "point[s] of resistance" that allow readers to envision medieval women's challenges to restrictive social norms, and one of the richest fields for such study has been the relationship between women and written culture.[1] In describing this dynamic, scholars often employ the famous lines from *The Wife of Bath's Prologue* quoted in the epigraph, which conveniently link women's resistance and writing.[2] The passage begins with the Wife's allusion to Aesop's

[1] The term "points of resistance" appears in the introduction to Ruth Evans and Lesley Johnson, *Feminist Readings in Middle English Literature: The Wife of Bath and All Her Sect* (London: Routledge, 1994), 2.

[2] Since Mary Carruthers, "The Wife of the Bath and the Painting of Lions," first appeared in 1979, this passage has figured prominently in discussions of gender and Chaucer. Carruthers's essay is reprinted with an afterword in Evans and Johnson, *Feminist Readings*, 22–53. See also Elaine Tuttle Hansen, *Chaucer and the Fictions of Gender* (Berkeley: University of California Press, 1992), esp. "The Wife of Bath and

fable in which a lion shown a picture of a man slaying a lion asks, "Who painted the lion?" and it concludes by underscoring the institutional exclusion of women from literate culture. According to the Wife, the proliferation of "books of wicked wives" is a natural consequence of the medieval battle between the sexes, and writing is a powerful weapon that men, through their monopoly on literary production, have kept from women. Critics are drawn to this passage largely because it appears to be a medieval version of recent debates concerning identity politics—which consider the racial, sexual, gendered, and economic positions of writers and readers. What makes this moment of gender-based dissent particularly appealing to scholars is not the Wife's breezy account of representational strategies and subject/object relations but her recognition of the "deep structure" of the lion's question. Like all rhetorical questions, the Wife's depends on the assumption that the answer is obvious to her audience. That is, the question and answer constitute a cultural law that everyone already knows: the answer to "Who painted the [woman]?" is of course "*Not* the woman." Everyone, the Wife asserts, recognizes this cultural rule, which Rita Copeland has referred to as the "law [that] women and books don't mix."[3] Alison, producing a narrative account of her "species," explicitly challenges her gender-based exclusion from written culture and confronts the *Prologue* and *Tale*'s audience with the alternate authority provided by her experience as a woman.[4]

Given the widespread circulation of texts like those in Alison's husband's "book of wicked wives" in the fourteenth century, it is hardly surprising that scholars sometimes see the Middle Ages as unrelentingly misogynistic and women's engagement with written texts as transgressive. It takes very little effort to find medieval authors who rail against women's involvement with written texts, and

the Mark of Adam," 26–57. Hansen offers an extensive review of criticism related to this passage (27 n. 4).

[3] Rita Copeland, "Why Women Can't Read," in *Representing Women: Law, Literature, and Feminism,* ed. Susan Sage Heinzelman and Zipporah Batshaw Wiseman (Durham, N.C.: Duke University Press 1994), 253.

[4] Hansen notes that Alison "has become a figure to be reckoned with by anyone interested in the history, both factual and literary, of women before 1500. Faced with the problem of women's absence and silence in the past, feminist historians and literary critics turn with enthusiasm to the Wife as a rare instance of woman as agent, speaker, and, most recently, reader" (*Chaucer and the Fictions of Gender,* 26). Many critics respond to the Wife as if she were a historical figure. See, for example, Lawrence Lipking, "Aristotle's Sister: A Poetics of Abandonment," *Critical Inquiry* 19 (1983): 61–81.

women's writing was especially condemned.[5] Male authors frequently remarked on the unsuitability of women's involvement with the written word—the chronicler Henry Knighton, for example, compares women's (and laymen's) reading with casting pearls before swine—and little evidence remains concerning women's education.[6] When writers did address women's role in society, they concentrated on ideals of religious devotion and ethical conduct—which were thought especially important for women because they had inherited their corrupt natures from their "mother" Eve—rather than on intellectual training.[7] It is therefore little wonder that Alison's denunciation of the clerical and masculine monopoly on textual production appears to embody the experiences of medieval women and that Chaucer's representation of women's exclusion from literate culture has been assimilated into studies of historical women. Following a strongly analytic impulse, scholars often assume, logically, that if cultural rules discouraged women from engaging in literate activities, then women who took part in literate culture did so in violation of those rules.

However, as I argue in this book, the relationship between women

[5] For a collection of medieval writing on the subject of woman, see Alcuin Blamires, *Woman Defamed and Woman Defended: An Anthology of Medieval Texts* (Oxford: Clarendon Press, 1992). See also Copeland, "Why Women Can't Read," 254–64; and Rowena E. Archer, " 'How ladies . . . who live on their manors ought to manage their households and estates': Women as Landholders and Administrators in the Later Middle Ages," in *Woman Is a Worthy Wight: Women in English Society c. 1200–1500*, ed. P. J. P. Goldberg (Stroud, U.K.: Sutton, 1992), 149–81.

[6] Knighton's description has become a commonplace in discussions of medieval women and writing. See, for example, Margaret Aston, "Lollard Women Priests?" in *Lollards and Reformers: Images and Literacy in Late Medieval Religion* (London: Hambledon Press, 1984), 49. Her essay includes a number of references to writers who object to women's learning, such as these lines from Hoccleve: "Some wommen eeke, thogh hir wit be thynne, / Wele argumentes make in holy writ! / Lewde calates! sittith down and spynne, / And kakele of sumwhat elles, for your wit / Is al to feeble to despute of it!" (51). See *Hoccleve's Works. The Minor Poems*, ed. F. J. Furnivall, EETS, e.s., 61 (London: Kegan Paul, Trench, Trübner, 1892), 13. Both Knighton and Hoccleve criticize lay reading generally and argue that women are the most pernicious of lay readers.

[7] Citing the writings of "educationalists" such as Philip of Novarre, Robert of Blois, and Giles of Rome, Archer remarks that "Selective reading may suggest that formal education of women was generally condemned." Such texts concentrated on "seclusion of women and good character formation. Sewing, spinning, and silk work were advocated chiefly as a remedy for idleness; reading, regarded with deep suspicion, was grudgingly conceded as a requirement strictly for the high-born lady; and writing was censured as subversion" (" 'How ladies,' " 151).

and writing in late medieval culture actually involved a contradiction between social impulses and practice. Although on a broad, cultural level medieval women were discouraged from interaction with the written word (for example, they were rarely formally educated and often discouraged from acquiring literate abilities), on an individual level they were often expected to take part in literate culture; therefore no equation between writing and "dissent" explains women's literate practice in fifteenth-century England. In fact, despite pervasive rhetoric against women's writing—and to a lesser extent against women's reading—there is little indication that women took part in text-based activities as expressions of *female* insurrection against male-dominated social forces. Rather, the women whose writing, reading, literary patronage, dictation, memorization, and recitation I study in this book both expected men to tolerate their textual engagements and, more surprisingly, were involved in literate practice at least in part because it served male-dominated social hierarchies, especially the patriarchally structured medieval family.[8]

Alternatively, in this book I argue that medieval women took part in literate culture through the authority of membership in family-based social groups and that such participation was part of a broader cultural shift in which social authority was increasingly based on the documentary abilities of the written word.[9] Underlying my argument is a critique of models that take the legal implications of "cultural law" at face value: because dissent-based models of medieval

[8] Even the rhetoric concerning women's involvement with the written word could be contradictory. See, for example, the well-known passage from Caxton's translation of the Book of the Knight of La Tour Landry in which the Knight maintains that women need not learn to write but rebukes men who refuse to let their wives and daughters read. *The Book of the Knight of the Tower,* trans. William Caxton, ed. Yvonne Offord, EETS, s.s., 2 (Oxford: Oxford University Press, 1971), 122. Julia Boffey mentions this passage in "Women Authors and Women's Literacy," in *Women and Literature in Britain, 1150–1500,* ed. Carol Meale (Cambridge: Cambridge University Press, 1993), 165; and Norman Davis refers to it in his introduction to *The Paston Letters,* 2 vols. (Oxford: Clarendon Press, 1971), xxxviii.

[9] Caroline M. Barron, "The Education and Training of Girls in Fifteenth-Century London," in *Courts, Counties and the Capital in the Later Middle Ages,* ed. Diana E. S. Dunn (Stroud, U.K.: Sutton, 1996), describes the centrality of written texts in the later Middle Ages: "Although the ability of both men and women to read may have been less widespread than some optimists have thought, there is no doubt that the society of the late fourteenth century was increasingly 'text-based.' English was used for letter-writing, proclamations, wills, accounts, court ordinances, fraternity rules, religious instruction; and, in this predominantly lay environment, women must, to some extent, have been drawn into this written vernacular culture" (143).

women's reading and writing categorize literate actions as either violations of the law or acts of gendered disobedience, they in effect discard the old law of oppression—which saw women as victims of patriarchy—only to replace it with the new law of dissent—in which women's literate action is an expression of gendered rebellion.[10] Instead of identifying women's literate practice as transgressive, this book explores the familial context from which women's literate engagement emerged and reconstructs the interplay between individuals and social structures in each of the book's four chapters. Rather than seeing literacy as static or symbolic, I draw on anthropological studies that consider literacy "not as a monolithic phenomenon but as a multifaceted one, whose meaning, including any consequences it may have for individuals, groups, or symbolic structures, is critically tied to the social practices that surround it and to the ideological system in which it is embedded."[11] This book moves away from legal models of literacy toward "practice" to describe the complex, sometimes contradictory, and socially shaped nature of medieval textual engagement.

By treating text-based action in terms of practice rather than law, this book tries to negotiate between the extremes of history divorced from individual action and individual action separated from history. To do this, I draw on a body of theoretical material that reflects on the relationships between structuring social orders and the ways that individual actors negotiate and reshape the world. Within practice theory, as anthropologist Sherry Ortner explains, "there is an insistence, as in earlier structural-determinist models, that human action is constrained by the given social and cultural order (often condensed

[10] Much of the recent work on Margery Kempe is based on this principle. See, for example, Lynn Staley, *Margery Kempe's Dissenting Fictions* (University Park, Pa.: Pennsylvania State University Press, 1994); and Ruth Shklar, "Cobham's Daughter: *The Book of Margery Kempe* and the Power of Heterodox Thinking," *MLQ* 56 (1995): 277–304.

[11] Niko Besnier, *Literacy, Emotion and Authority: Reading and Writing on a Polynesian Atoll* (Cambridge: Cambridge University Press, 1995), 2–3; Besnier, drawing on Brian V. Street, *Literacy in Theory and Practice* (Cambridge: Cambridge University Press, 1984), divides studies on literacy into those that follow an "autonomous" model in which there are "certain inherent properties of literacy" that "cause basic changes in the structure of societies" (2) and those that depend on an "ideological model" in which literacy is viewed as social practice (3). Since M. T. Clanchy, *From Memory to Written Record* (Cambridge: Harvard University Press, 1979) appeared, studies of literacy in medieval England have moved decisively toward ideological models.

in the term 'structure'); but there is also an insistence that human action *makes* 'structure'—reproduces or transforms it, or both."[12] According to this theoretical model, practices are produced through relationships between the individual, who has his or her own set of "dispositions"—developed over time and particularly inflected by childhood experiences—that follow regular patterns without following a consciously articulated plan of action, and society's structures and conditions.[13] Practice theory provides a framework for studying medieval women and literacy that is flexible enough to include both the strictures against female literate involvement and women's participation in text-based practices without insisting that such involvement was necessarily subversive of gender hierarchies. By focusing on the relationship between structure and individual, it allows me to consider women's involvement in literate culture less as a matter of violation (or oppression) and more as a process of negotiation and adjustment. These negotiations may include conscious strategizing by the individual against prevailing systems, but even this strategizing is part of a socially complex system, not a simple case of conscious "intention" in which the individual is free to transcend social forces. To convey the complexity of the relationship between the individual and social structures, I have found Ortner's notion of "serious games" very helpful because it offers a way to escape binary views of the shaping power of social life on the individual:

> The idea of the "game" . . . capture[s] simultaneously the following dimensions: that social life is culturally organized and constructed, in terms of defining categories of actors, rules and

[12] Sherry B. Ortner, *Making Gender: The Politics and Erotics of Culture* (Boston: Beacon Press, 1996), 2.

[13] Like Ortner, there are a number of scholars, primarily sociologists and anthropologists, who fall under the rubric "practice theorist," and although they use a variety of terms for Ortner's dispositions—the best known is Pierre Bourdieu's *habitus*—and differ in their sense of the degree to which these dispositions reflect social structures, they all offer loose theories of action as both embedded in cultural networks and predicated on individual responses. For a very useful elucidation of Bourdieu's ideas about the habitus, see John B. Thompson's introduction to Pierre Bourdieu, *Language and Symbolic Power,* trans. Gino Raymond and Matthew Adamson (Cambridge: Harvard University Press, 1991), esp. 12–14. I have found Ortner helpful because she is explicitly concerned with the relationship between practice theory and feminism. In addition, I have worked closely with Talal Asad's practice-based discussion of religion and ritual in *Genealogies of Religion: Discipline and Reasons of Power in Christianity and Islam* (Baltimore: Johns Hopkins University Press, 1993), 1–167.

> goals of the games, and so forth; that social life is precisely social, consisting of webs of relationship and interaction between multiple, shiftingly interrelated subject positions, none of which can be extracted as autonomous "agents"; and yet at the same time there is "agency," that is, actors play with skill, intention, wit, knowledge, intelligence.[14]

Practice theory in this way produces a less romantic version of women's literate engagement than does the model of rebellion associated with figures such as the fictional Wife of Bath, but it also allows for a more complicated presentation of individual action than has otherwise been available: it insists on the presence of social structure, individual players, and unequal power and resources in discussions of text-based activity.

Further, "literate practice" avoids the sense of stasis associated with "literacy," that is, the term allows me to resist the notion that the individual either is or is not literate, and to avoid a related idea, that individuals' literate investments never change. I titled this book *Reading Families* because each of its chapters is concerned with the ways that women, sometimes as individuals, sometimes as groups, analyzed and responded to the familial structures around them through interactions with the written word. By "reading" responses to their literate engagements, medieval women shaped and modified their literate practice pragmatically and imaginatively. Sometimes this led to moments of crisis in which they recognized the social contradiction that formed the basis of their literate involvements—a clash between their own experiences and the increasingly text-dependent culture of late medieval England, which required even those who were "illiterate"—and who often continued to be designated as illiterate—to engage in textual interactions. Sometimes, it led to deeper identification with "masculine" social imperatives through involvement with the written word. Sharply divorced from the normative connotations of literacy, the term "literate practice" describes the range of activities engaged in by individuals at varying times as well as the diversity of social meanings of those activities as associated with and reshaped by literate agents.[15]

14 Ortner, *Making Gender,* 12.

15 See Jonathan Boyarin, ed., *The Ethnography of Reading* (Berkeley: University of California Press, 1993), a collection of essays that studies reading as a diverse and multivalent practice. Johannes Fabian's "Keep Listening: Ethnography and Reading,"

Finally, my use of the term indicates this project's attention to a range of disparate, text-based practices, including literary patronage, dictation, memorization, and recitation—as well as reading and writing—and by using it, I indicate my concern with both the place that textual interactions held in fifteenth-century women's lives and the particular text-based actions in which women took part. In the Middle Ages even those persons designated as literate were not uniformly skilled: people incapable of actually reading for themselves could experience texts aurally; those unable to write could claim to do so through an amanuensis; and even a "knowingness," as Steven Justice calls it, of the importance of the written word surely has some relationship to literacy.[16] Although a great deal has recently been written about medieval women and writing, most studies are ultimately concerned with authorship: they look in particular at Margery Kempe and Julian of Norwich as literary foremothers and study their books increasingly as evidence of writerly autonomy and literary influence.[17] This book, on the other hand, is concerned primarily with the ways that the written word influenced women's lives in more mundane ways. Rather than dismissing all other textual engagement as trivial, this book looks at different text-based technologies available to medieval women and situates literate practice in the historical conditions of particular social configurations—legally driven East Anglia, reformist Norwich, royally connected London and its environs.

Historicist critics rightly point out that there is no single, uniform pattern that defines the medieval family: what constituted the family differs for each genealogical unit, depending on numerous factors including social class, region, political climate, and extra-familial affiliations, and for this reason it seems clear that what propelled women

80–97, is especially useful on the social/anthropological history of the study of literacy.

[16] " 'Literacy,' clearly, must mean something different from the mere ability to make and construe the written word. . . . The scope of the literacy the rebels claimed had more to do with their claims to familiarity with and investment in the documentary culture . . . more to do with the place of writing in their collective lives" (Steven Justice, *Writing and Rebellion: England in 1381* [Berkeley: University of California Press, 1994], 52).

[17] Recent examples are Staley, *Margery Kempe's Dissenting Fictions;* and Denise Baker Nowakowski, *Julian of Norwich's Showings: From Vision to Book* (Princeton: Princeton University Press, 1994).

into literate practice differed according to these differing familial constellations and individual responses. Nevertheless, certain observable tendencies in medieval society lead me to give preeminence to familial relations. As historian Joel Rosenthal points out, late medieval family relationships

> were mostly about men: fathers, sons, brothers, and, when better alternatives failed, nephews and cousins. The social role of women was almost never as important as their biological role, and even when an individual woman became the key in the transmission of a patrimony or the preservation of a lineage, her individuality was soon subsumed by the males whom she bore to the new patrilineage.[18]

Under their husbands' or fathers' authority, according to medieval law, women were defined as dependents, and although the circumstances of this dependence varied greatly according to social class and familial situation, Rosenthal's observation applies to medieval women generally and not merely to the socially privileged.[19] In looking at the way that family affiliations intersected with women's literate practice, I argue that women were largely defined by their incorporation into men's families, that is, by their membership in male-dominated and male-centered genealogical groups, but that these definitions were flexible, infinitely variable, and open to amendment.[20]

[18] Joel T. Rosenthal, *Patriarchy and Families of Privilege in Fifteenth-Century England* (Philadelphia: University of Pennsylvania Press, 1991), 175.

[19] Scholarship on the family in the Middle Ages is vast. In "Medieval Women, Modern Women: Across the Great Divide," in *Culture and History, 1350–1600: Essays on English Communities, Identities, and Writing,* ed. David Aers (Detroit, Mich.: Wayne State University Press, 1992), Judith Bennett provides a useful summary of medieval historians' approach to the subject: "In the last decade, medievalists have repeatedly attacked the model that posits, based largely on the arguments of Philippe Ariès and Lawrence Stone, an early-modern emergence of affective family relations. Studies by Barbara Hanawalt, Lorraine Attreed and others have demonstrated not only that medieval people recognized the special nature of childhood but also that medieval family relations could be quite warm, intimate, and affectionate" (148).

[20] David Herlihy points out that literary and philosophical writings from the Middle Ages show that affection bound family members together: "Unmistakeably, these authors assume that persons who live together will normally love together and that this love is the first to be learned and the last to be relinquished"; see David Herlihy, "Family," in *Portraits of Medieval and Renaissance Living: Essays in Memory*

Although medieval women may have participated in literate activities through various communal groups, the family was the most important of these social formations. Among the more significant nonfamilial institutions that shaped women's lives were the parish and, for certain women, guilds. R. N. Swanson notes that parishes provided some opportunities for members of their lay community to acquire elementary training in reading and writing to enable their participation in services, and Beat Kümin suggests that this training allowed even women very occasionally to serve as church wardens, the lay officers who attended to parish needs and kept accounts of expenses.[21] Guilds may have offered women the opportunity to acquire some literate skills because guilds, like parishes, kept records of their proceedings and depended on the literate abilities of some of their members. However, whatever the extent of these educational opportunities in the parish and the guild was, participation in these communities was closely associated with familial arrangements. Kümin, for example, points out that even when parishes appointed women as wardens, they did so because the women were widows of the men who had held those offices.[22] Similarly, Judith Bennett observes that women's guild activity was critically tied to marital status: married women entered their husbands' guilds as "sisters," and widows assumed privileges from their deceased husbands but could lose those privileges upon remarriage.[23] Religious participation itself was, as Jonathan Hughes has observed, familial, and kinship ties offered members of communities spiritual security.[24] Although women were

---

of David Herlihy, ed. Samuel K. Cohn Jr. and Steven A. Epstein (Ann Arbor: University of Michigan Press, 1996), 18–19.

21 R. N. Swanson, *Church and Society in Late Medieval England* (New York: Blackwell, 1989), 304. Cited in Beat Kümin, *The Shaping of a Community: The Rise and Reformation of the English Parish, c. 1400–1560* (Brookfield, Vt.: Scolar Press, 1996), 61. For Kümin's discussion of female churchwardens, see *Shaping of a Community,* 40.

22 Kümin, *Shaping of a Community,* 40. See also Katherine French, *The People of the Parish: Community Life in a Late Medieval Diocese* (Philadelphia: University of Pennsylvania Press, 2000).

23 Bennett, "Medieval Women, Modern Women," esp. 160. See also on this subject Caroline M. Barron, "Introduction: The Widow's World in Later Medieval London," in *Medieval London Widows, 1300–1500,* ed. Caroline M. Barron and Anne F. Sutton (London: Hambledon, 1994), xiii–xxxiv; and Mavis E. Mate, *Daughters, Wives, and Widows after the Black Death: Women in Sussex, 1350–1535* (Woodbridge, Suffolk: Boydell, 1998).

24 Jonathan Hughes, *Pastors and Visionaries: Religion and Secular Life in Late Medieval Yorkshire* (Woodbridge, Suffolk: Boydell, 1988), 5–37.

clearly involved in communal groups that extended beyond their immediate families, this involvement was predicated on family relationships, and those relationships, as Bennett points out in a discussion of the family economy, "reflected the patriarchal authority of men in medieval society."[25] As a consequence, women's participation in literate culture was first and foremost responsive to familial demands and influences.[26]

The patriarchal family (both secular and religious) exerted its force on medieval women by presenting them with the "naturalness" of that order, primarily through the discourse of generation, and familial unity was posed as a higher—because more sacred, natural, and beneficial—order than that which a sense of collective, gendered identity might have provided. Although women were, as a group, identified as possessing particular traits and propensities, they seem rarely to have perceived this gendered categorization as an impetus for subversive action. Instead, medieval women—who engaged in literate practice as individuals dominated by social orders but who seem to have been only minimally aware of this domination as a structural problem—experienced little conflict in ignoring gender rules concerning literate engagement. For most women, participation in practices that were culturally specified as masculine was possible only if they understood themselves as agents whose actions were not tightly defined by the rules of gender. For many women and the more dominant individuals around them—a group composed primarily of their husbands, sons, and fathers—the advantages of such misrecognition clearly outweighed the disadvantages. Women of privileged circumstances such as Margaret Beaufort and Margaret Paston were especially unlikely to recognize gender as a classification that superseded all other princi-

[25] Bennett, "Medieval Women, Modern Women," 152.

[26] There is some evidence of formal schooling for girls. See, for example, Barron, "Education and Training of Girls in Fifteenth-Century London," 139–53; and Caroline M. Barron, "The Expansion of Education in Fifteenth-Century London," in *The Cloister and the World: Essays in Honour of Barbara Harvey*, ed. John Blair and Brian Golding (Oxford: Clarendon Press, 1996), 219–45. Barron's central piece of evidence for girls' education is a statute from 1406 that guaranteed "the right 'of every man or woman, of whatever estate or condition he be, to set their son or daughter to take learning at any manner of school that pleaseth them' " ("Education and Training of Girls in Fifteenth-Century London," 139). On education in the Middle Ages, see also Jo Ann Hoeppner Moran, *The Growth of English Schooling, 1340–1548: Learning, Literacy, and Laicization in Pre-Reformation York Diocese* (Princeton: Princeton University Press, 1985); and Nicholas Orme, *Education and Society in Medieval and Renaissance England* (London: Hambledon, 1989).

ples of social division, such as age, regional affiliation, or economic class, because acceptance of this as a primary identifying characteristic meant embracing a full range of less advantageous affiliations (intellectual and spiritual weakness, for example).[27]

However, although women formed little common cause with one another through their gender-based limitations, they did not "forget" their sex—that is, escape from the effects of gender-inflected social understandings and act in an independent, "manly" fashion, a common description of saintly female behavior in Church fathers' writings from the earlier Middle Ages.[28] As medieval society became increasingly dependent on texts, women, like men, adapted to the situation by cultivating literate skills, or at least by gaining access to literate mediators. Barred from professional training available to men, women's means of acquiring text-based knowledge were generally unofficial, that is, non-institutional, and haphazard, and, given the importance of women's literate involvement in family affairs, the resulting lack of literate competency—in terms of the ability to wield a pen or to read—was sometimes staggering. Margaret Paston, wife of the influential Norfolk lawyer John Paston and "author" of hundreds of letters, despite her seeming inability to write, exemplifies the difficulties in thinking about the social restrictions on medieval women's involvement in written culture as skill-based. Norwich Lollard women such as Margery Baxter placed a high value on vernacular books, helping literate members to transport them, but were often unable to read themselves. And even a "fully literate" woman such as Margaret Beaufort bemoaned her limited facility with Latin but also oversaw the production of printed works in that language.

Although the English medieval family was the context for women's involvement with the written word in the fifteenth century, it did not necessarily constitute a "textual community" of the kind described by Brian Stock in *The Implications of Literacy.*[29] From his analysis of religious/heretical groups from the High Middle Ages,

[27] For an interesting discussion of the varying importance of gender in relation to other social factors, see Toril Moi, "Appropriating Bourdieu: Feminist Theory and Pierre Bourdieu's Sociology of Culture," *New Literary History* 22 (1991): 1017–49.

[28] See Jane Tibbets Schulenberg, *Forgetful of Their Sex: Female Sanctity and Society, ca. 500–1100* (Chicago: University of Chicago Press, 1998), 1.

[29] Brian Stock, *The Implications of Literacy: Written Language and Models of Interpretation in the Eleventh and Twelfth Centuries* (Princeton: Princeton University Press, 1983), esp. 88–92.

Stock coined the phrase to describe the ways members of such groups shared interpretive understandings of core texts, usually through the interpretive mastery of an individual, and the term has become commonplace in discussions of medieval literacy. Felicity Riddy, for instance, describes reading communities as subcultures composed of medieval women readers focused on certain kinds of texts.[30] Some English women readers in the fourteenth and fifteenth century—particularly elite readers—were clearly involved in such communities, but in this book I suggest that this involvement is a secondary development of the familial impetus toward literate practice. I argue that the social space in which medieval women developed literate habits was defined by familial relationships and not by textual predilections. As I discuss in chapters 3 and 4, even when women seemed to belong to particular interpretive communities, such as the Lollard sect or the Bridgettine order, they participated in those communities through family-based identification. Like Riddy and Carol Meale, who both associate medieval women's reading and writing with households and kinship, and Claire Cross, who describes Lollards as belonging to a "family sect," I endeavor to demonstrate how literate concerns were shared in local and family circles.[31] However, I also see familial understanding as extending to imaginative structures that shaped literate practice. In this book I argue that the fifteenth-century family was both the context for women's introduction into literate culture and an imaginative category through which women understood and reshaped their experiences in the world. For this reason, one of my primary concerns is to look at the way women's literate practices shifted and were re-shaped by the changing circumstances of their familial relations: fifteenth-century Englishwomen tended to reread family situations through and as a consequence of their literate investments, and this book focuses on the dynamic shifts in familial groups, including marriage, death of a spouse, motherhood,

[30] Felicity Riddy, " 'Women talking about the things of God': A Late Medieval Sub-Culture," in *Women and Literature in Britain,* 104–27.

[31] See Carol M. Meale, " 'Alle the bokes that I haue of latyn, englisch, and frensch': Laywomen and Their Books in Late Medieval England," in *Women and Literature in Britain,* 128–58; and Claire Cross, " 'Great reasoners in scripture': The Activities of Women Lollards, 1380–1530," in *Medieval Women,* ed. Derek Baker (Oxford: Blackwell, 1978), 359–80. Anne Clark Bartlett also describes the relationship between women readers and male, clerical authors as familial; see *Male Authors, Female Readers: Representation and Subjectivity in Middle English Devotional Literature* (Ithaca, N.Y.: Cornell University Press, 1995).

and sisterhood (natural and religious) as they shaped and were reshaped by text-based concerns.

In addition to considering how women "read" family relationships and how this interpretive process reshaped literate practices, this book looks directly at the specific nature of women's textual habits and the works they read and wrote. This technique is commonly used in studies of canonical authors and their works: when we read Chaucer, for example, we also think about poets whom he read (Dante, Boccacio, "Lollius") and how he read them. In contrast, discussions of medieval literacy have tended to concentrate on bibliographic details such as book and manuscript ownership, patronage, and textual circulation, with little room for consideration of the actual contexts of the writings produced, consumed, and distributed.[32] Yet, as I insist in this book, to consider how and why an individual read or wrote, valued or feared, plagiarized or translated, particular works, we need to know what those texts *were* as well as where they came from. We need, in other words, to take seriously what we take for granted in studying canonical authors: both to ask what thematic, formal, and explicitly textual characteristics attracted women as readers, writers, patrons, and listeners and to think about what women did with written texts once they came into contact with them.

This book moves from a discussion of women's literate practice as physically located in actual, individual, familial structures—beginning with Margaret Paston's letters, which were written expressly at her husband's request—toward an increasingly imaginative understanding of familial/textual relations—ending with devotional texts that describe the spiritual "daughterhood" of the Bridgettine readers at Syon Abbey. Corresponding with the movement of the chapters toward imaginative, familial structures is an increasing concern with the materiality of literate practice. That is, as the "family" that shaped textual interaction became increasingly abstract, the texts involved become more concerned with the connection between literate practice and bodily experience.

Chapters 1 and 2 consider two individual women, Margaret Paston, the wife of the Norwich lawyer John Paston, and Margaret Beaufort,

[32] Meale's anthology is an important example of this kind of criticism. Another useful, recent source is Karen Jambeck, "Patterns of Women's Literary Patronage: England, 1200–ca. 1475," in *The Cultural Patronage of Medieval Women,* ed. June Hall McCash (Athens: University of Georgia Press, 1996), 228–65.

the mother of the first Tudor king, Henry VII, in terms of explicit familial/textual relationships. In "Husbands and Sons: Margaret Paston's Letter-Writing," I argue that the letters Margaret Paston dictated were written as evidence, like a title or deed, that proved the author's worth to her husband and verified her interpretive legitimacy. Tracing her letter-writing from the early years of her marriage to her husband's death, chapter 1 describes how Margaret Paston's textual authority was challenged by her son, and illustrates some of the ways that family structures and literate practices ultimately came into conflict. Chapter 2, "Margaret Beaufort's Literate Practice: Service and Self-Inscription," establishes a link between aristocratic women's administrative responsibilities and personal investment in written texts. Although Margaret Beaufort's life is typically defined in relation to her son, Henry VII, this chapter imagines a relationship between the literate practices of her mother and mother-in-law and those of Margaret herself. I conclude that Margaret became directly involved in the late-fifteenth-century print trade in response to ideas about books and writing that she learned both from women in her family and through religious affiliations.

Chapters 3 and 4 look at women's literate practice within two religious communities. The first was the Lollard circle that met in and near Norwich in the first half of the fifteenth century. In "Children of God: Women Lollards at Norwich," I argue that Lollard women viewed themselves as "children of God" and claimed literate authority through divine kinship, asserting that God was their Father and the scriptures (rather than the Church) their mother. This chapter demonstrates that the family-based model of literacy extended beyond circumstances of literate education and textual transmission to imaginative structures: Lollard women resisted clerical control of their engagement with the scriptures, and they read and wrote as mothers or daughters or sisters within their individual families. Chapter 4, "Reading at Syon Abbey," is about the Bridgettine double monastery founded by Henry V in 1415. As the fifteenth century wore on, ownership of books became increasingly common at Syon, despite legislation against personal property. This chapter considers the complex dynamic between Bridgettine imitation, liturgical reading, and secular, aristocratic culture, which made material books so important at Syon by 1500.

As literary scholars, our interest in the production of imaginative or aesthetic works need not blind us to the important and meaningful ways that medieval women engaged in literate practice. By participating in activities that included reading, dictating letters, memorizing scripture, owning and sharing books, translating, and patronizing printers, women responded to and reconfigured the familial and social circumstances in which they lived. If we want to know why the written word was central to late medieval culture, it may be less important to concern ourselves with a handful of "great" texts than it is to study medieval people's daily involvement with writing. This book attempts to reconstruct some of the ordinariness of (which is not to say insignificance of) medieval women's relationship to written texts and to examine the seeming naturalness of their engagement in literate endeavors.

Finally, a note about quotations and names. As is increasingly customary, I have eliminated all yoghs and thorns from Middle English quotations. As is becoming less common, I have referred to my subjects by their first names (for example, "Margaret" rather than "Paston" for Margaret Paston). This should be in no way understood as an act of condescension—indeed, I also refer to John Paston by his first name—but rather as an attempt not to confuse the reader. Family names are shared by a number of my subjects, and I found it easiest to use first names for this reason. Historical figures who are perhaps more familiar to readers and who have been traditionally called by their last names are referred to in that way (Reginald Pecock is "Pecock" and not "Reginald"); the distinction between persons who are called by a first name and those called by a last is strictly utilitarian.

CHAPTER 1

Husbands and Sons:
Margaret Paston's Letter-Writing

Among the more surprising aspects of late medieval English culture is the alacrity with which some women recognized the practical value of writing, despite receiving no instruction in literate modes. Margaret Paston, for example, who from all evidence seems to have been unable to wield a pen for herself and who may have been unable to read, in 1466 dictated a letter addressed to her son John Paston II in which she affirmed the paramount value of written documents.[1] She advises John that he

> be ware that ye kepe wysly youre wrytyngys that ben of charge, that it com not in here handys that may hurt you heraftere. Youre fadere, wham God assole, in hys trobyll seson set more by hys wrytyngs and evydens than he dede by any of his move-

[1] Norman Davis reflects on the relationship between Margaret's seeming inability to write and the ability to read: "Margaret could certainly read, as we learn from her son Sir John's injunction to his brother in a letter of 1470: 'I praye yow *schewe* ore rede to my moodre such thynges as ye thynke is fore here to knowe, afftre yowre dyscression.' But it does not follow that she could write; and another indication that she did not may be seen in a suggestion made by the youngest John in 1477. He has prepared a draft of a letter to be sent in her name, and he introduces it thus: 'Wherfor, modyr, if it please yow, myn advyse is to send hyr answer a yen in thys forme folowing, *of some other manys hand*' " (Davis, "The Language of the Pastons," Proceedings of the British Academy, vol. 40 [London: Geoffrey Cumberlege, 1955], 121). Although I am inclined to agree with Davis that Margaret could read—several other passages in the letters suggest that Margaret could understand a written text by looking at it—it should be noted that she refers to her letters as texts that she has "written," although they were actually transcribed by an amanuensis.

abell godys. Remembere that yf tho were had from you ye kowd neuer gyte no moo such as tho be for youre parte.[2]

Although Margaret makes her claim in the name of John II's recently deceased father, the protective language is her own, and the dramatic comparison between legal documents and one's most precious possession leaves no doubt about the value she herself placed on the written word. Presenting her husband as a veteran of legal struggles, Margaret reminds her son that most of the world's skirmishes take place in the courts and that he, as the new head of the family, should demonstrate the same diligent care for written documents that his father had shown. If she saw any irony in the coupling of her paramount faith in written evidence with her own inability to write, she never reveals it in the more than one hundred letters dictated over the course of her adult life. For Margaret Paston, both her inability to write and her dependence on written documents were essential parts of her life in fifteenth-century Norfolk; the incongruity between her skill and her faith was no cause for reflection or consternation.

Margaret's attitude toward her own writing is so matter-of-fact that it has led twentieth-century historians to underestimate the strangeness of her participation in literate culture. For instance, a recent biography of the Pastons, Joseph Gies and Frances Gies's *A Medieval Family,* suggests that Margaret's reliance on written correspondence was typical of fifteenth-century women.[3] Carried away

[2] *Paston Letters and Papers of the Fifteenth Century,* ed. Norman Davis, 2 vols. (Oxford: Clarendon, 1971), no. 198. Most subsequent references to the Paston letters are given parenthetically in the text and use Davis's numbering.

[3] Frances Gies and Joseph Gies, *A Medieval Family: The Pastons of Fifteenth-Century England* (New York: HarperCollins, 1998). Although this is a "popular" biography, it is carefully researched and provides a good outline of events in the family's history. Aside from the work of Norman Davis, whose edition of the Paston letters is standard and who has written extensively on the language of the letters, and that of Colin Richmond, whose remarkable accounts of the family's history, *The Paston Family in the Fifteenth Century: The First Phase* (Cambridge: Cambridge University Press, 1990), and *The Paston Family: Fastolf's Will* (Cambridge: Cambridge University Press, 1996), are deeply concerned with archival information, most book-length studies of the family are written for general audiences. See, for example, H. S. Bennett, *The Pastons and Their England: Studies in an Age of Transition* (1922; reprint, Cambridge: Cambridge University Press, 1991). Non-medievalists interested in the family's correspondence have included Horace Walpole, who wrote that it "make[s] all other letters not worth reading"; Virginia Woolf, who imagined John Paston II's "strange intoxication" when reading Chaucer and Lydgate—which constrasts sharply with her picture of Margaret's literate habits: "Mrs. Paston did not talk about herself" in her letters; and Robert Louis Stevenson, whose *Black Arrow* is based on

by biography's predilection for coherence and causality, *A Medieval Family* uses the lines from Margaret's letter quoted above to account for the existence of the massive Paston archive, which includes more than one thousand letters and documents written by members of the family and their associates, identifying her comments as an expression of the family's habit of safekeeping written texts.[4] Uninterested in the specific circumstances of Margaret's letter-writing, the biographers, neatly heightening and minimizing fifteenth-century women's social efficacy, remark that "for a woman like Margaret Paston to provide the nexus of communication for husband, children, kinsmen and friends was *natural*" (italics added).[5] They assume, in other words, that Margaret sent her son nagging letters about keeping track of his papers because this is what mothers do. The Gieses' portrayal of fifteenth-century family relationships approximates present-day models of family dynamics, and Margaret Paston's letter-writing is shown to be a method, familiar to readers throughout history and seemingly available to all medieval women, by which a parent seeks to influence her potentially rebellious child.

Anyone acquainted with the details of Margaret's relationship with her children will readily agree that she was bent on controlling at least some aspects of their lives. From disowning her daughter Margery upon Margery's marriage to family steward Richard Calle to threatening her elder sons periodically with the possibility of emending her will, Margaret expressed her opinions about her children's lives with certainty and purpose. But sensing that she was a controlling—or at least interfering—mother and assuming that her epistolary habits were a natural extension of maternal solicitude are very different things, and it is the second assumption with which I disagree. Although it came to seem natural to Margaret and her family for her to compose letters, it was nevertheless unusual (although coming to be more usual) that a gentlewoman in the fifteenth century had done so with such prolixity.[6] Accounts such as the Gieses' fail to

---

his reading of the letters. See W. S. Lewis, ed., *Horace Walpole's Correspondence* (New Haven: Yale University Press, 1965), 558–59; Virginia Woolf, *Collected Essays* (London: Hogarth Press, 1967), 3:7, 4, 1–17; and *The Letters of Robert Louis Stevenson*, ed. Sidney Colvin (New York: Charles Scribner's Sons, 1911), 2:127, cited in Sister Mary Alicia [Julia Elizabeth Allehoff], "The Influence of the Paston Letters on Stevenson's *Black Arrow*" (master's thesis, University of Washington, 1930), 24.

4 Gies and Gies, *A Medieval Family*, 8–20. On the relationship between individuals and the Paston family as a social unit, see Richmond, *Fastolf's Will*, 47.

5 Gies and Gies, *A Medieval Family*, 9.

6 By the mid-fifteenth century, women, especially those who were members of

historicize the process of writing, assuming for instance that both material conditions such as the ready availability of writing materials and emotional configurations such as the use of letters to express maternal disapprobation that are common in the late twentieth century were common in the fifteenth century.[7] This chapter, rather than ascribing literate engagement to transhistorical, maternal habits, looks at some of the social conditions that led Margaret Paston, despite her astonishing lack of training in literate skills, to employ literate strategies in her daily life and to put increasing trust in the power of her own written evidence. In short, it demonstrates that it was her marriage to John Paston, who—like his father and grandfather—studied law and its ability to shape reality through documentation, that initiated Margaret into literate culture; it was as part of this family

---

families with extensive business interests, started writing letters. Several letters are extant, for example, from the Stonor women, a few from the Cely women, and a number from women associated with the Pastons. Alexandra Barratt, writing about women who corresponded with the Pastons, notes that despite dictating many of the letters, "All the [women] writers use writing unself-consciously for a variety of practical purposes in a way that indicates a thoroughly literate mentality. They are familiar with the idea that written records are valuable, that writing can have practical effects, and that it is a substitute for 'presence' " (Barratt, in *Women's Writing in Middle English,* ed. Alexandra Barratt [London: Longman, 1992], 239). By the end of the fifteenth century the exchange of letters appears to have become a matter of course. For example, in 1474 Richard Cely writes his son Robert a letter in which he mentions that Robert's wife had complained that Robert had not "wryt to here." Similarly, Thomas Betson, who eventually married Katherine Riche, remarks in a letter from 1477 that he is "wrothe with Kateryne, by cause she sendith me no writtynge." See *The Cely Letters, 1472–1488,* ed. Alison Hanham, EETS, 273 (London: Oxford University Press, 1975), no. 2. For the Stonor letters, see *Kingford's Stonor Letters and Papers, 1290–1483,* ed. Christine Carpenter (Cambridge: Cambridge University Press, 1996), no. 185.

7 The idea of gender as socially and culturally constructed has become increasingly important in medieval studies. Recent works such as Marilynn Desmond, *Reading Dido: Gender, Textuality, and the Medieval Aeneid* (Minneapolis: University of Minnesota Press, 1994), draw on feminist theory to explicate medieval literary reception. Jane Chance, ed., *Gender and Text in the Later Middle Ages* (Gainesville: University Press of Florida, 1996), is a collection of essays that seeks to "reconstruct . . . a medieval feminine aesthetic" (19) and draws on theories of social construction to do so; see esp. Jane Chance, introduction in *Gender and Text in the Later Middle Ages,* 1–21. Collections such as Karma Lochrie, Peggy McCracken, and James A. Schultz, eds., *Constructing Medieval Sexuality* (Minneapolis: University of Minnesota Press, 1997), consider the relationship between contemporary theories of sexuality and gender and medieval understandings of gender relations. My discussion of gender is underwritten by the idea that feminine and masculine roles are constructed differently at different historical moments, even when those roles depend on biology for their constitution.

that she developed and adapted her own literate strategies, learning to reshape her familial position through the authority granted by written evidence.[8]

I argue that Margaret Paston adopted many of her husband's textual strategies to suit her own purposes as she lived her married life, but before doing so I must describe the social problem that dogged the Paston family throughout the fifteenth century, and I must do so for two related reasons. The problem was the pervasive suspicion in late medieval Norfolk that the family was not "gentle," specifically, that a recent Paston ancestor had been married to a bondwoman; the reasons that this mattered for Margaret's literate practice are first that this difficulty made the family eager to "marry up"—Margaret's pedigree was impeccably gentle—and second that this marriage, as I demonstrate, led to her letter-writing. The suspicions surrounding the Pastons' status are by now well known to scholars interested in the family, having been extensively documented by Colin Richmond and Caroline Barron, but they have generally been presented as either illustrations of changes in the Middle Ages' feudal structure or as so particular that little can be generalized from them about medieval culture.[9] Rather than considering political interactions among the ruling classes or dwelling on the particulars of the marriage agreement, I am interested in what this family history tells us about the explicitly text-based nature of these social changes and, ultimately, what those changes meant for women's participation in literate culture.[10]

The story of the Pastons' attempt to revise their family history is told by two documents that survive from the fifteenth century. The first is an anonymously authored text known as "A Remembraunce of the wurshypfull Kyn and Auncetrye of Paston, borne in Paston in Gemyngham Soken," which Norman Davis identifies as having been

[8] Recent studies of medieval women and reading or writing have either assumed or insisted that women's literate activities are empowering acts that allow women to resist patriarchal domination. Laurie Finke, for example, frames her discussion of medieval women's writing by locating her analysis "of women as an oppressed group within a theory of oppression that describes a dialogic interplay between the oppression of the powerful and the resistance of the oppressed" (Finke, *Women's Writing in English: Medieval England* [London: Longman, 1999], 3).

[9] On the family's gentility, see Richmond, *First Phase,* 1–22; and Caroline Barron, "Who Were the Pastons?" *Journal of the Society of Archivists* 4 (1972): 530–35.

[10] Richmond treats the marriage arrangements in detail; see *First Phase,* 120–34.

produced during John Paston I's lifetime.[11] The "Remembrance" might appear to modern readers to be a memorial to the family's honest origins, an account composed by a successful descendant intent on honoring the hard work of his forebears. It, for example, praises the family's industrious ancestors such as the "good pleyn husbond" Clement Paston, who "lyvvyd upon hys lond that he had in Paston, and kept ther on a plow alle tymes in the yer" and "rodd to mylle on the bar horsbak wyth hys corn under hym, and brought hom mele ageyn under hym." But if a fifteenth-century Paston composed this memorial, his admiration for Clement's quiet industry came at the expense of the living Pastons. In admiring Clement's wholesome, agrarian life, the "Remembrance" declares that Clement was married to a certain Geoffrey of Somerton's sister, "qwhych was a bond womanne to qwom it is not unknowyn."[12] By the fifteenth century, "gentleness," which was celebrated throughout the Middle Ages, had come to be associated increasingly with lineage, and an affiliation between the family's line of descent and bondage was information that the Pastons would omit from a written document; the author of the "Remembrance," whoever he or she was, only contributed to the family's difficulties by celebrating their humble origins and mentioning the apparently well-known servitude of Clement's wife.[13]

[11] *Paston Letters* 1:xli–xliii. Davis notes that the manuscript copy of the "Remembrance" has been lost. James Gairdner, whose last edition of the letters appeared in 1904, had not seen it, but William Frere, who found it among his uncle Sir John Fenn's papers, had it in 1823. Fenn had brought out an edition in two volumes of 155 of the Paston letters, at Horace Walpole's suggestion, in 1787 and then two more volumes, with a fifth ready for publication before his death in 1794, which Frere published in 1823. Davis reproduces Frere's text of the "Remembrance."

[12] *Paston Letters* 1:xli, xlii.

[13] The problem of defining who was "gentle" continues to occupy medieval historians and literary scholars. This is because, as Jennifer Ward observes of fourteenth- and fifteenth-century England, "there could be said to be a hierarchy of knights, esquires and gentry, but it has to be emphasised that these were by no means rigidly exclusive groups. Moreover, a distinction has to be drawn between the country gentry, who were men of wealth and standing, and the gentry whose outlook was confined to the parish or their immediate locality" (Ward, *Women of the English Nobility and Gentry, 1066–1500* [Manchester: Manchester University Press, 1995], 3). Christopher Dyer, *Standards of Living in the Late Middle Ages: Social Change in England c. 1200–1520* (Cambridge: Cambridge University Press, 1989), also remarks on the permeability and changeableness of such designations; see esp. 13–21. Christine Carpenter, *Locality and Polity: A Study of Warwickshire Landed Society, 1401–1499* (Cambridge: Cambridge University Press, 1992), comments on the complex nature of status in late medieval England and notes that "despite the precision of titles listed in the statutes" that "the exact dividing line at the bottom end of the landowning scale between the well-born and the rest was yet to be drawn" (45). Unlike historians,

The "problem" of social climbing was addressed repeatedly in the Middle Ages through ordinances such as the fourteenth century's sumptuary laws legislating particular dress for specific classes, and the material and cultural advantages associated with the higher end of the social scale were widely recognized.[14] Yet by the fifteenth century, the social arrangement by which families were designated as gentle had become increasingly permeable in large part because of the transformative power of writing. In obvious contrast with the "Remembrance" 's memorial to humble beginnings, another text that provides information about the Pastons' origins, a proclamation by Edward IV recorded in 1466, celebrates their illustrious past. Far from being servile, the Paston line is proved noble in this document; the proclamation announces that the Pastons have demonstrated their gentility by providing "evident proofe how they and their ancetors came linealy descended of right noble and worshipfull blood and of great lords sometime liveing in this our realme of Ingland" (no. 897). It even mentions an Anglo-Norman ur-ancestor, Wulfstan de Paston, whose antiquity and nobility supplant contemporaries' knowledge of the servility associated with the "Remembrance" 's not-long-dead bondwoman. In 1466, status came from a continuously elevated lineage, not from the memory of fortitude and hard work, and the Pastons' claim about their bloodline is important not only because it provided the family with noble antecedents but also because it fixed that claim in writing.

Although the "Remembrance" referred to common knowledge to authorize its claims, Edward's proclamation records the Pastons' text-based strategy of demonstrating gentility through written evidence, noting that they have offered "divers great evidences and court rolles, how that they and their ancestors had been possessed of a court and

---

literary scholars have tended to explore representations and social definitions of gentle behavior. See, for example, Felicity Riddy, "Engendering Pity in the *Franklin's Tale*," in *Feminist Readings in Middle English Literature: The Wife of Bath and All Her Sect*, ed. Ruth Evans and Lesley Johnson (London: Routledge, 1994), 56.

14 Paul Strohm observes that such statutes did not address a "mere concern with apparel or ornament" but rather express "an urgent unease about the forms of appropriate relation between persons" (Strohm, *Hochon's Arrow* [Princeton: Princeton University Press, 1992], 60). Dyer alludes to the sumptuary law of 1363 in which certain individuals below the esquires were "described as 'gentle' . . . but who had not yet been accepted as a definite group of 'gentlemen' " and cites a 1379 schedule that declares " 'merchants, citizens and burgesses, who have goods and chattels to the value of £1,000 . . . may . . . wear [clothing] in the same manner as esquires and gentlemen who have land and rent to the value of £200 a year' " (Dyer, *Standards of Living*, 13, 14).

seniory in the towne of Paston, and of many and sundry bondmen, sithen the time that no mind is to the contrary."[15] This is of course a claim about social relations: the Pastons asserted not merely that they were free but that they and their ancestors had been masters of bondsmen. Yet this claim also indicates the extent to which such social assertions depended on textual evidence. Gentility was loosely defined in the Middle Ages, most famously as those who possessed the right to bear arms, and in the late fifteenth and early sixteenth centuries attempts to offer other definitions, such as that suggested by Edward's proclamation (that gentility was dependent upon the possession of a manor and the maintenance of bondsmen), were common.[16] However, the document itself appears to be less concerned with establishing the facts that prove the family has fulfilled the terms of gentility than it is in claiming that the Pastons hold valid, written evidence for their position. The proclamation's persuasive strategy rests on both the authority and quantity of documentation that the family provided, suggesting that written evidence was increasingly understood as more powerful than popular knowledge or appeals to collective memory.[17]

Edward's proclamation was the result of years of hard work on the part of John Paston and his eldest son, John II. John I, counting on the family's Yorkist affiliations, had bet on Edward IV's willingness to support the Paston cause, and sent his son to attend the new king only months after Edward entered London in 1461 and claimed the

15 *Paston Letters,* no. 897. Clanchy explains that the term "time out of mind" came to have a precise defintion: "By statutes in 1275 and 1293 the date of Richard I's coronation (3 September 1189) was fixed as the legal limit of memory. This meant that a litigant was not required to go any further back into the past than that date when proving a claim" (Clanchy, *From Memory to Written Record,* 152).

16 P. R. Coss notes, in "The Formation of the English Gentry," *Past and Present* 47 (1995): 38–64, that historians sometimes fail to distinguish between the gentry and gentility. The gentry are often identified as "all those who are accepted as, or who lay claim to being, gentle"; according to Coss such equations fail to note that some of those people who were identified at a particular moment as members of the gentry had already "been regarded as gentle for some time" (41).

17 Richard Firth Green, *A Crisis of Truth: Literature and Law in Ricardian England* (Philadelphia: University of Pennsylvania Press, 1999), remarks on the relationship between uses of documentation and memory: "Clanchy's work, in particular, should have prepared us to recognize that the peculiarity of bastard feudalism lies not in its employment of one kind of legal document as against another, but in its supplanting the ancient bonds of the commemorative act of homage and oath of fealty by the newer constraints of a written covenant" (156). See also Clanchy, *From Memory to Written Record,* esp. "Trusting Writing," 294–327.

throne.[18] In August 1461, John II wrote to John I of his efforts to obtain Edward IV's aid through the influence of the Lord of Essex and his man, Baronners. Anxious to obtain particular "court rolls of Gemyngham" held by the Crown, which Barron and Richmond suggest contained evidence, or possible evidence, of the Pastons' lowly origins, John I had urged his son to use their social connections to persuade the young king to help.[19] At their urging, Baronners discussed the issue with Edward, and John II reported that Baronners claimed Edward would forward the rolls to the Pastons. John II wrote to his father that the king said he "wold hold wyth yowe jn yowre rygth." But that assurance came only after Edward had toyed with them concerning the rolls from Gemingham: when Baronners asked Edward about the existence of "the bille copye of the cort rolle," Edward "smyllyd and seyd that such a bylle there was" (no. 231). The king's smile, and John II's inclusion of the detail in the letter to his father, suggests how ambiguous the aims of even pragmatic textuality are. Documents that attest to legitimate origins depended on an audience devoid of cynicism concerning the relationship between truth and textuality; if this were not the case, why would men such as John I work so feverishly to gather written evidence? If it was commonly known that legal evidence was forged, falsified, or even conveniently forgotten, there seems little reason to trust in that documentation. But the desperate scramble for authentic documentation—and the Pastons were by no means the only medieval family to embark on such an endeavor—depended simultaneously on the recognition that writing both created and reflected truth.

The question is not whether the Pastons were lying about their origins but rather why they turned to documentary authority to establish their claims to gentility.[20] The answer seems to lie in their reliance on legal models that functioned through authorized evalua-

[18] Richmond describes John's attempt to place John II at the Yorkist court as "part of the strategy to defend the Fastolf estates," and, further, as a necessary shift of allegiance (*Fastolf's Will,* 113, 114). The Pastons supported the restoration of Henry VI in 1470, with John II and John III fighting for him (and losing) at Barnet in 1471. Richmond notes that such variable choices were pragmatic rather than strategic (*Fastolf's Will,* 118).

[19] Richmond, *First Phase,* 10–22; Barron, "Who Were the Pastons?" 530–35.

[20] Barron makes an interesting case for the difference between John and Margaret's caution concerning documentation: Margaret had written John a letter that described an episode in which one the Pastons' neighbors referred to them as "charles [churls] of Gemyngham," an allusion to their servile origins; Barron suggests that John subsequently cut the word out of the text of the letter because he did not want

tions of evidence. John I's concern with establishing a gentle identity as well as with securing the legitimate title to his estates from Fastolf was intimately bound up with documentary evidence: having textual proof did not assure successful acquisition of property rights, but not having it might assure failure.[21] John II's description of Edward's grin highlights the strange relationship between his desire for essential, unmediated origins and the recognition that such origins need to be constructed, textualized, and institutionalized.[22] Like medieval Christianity, fifteenth-century law depended on notions of authoritative exegesis that structured reality. John I sought Edward's support for their claim because Edward, who could evaluate social and documentary evidence, had the ultimate authority over interpretation of legal claims such as that of the Pastons.[23] Imaginable in their social milieu as gentle because they possessed the accoutrements of breeding such as the manor house and estates, the Pastons' claim to innate, timeless gentility seemed plausible enough to be true, and by 1466 it became a matter of historical record. Because the Pastons already counted among those people who were conceivably gentle, Edward IV, untroubled by the family's dubious pedigree, granted the documents the meaning that the family desired.

Among the most important ways to count among those considered gentle was to marry into families that were unquestionably gentle. Unlike social phenomena such as knighthood that depended on rites of institution, gentle status in the fifteenth century generally rested on an accumulation of diverse bodies of cultural evidence. For this reason, institutions that offered themselves as rites of consecration

---

it associated with the family even as part of a quotation. See Barron, "Who Were the Pastons?" 533–34.

[21] Richmond, *First Phase,* 15; concomitant with a vast buildup of accumulated properties was the Pastons' determined demonstration of not just participation in a particular social sphere but of "natural" gentility.

[22] The same relationship between truth and textuality characterizes the Pastons' submission to legal systems; such systems demand that citizens forget the constructed nature of legality and instead view the law as eternal even as new laws are being created. The Lancastrians were notorious for their legalism; see Alison Allan, "Yorkist Propaganda: Pedigree, Prophecy and the 'British History' in the Reign of Edward IV," in *Patronage, Pedigree and Power in Later Medieval England,* ed. Charles Ross (Gloucester: Sutton, 1979), 171–92. The "Remembrance" represents a recognition of the relationship between origins and textuality that the Pastons could not afford to embrace and which Edward's proclamation helped them to try to forget.

[23] On the king's legal prerogatives, see E. W. Ives, *The Common Lawyers of Pre-Reformation England. Thomas Kebell: A Case Study* (Cambridge: Cambridge University Press, 1983), esp. "The Crown and the Profession," 222–46.

within the system were especially important in creating distinctions, and marriage, which could simultaneously signify and enhance social worth, was especially important.[24] When nineteen-year-old John I married eighteen-year-old Margaret, John did not know that his son would win the favor of the king twenty-six years later. But he, and as importantly, his father William, like everyone in Norfolk, knew that no doubts would arise concerning Margaret's pedigree—her family was known to be gentle since "time out of mind"; there was no chance that this alliance would rupture the fragile semblance of gentility that the Pastons had managed to scrape together. Although it brought with it long-term financial and real estate gains, it was, as Richmond observes, "neither an immediate nor a simple financial coup." Rather, the marriage was a social investment, and this was noted by John I's mother, Agnes, in a letter to her husband, William. Agnes describes Margaret's first date with John I in this way: "I sende yow gode tydynggys of the comyng and the brynggyn hoom of the *gentylwomman* that ye wetyn of . . . as for the furste aqweyntaunce be-twhen John Paston and the seyde *gentilwomman,* she made hym *gentil* chere in *gyntyl* wyse" (italics added).[25] As Richmond states, John's marriage to Margaret "strengthened the Pastons' place in Norfolk society. With this alliance they arrived, or thought they had."[26] On a social level, the match was an attempt to gather and produce evidence, much like the documents shown to Edward years later, that would prove and enhance the Pastons' social value.[27]

My point in discussing the Pastons' efforts at securing gentle status is that they can show us the problem with imagining that Margaret Paston's letter-writing was an obvious tool for approaching fam-

[24] Concerning acts of institution, see Pierre Bourdieu, *Language and Symbolic Power,* trans. Gino Raymond and Matthew Adamson (Cambridge: Harvard University Press, 1991), esp. 121–22. Bourdieu asserts that "Acts of social magic as diverse as magic or circumcision, the attribution of titles or degrees, the conferring of knighthoods, the appointment to offices, posts or honours, the attribution of a quality label, or the corroboration by a signature or initials, are all acts which can only succeed if the institution . . . is guaranteed by the whole group or by a recognized institution" (125).

[25] *Paston Letters,* no. 13.

[26] Richmond, *First Phase,* 134.

[27] Edward's proclamation makes explicit reference to the status of marriage partners as proof of the family's gentility: "Also they shewed how that their ancetors had in old time and of late time married with worshipfull gentlemen, and proved by deeds of marriage and by other deeds how their ancetors had indowed their wives" (*Paston Letters,* no. 897).

ily issues. First, although it is true that several letters from John's mother Agnes are still extant, such as the one quoted above, the bulk of the family's correspondence resulted from male family members' legal and financial concerns. Personal remarks such as Agnes's commentary on Margaret in the above-quoted letter, for example, are far less common to the Paston archive than are letters detailing business affairs. Clanchy has demonstrated with remarkable clarity the documentary basis of the growth of literate modes earlier in the Middle Ages; if any use of written language was taken for granted by the Pastons, it was writing's evidentiary capability.[28] Yet, as I hope my comparison of the two documents relating to the family's gentility has shown, even evidentiary, textual strategies were not obvious, natural approaches to social problems because textual evidence alone could not replace notions of inherent gentility. Further, because even the status of such evidence was equivocal—one document might replace another, for example—faith in written language's transformative power had obvious, anxiety-inducing consequences: documentary evidence sometimes depended on social circumstances more than on the language of the text for its interpretation.[29]

Like the meanings associated with written texts, women's initiation into literate culture depended on the pragmatic value of writing for given situations. Unlike their male counterparts who were being trained more and more frequently in literate modes for professional reasons, women interacted with texts in unsystematic and unofficial ways up through the fifteenth century. In fact, on a broad, cultural level, women were often discouraged from becoming fully literate. This is shown, for example, by the now well-known comments the Knight of La Tour Landry addresses to his daughters in the *Book of the Knight of the Tower:* "as for wrytyng, it is no force yf a woman can nought of hit."[30] In the context of the *Book,* he encourages his

[28] See Clanchy, *From Memory to Written Record,* esp. "The Proliferation of Documents," 44–80. Richmond speculates about John's relationship to the law, asking "what else could [John], and everyone else of his class, live by but the law?" (*Fastolf's Will,* 144).

[29] One of the central concerns of Green's *A Crisis of Truth* is the way in which during the "half century following the Black Death . . . an increasing willingness to trust writing generated a corresponding crisis of authority, both intellectual and political" (123). Green builds a case concerning developments in common law during the fourteenth century to demonstrate the ways that a "crisis of authority" shaped late medieval literature.

[30] *The Book of the Knight of the Tower,* trans. William Caxton, ed. Yvonne Offord, EETS, s.s., 2 (London: Oxford University Press, 1971), 122.

daughters to read but sees no reason for them to learn to write for themselves. Other authors, especially religious writers such as the chronicler Knighton, forbade both women's reading and writing, and even secular poets such as Chaucer poke fun at women's lack of education.[31] Although there was no uniform policy concerning women's engagement with written texts, the general, cultural sense at the turn of the fourteenth into the fifteenth century, despite the fact that women did indeed take part in literate culture, was that women should not be fully literate.[32] Medieval women's literacy, like many things, involved a disjunction between general, cultural understandings and actual practice. Because the pragmatic value of writing was so high in the later Middle Ages, women, despite such cultural dismissals, were called on to use written texts in a variety of ways. Not just the ability to read and write but even knowledge of literate ways of transacting business became increasingly valuable as legal, financial, and religious institutions came to rely on written documentation in the fifteenth century, and once this was the case, women were encouraged to assist their families by employing literate strategies.[33]

Margaret Paston's introduction to literate culture through her husband's legal/literate practice demonstrates how the demands of daily life led women in the later Middle Ages to work with written texts even when they possessed few literate skills themselves. Letter-writing, defined as it is as a practical device for communicating over distance, is perhaps the most easily adopted mode of active, textual production. It was also one, at least in the Middle Ages, that required no actual knowledge of the written alphabet on the part of the author. Because even fully literate men such as John Paston often had scribes write down their compositions for them, it remains unclear in many cases just how much personal letters reflect the actual words of the

[31] In the *Nun's Priest's Tale*, Chauntecleer expects of course that Pertelote won't understand his Latin when he translates "In principio, / Mulier est hominis confusio" as "Womman is mannes joye and al his blis" (*The Riverside Chaucer*, ed. Larry D. Benson, 3d ed. [Boston: Houghton Mifflin, 1987], ll. 4353–54). On the Prioress's English ("After the scole of Stratford atte Bowe") French, see the *General Prologue* (*Riverside Chaucer*, l. 125).

[32] See Rita Copeland, "Why Women Can't Read: Medieval Hermeneutics, Statutory Law, and the Lollard Heresy Trials," in *Representing Women: Law, Literature, and Feminism*, ed. Susan Sage Heinzelman and Zipporah Batshaw Wiseman (Durham, N.C.: Duke University Press, 1994), 253–86.

[33] Steven Justice makes a similar point about the literacy of the rebel letter writers in the 1381 Rising (Justice, *Writing and Rebellion: England in 1381* [Berkeley: University of California Press, 1994], 52).

author and how much, if at all, they involved scribal intervention. This ability to compose without wielding a pen vexes present-day scholars who wish to establish the number of persons who could actually write in earlier periods; its effect on people in the Middle Ages, however, was to make composition both practically and imaginatively possible to anyone with access to a scribe. For this reason, among women of Margaret Paston's social standing it was less the inability to maneuver a pen that kept women from writing and more the sense that there was no need for them to do so.[34] This is not to discount the struggles of exceptional women such as Margery Kempe who identified with traditions of revelatory, spiritual writing and who experienced great difficulty in finding suitable scribes; on the contrary, it is only to suggest that women, like men, came to be involved in literate culture only when they believed that such activity was in some way necessary (necessity being broadly and not merely pragmatically defined) to their lives.[35] For Margaret Paston, this necessity arose from her husband's professional situation, and her access to scribes was predicated on his professional practices as well as her social affiliation.

The fact of her married life that led Margaret Paston to write letters was that she and her husband were frequently separated by physical distance. The Paston estates were in Norfolk, but the center of legal affairs in England was London, and John I's business kept him in that city for months at a time while Margaret remained at home to manage household affairs. Letter-writing under these conditions became a means of informing her husband about affairs at home.

Even without the added complication of John's absence, Margaret would have been responsible for running the daily business of domestic life such as keeping the household stocked with food, making sure

[34] By the middle of the fifteenth century, the number of women learning to write appears to have risen dramatically. Evidence from the Paston family is interesting in this regard: Margaret Paston appears not to have been able to write; her daughter was able to sign her name (although rather awkwardly).

[35] V. H. Galbraith makes a similar observation about literate abilities and necessity in relation to the medieval kings of England: "the ruling class remained so long illiterate [because] [i]t could get along without reading or writing, and in general did not hanker after them. . . . These men, however, were not necessarily uneducated, as historians of a hundred years ago tended to think. . . . A modern defence would rather argue that the medieval potentate did not read or write (if indeed he could not) because he had neither the need nor the wish, having others to do these things for him" (Galbraith, *Literacy of the Medieval English Kings,* Proceedings of the British Academy, vol. 21 [London: Humphrey Milord, 1935], 4–5).

that the children—once they had them—had adequate clothing, and supervising the servants. As John reminds her in a letter written in 1465, she should "wekely take a sad communicacion of such thynges as be for to do, or oftenner and nede be" as part of the "god gouernaunce" of the household and toward the "guydyng of other thynges touchyng" her husband's "profit" (no. 72). Margaret's job, in other words, was not merely to manage affairs but to report on that management to her husband. If he had been home, Margaret would have given him an account of these affairs verbally. Unfortunately for John, his letter was written from prison in 1465; Margaret's only means of communicating with him was to write in response.[36]

For John, letters were obvious instruments for performing such tasks, but this assumption was of course no more necessary than the earlier medieval faith, described by Clanchy, in verbal accounts over written ones.[37] Rather, John's literate practice was shaped by his professional and familial situations, and these conditions in turn shaped Margaret's textual interactions. As a lawyer trained in textual methods, John's habit of depending on written texts to prove facts is easily explained by the fifteenth century's ever greater dependence on documentation. His expectation that Margaret should send him letters, however, had more to do with his parents' practice of exchanging letters, such as the one Agnes sent to William describing Margaret's gentility, than with a professional, interpretive model.[38] John seems to have assumed that his wife would, like his mother, send her husband written messages when he needed them, and there are two important conditions underlying such an assumption. The first is that it must have mattered little to John that Margaret was probably unable to write herself: this meant that he was certain she could convey her message through a scribe, that is, that there were plenty of persons

[36] Between 1461 and 1465 John went to prison three times, and all three occasions were related to his attempts to hold disputed property left by Sir John Fastolf. See Richmond, *Fastolf's Will*, esp. 125, on the imprisonments. The direct cause of John's first imprisonment was disobedience of Edward IV's summons—John's brother Clement writes his brother "in great haste" that if he does not appear, Edward has threatened to have him killed. See *Paston Letters*, no. 116.

[37] Clanchy, *From Memory to Written Record*, 260–78, 294–327.

[38] Barratt, in *Women's Writing in Middle English*, states that there is "good reason to believe that Agnes Paston . . . wrote one of her surviving letters, and part of another for her husband, in a clear and expert hand" (239). Margery Paston, as I mentioned earlier, was able to sign her name (although according to Davis her signature was in a hand "halting and uncontrolled," and she "certainly could not have written a whole letter reasonably legibly in a reasonable time") (*Paston Letters* 1:xxxvii).

around who could write for her. The second is that what Margaret had to say was important to her husband. There was in fact no need for John to depend on letters from his wife for information about business affairs because John had numerous servants and associates who sent him such information. Rather, he apparently wanted to know what Margaret herself knew about his affairs. Having grown up in a household in which his mother provided his father with written information about their concerns, John assumed that his own wife would perform the same role.

This illuminates John's expectation that his wife would write letters and even, given the widespread use of scribes to compose letters, accounts for Margaret's easy, imaginative adaptation to her husband's demands. It does not, however, tell us how Margaret knew what to write; in other words, it explains only that she wrote and not how she understood the function of letters or consequently how that understanding and its generic expectations informed her writing. Although her letters followed the *ars dictaminis* model of epistolary construction—a loose, formal arrangement that included traditional greetings and modes of courteous inquiry that would have been recognized by most readers of letters in the later Middle Ages—what mattered even more in terms of the content of the letters was her sense of what her husband expected from her. Margaret's letter-writing depended on a relationship between her sense of the value of her writing, which developed over time and through the conditions of use, and what we might call the market for her correspondence, that is, the audience (first her husband and later in her life her son John Paston II) for whom the letters were written. As we shall see, her earliest audience, her husband John, valued writing because it could be used as proof; Margaret's earliest letters show us an author who came to depend on the written word to document her conduct.

Margaret's literate practice was based in an ideology that understood women's writing as collaborative and women's identities as publicly constructed. Her first extant letter, speculatively dated by Norman Davis to 1441, is an early example of Margaret's adoption of literate modes as a response to her husband's legal/literate agenda. Specifically, Margaret's letter equates the act of writing with the fulfillment of social obligations. Dictated to an anonymous scribe in Norwich and sent to her husband at Peterhouse, Cambridge, where he was finishing up his studies, the letter is generally unexceptional in its contents—it makes brief mention of an attack by "Flemyns" who were repulsed and drowned, contains a vague allusion to a political affair in Norwich, and refers to a Paston associate.[39] Margaret's letters are filled with information of this sort, elliptical comments about political and social events that may have interested her husband and about which he would have had little knowledge while he was away from home because the dissemination of news depended primarily on informal modes of transmission.[40] But this information is not static, not simply factual. Rather, the letter offers its news explicitly as a response to a text that she had received from her husband, that is, it presents news as an entity much like an object of exchange. Referring back to John's last letter, Margaret writes, "I thanke yow hertely for my lettyr, for I hadde non of yow syn I spake wyth yow last" (no. 124). It is unclear when they had last seen one another, and because there are only a few letters from the first two years of her marriage, it seems likely that she did not at this point compose letters frequently, but she nevertheless understood letters as similar to gifts, that is, as items exchanged between two people that demanded some kind of appropriate response.[41]

Modern readers are used to "owing" someone a letter, but it was a new experience for fifteenth-century laypersons. One might owe money, or allegiance, or respect, but to feel obliged to offer a written text in return for another written text was far less common in the late Middle Ages, given among other things the relative scarcity of writing materials (in a letter written on a sheet of paper with a large chunk cut off, Margaret mentions that "paper is deynty").[42] Further,

[39] The content of the letter is obscure. Samuel Davey, " 'The Paston Letters,' with Special Reference to the Social Life of the Fourteenth and Fifteenth Centuries," in *Chaucer Memorial Lectures, 1900,* ed. Percy W. Ames (London: Asher and Co., 1900), cites Margaret's letter concerning this attack by 1,100 Flemings and piracy: "Not only at this time were there land thieves, but water thieves as well. The English Channel was infested with pirates and robbers; for men took to piracy at sea, as they did to poaching on land. . . . In Chaucer's time, the Merchant, in 'The Canterbury Tales,' wished the sea were guarded 'betwixteen Middlebury and Orwell' for the safety of his goods" (74).

[40] On the dissemination of news, see C. A. J. Armstrong, "Some Examples of the Distribution and Speed of News in England at the Time of the Wars of the Roses," in *England, France, and Burgundy in the Fifteenth Century* (London: Hambledon, 1983), 97–122.

[41] Physically, the letters may have looked a little like small gifts. H. S. Bennett describes them thus: "the letters were folded into small oblong packets, about 3 or 4 inches long, and 2 or 3 inches wide, and fastened by a thread, or a thin strip of paper through the folded thicknesses. Then the ends of the threads or paper were sealed, and the address added" (*Pastons and Their England,* 127).

[42] *Paston Letters,* no. 142. Davis cites this letter in the introduction in his account of the physical state of the letters, see *Paston Letters* 1:xxxiii–xxxv. Bennett ex-

quantitative measures are not the only ones applied in such exchanges. Rather, like any reciprocal arrangement, the exchange of letters demanded that the letter sent in return approximate the value of that which had been sent, and Margaret's first letter suggests an uneasiness about the quality of her reply. Not only is the hand of this first letter "crude and unpractised," according to Davis, but the text of the letter itself seems to have been broken off as if the scribe or compositor had become tired of writing.[43] The vague, fragmented quality of the news items contained in the letter is matched by phrasing in the closing lines that suggests both inexperience in composition and uncertainty about the content of the letter. Implying that she has not quite finished her task but nevertheless needs to draw the letter to its conclusion, Margaret writes, "No more I wryte to yow atte this tyme, but the Holy Trenyté hawe yow in kepyng."[44] Treating the letter's contents in quantitative terms and the time of writing as a finite but iterable moment, Margaret's concluding sentence suggests that her letter is in some way incomplete. Implicit in this remark is the sense that what has been written is not adequate, and for this reason she promises more letters in the future: if her reader does not feel satisfied with this particular epistle, he can look forward to receiving additional (potentially more gratifying) letters later. Although all exchanges, as sociologists such as Marcel Mauss have argued, depend on an "obligation to *reciprocate*," letter-writing is an "extension" of this system because it involves both symbolic and communicative reciprocation.[45]

To report successfully on household management, Margaret needed to know what to include in her letters. She needed in other words to imagine what would interest her audience at a given moment and to present that information effectively. It may seem that

---

plains that the quality, as well as quantity, of paper available in the fifteenth century varied greatly: "Some of [the writing paper upon which the Pastons wrote their letters] is of a fine texture, with a fairly smooth surface, while some sheets are coarse and thick. The paper is tough and strong for the most part, and is all handmade" and imported from France or northern Italy (*Pastons and Their England,* 125–27).

43 *Paston Letters,* no. 124. Davis makes no suggestion that this could be Margaret's own writing—it is a (perhaps remote) possibility given the amateur nature of the hand.

44 Ibid., no. 124. It should be noted, however, that other writers including John I also use this kind of closing. See, for example, John's last letter to Margaret, which closes with this rhyme: "Nomore to yow at this tyme, but God hym saue that mad this ryme" (no. 77).

45 See Marcel Mauss, *The Gift,* trans. W. D. Halls (1950; reprint, New York: W. W. Norton, 1990), 18.

this arrangement made her letters wholly dependent on the transmission of factual information because John wanted news from home, but as historicist critics have shown, there is no simple dispersing of facts through writing.[46] Rather, written accounts always involve a selection of details that is necessarily interpretive, and Margaret *read* both John and her experiences at home as she produced her written texts. A good example of this is Margaret's well-known letter from 1441 in which she alludes to her pregnancy. Although the fact of her condition was already known to her husband, she nevertheless writes a letter that announces and then interprets her situation for him. The letter appears at first glance to be a quick note instructing John to send supplies home from London. As Margaret explains, she has "no govne to werre this wyntyr" except one that she is "wery to wer" (no. 125), and therefore she asks her husband to purchase some fabric from which to make a new dress. But more than simply requesting goods, much as she might have done orally, Margaret wrote a letter that identified her request with her exemplary performance as John's wife.

She did this by linking her written letter first with her request for a belt and then with a ring she had given her husband. Mentioning to John that his father had promised her a new belt and then made a "skevsacion" for having broken the promise, she begs her husband for one, not because she is tired of her old belts but because she "hadd neuer more nede ther-of" since she has grown "so fetys." That she has become "fetys," that is, "shapely," is of course a little joke for her husband and the first reference to her pregnancy in the letter. Alluding ironically to the word's traditional use to describe a fine lady's body, Margaret lets her husband know that her own body has taken on an entirely different kind of shape.[47] But that there is more to this punning than playfulness becomes clear at the letter's close, where she asks that John wear a ring she had given him bearing the image of Saint Margaret, who was traditionally associated with childbirth, as a "rememravnse."[48] Wittily, she suggests that the large belt to circle

[46] On the relationship between texts and history, see, for example, Strohm, *Hochon's Arrow,* esp. 3–9; and Justice, *Writing and Rebellion,* esp. 255–61.

[47] For literary uses of "fetys," see, for example, Chaucer's translation of the *Romance of the Rose:* "Fetys she was, and smal to se" (*Riverside Chaucer,* l. 1017); and *William of Palerne: An Alliterative Romance,* ed. G. H. V. Bunt (Groningen: Bouma's Boekhuis, 1985): "He hath oft herde sayd of youre semly dougter, how fair, how fetis sche is" (l. 1446).

[48] Keith Thomas notes that "Pregnant women could use holy relics—girdles, skirts, and coats—kept for the purpose by many religious houses, and they were

her swollen stomach and the ring for John's finger are linked: according to Margaret, John has left her "sweche a rememravnse" that she thinks of him "bothe day and nyth" when she would like to sleep (no. 125). In this way the letter itself becomes, like the ring, like her body, a remembrance for her husband that has explicitly extrinsic meaning.

What these signs all meant was that an heir to the Paston estates was about to be born, and the importance of this event and its relationship to Margaret's own person were marked in her letters. Childbearing was understood as a woman's most important contribution to domesticity in the early years of her marriage; Margaret's pregnancy demonstrated her successful compliance with social norms.[49] John Paston's interest in his first son's birth was perhaps more intense even than the usual high hopes that a first child's arrival elicited because the birth offered immediate financial advantages to his father: according to the terms of the indenture drawn up between John and the feofees (trustees) of Margaret's grandfather's estate, John's access to financial benefits from certain Mautby properties was contingent upon the birth of a male heir.[50] More generally, of course, John II's nativity ensured the continuation of the Paston line, and his birth was greatly desired by both his paternal and maternal relations.[51]

All of this would have been true with or without Margaret's letter, and I am certainly not claiming otherwise. I am suggesting rather

---

urged by midwives to call upon St. Margaret or the Virgin Mary to reduce the pangs of labour" (*Religion and the Decline of Magic* [New York: Charles Scribner's Sons, 1971], 28).

[49] On late medieval marriage and sexual relations, see, for example, P. J. P. Goldberg, *Women in England c. 1275–1525* (Manchester: Manchester University Press, 1995), 9–19; Keith Dockray, "Why Did Fifteenth-Century English Gentry Marry?" in *Gentry and Lesser Nobility in Late Medieval Europe,* ed. Michael Jones (Gloucester: Sutton, 1986), 61–80. On kinship and family relations more generally, see David Cressy, "Kinship and Kin Interaction in Early Modern England," *Past and Present* 113 (1986): 38–69. Cressy emphasizes both the significance of "nuclear" family relations and kinship relations "beyond the household," which he defines as "contextual and informal" (67) but nevertheless extremely important. See Zvi Razi, "The Myth of the Immutable English Family," *Past and Present* 140 (1993): 3–44, for a discussion of the changes that took place in the familial organization in English villages between 1200 and 1700, which he sees as directly related to land markets and mobility.

[50] Richmond, *First Phase,* 121.

[51] Simon Payling states, "it needs to be emphasized that the marriage of a daughter represented an opportunity just as did that of a male heir" ("The Politics of Family: Late Medieval Marriage Contracts," in *The McFarlane Legacy: Studies in Late Medieval Politics and Society,* ed. R. H. Britnell and A. J. Pollard [Stroud: Sutton, 1995], 23).

that she wrote the letter as an aspect of literate practice in which written texts functioned as documents that testified to the validity of social interpretations of physical facts. In this case, the social fact was the significance of her pregnancy for her husband's prestige. Margaret was concerned with her family's welfare, and in her letters to John she conveyed information pertinent to the Pastons' social and financial standing. This was also true in letters written by other women from the period, such as Margery Cely's 1484 letter to her husband George or Jane Stonor's 1472 letter to her daughter.[52] Yet the familial context for medieval women's social interactions has often been ignored by critics concerned with establishing the historical significance of women's participation in literary culture. For example, Wendy Harding, one of the few literary scholars to approach Margaret's letters, suggests that "in relying on antiphrasis, euphemism, and allusion, Margaret ensures that her pregnancy remains unwritten . . . [her] maternity remains outside the order of history and writing."[53] But it seems to me that just the opposite is true: Margaret's letter conveys information about her pregnancy precisely because it was a subject that was important to her and her husband's economic and social interests; letter-writing offered the best means of presenting the important aspects of the pregnancy. Margaret is not, as Harding claims, making an effort "to keep the maternal body out of circulation" but rather emphasizing what matters to her and her husband: in asking him to wear his St. Margaret ring, which functioned as a public announcement that the wearer's wife was pregnant, Margaret's letter documents the social importance of her condition by pointing outward toward the outside world's recognition.[54] This does not mean that these concerns were separate from some "private" expression of emotion. Rather, Margaret's emotional investment in the pregnancy was inseparable from what the birth of an heir would mean for her and her husband, and the letters were written as documents attesting

[52] Margery Cely's letter to George, written in 1484, is primarily concerned with her desire to hear from her husband and her longing for him to come home, but she is also careful to note that he should be "of good cher" because all of his "goodys are in sanfte at home" (*Cely Letters*, no. 222). Jane Stonor's letter concerns her daughter's position in Queen Elizabeth Woodville's household. Jane's daughter seemed to think that the queen no longer wanted her in the household; Jane assures her if that is the case, she may come home but that she needs "writyng fro the quene with her awn hand" to this effect (*Stonor Letters*, no. 120).

[53] Wendy Harding, "Medieval Women's Unwritten Discourse on Motherhood," *Women's Studies* 21 (1992): 199, 201.

[54] Harding, "Medieval Women's Unwritten Discourse," 201.

to her commitment to her family's welfare. Prestige-based arrangements depend on validation from external sources, and Margaret's letter, emphasizing the impossibility of concealing her condition, acknowledges this. Like expensive clothing or lavish homes, pregnancy is a sign whose significance is recognizable to neutral observers, and writing about that observation enhanced Margaret's worth in her husband's eyes.[55]

Although Margaret's letter expresses intense awareness of the importance of her pregnancy for her husband personally, it also offers public approval of her status. The letter is not after all an announcement of her pregnancy, of which John already knew. Rather, it draws attention to a specific, observer's view of her situation. Halfway through the letter, she mentions that her mother-in-law (Agnes Paston) had "dyskevwyrd" her (discovered her, that is, disclosed her state) to John of Dam, one of the Pastons' associates; Margaret wrote that John of Dam, upon hearing of the pregnancy, said that he "was not gladder of no thyng that he hard thys towlmonth than he was ther-of" (no. 125). The older woman's revelation of this detail to someone outside of the family is telling in its ability to convey the familial hopes surrounding the birth of Margaret's first child, and John of Dam's congratulations make it clear that this anticipation extended beyond the immediate family to those affiliated more broadly with the Pastons' financial and social aims. As Margaret records this public response to her pregnancy for her husband, she goes on to emphasize the pellucidity of her bodily state and its social meaning. Shifting her focus in the letter from an enclosed, intimate, and perhaps primarily female world in which pregnancy might be seen as a personal matter, Margaret states that she can no longer "leve be [her] crafte" and that she is "dysscevwyrd of alle men that se" her. In this way the letter functions as a witness to her social importance, a document that shows her husband the manner in which she reinforces his success visibly and publicly. Taking what might seem a personal matter and writing about its public ramifications, she composes a letter that becomes a testament on her own behalf. As such, the letter was not written from a "protected base of autonomy and power in

[55] On legitimation and self-recognition, see Bourdieu, *Language and Symbolic Power,* 117–26. Bourdieu concludes, "The act of institution is thus an act of communication, but of a particular kind: it *signifies* to someone what his identity is, but in a way that both expresses it to him and imposes it on him by expressing it in front of everyone (*kategorein,* meaning originally, to accuse publicly) and thus informing him in an authoritative manner of what he is and what he must be" (121).

which the individual self can act alone," as Sarah Stanbury suggests that medieval women's letters were, but, rather, out of the sense that writing about her pregnancy, because it was a public concern, was an important way to demonstrate her "mastery" over cultural norms.[56] Margaret's authority was based not in her ability to act individually, apart from her husband, but rather to work in concert with him. Her letters record her success in this regard.

Far from expressing independence, either personal or social, Margaret's letters are determinedly focused on her relationship to the public sphere and its ability to shape her family's future. Nor was this focus idiosyncratic. Rather, medieval women's letters were "collaborations" in which the author implicitly and explicitly adapted her writing to the immediate and very public conditions of its production.[57] We can see this if we look at the most widely anthologized of the Paston letters, the so-called Valentine letter. This letter was written by Margery Brews (not Margaret Paston) before her marriage to John Paston III, Margaret's son and John II's brother. The 1477 letter, addressed to "my ryght welbelouyd Voluntyn John Paston," includes what might be considered one of the earliest love lyrics by an Englishwoman. The letter seems to support the idea that women's letters were written from a "private sphere" and that they were concerned with the expression of intimate emotions. Margery declares her undying affection for John in verse form:

> For ther wottys no creature what peyn that I endure,
> And for to be deede I dare it not dyscure . . .
> And yf ye commande me to kepe me true where-euer I go
> Iwyse I will do all my myght yowe to love and neuer no mo.
> And yf my freendys say that I do amys, thei schal not me let so
> for to do,

[56] Sarah Stanbury, "Women's Letters and Private Space in Chaucer," *Exemplaria* 6 (1994): 271–85, 280. Norman Davis, "The Litera Troili and English," *Review of English Studies* 16 (1965): 233–44, describes the relationship between the formal model of the *ars dictaminis* tradition and the letters in *Troilus and Criseyde.*

[57] Joan Ferrante uses the term "collaboration" to describe the relationship between female readers or patrons and male writers: "[A] woman might set [a] man a program of activity, forcing him to work out his ideas or do more research, or she might frame the structure of his work by the questions she asked; and he responded because the subject interested him and he trusted her to be a sympathetic audience to ideas as he developed them or to be a purveyor of his ideas to a wider public" (Ferrante, *To the Glory of Her Sex: Women's Roles in the Composition of Medieval Texts* [Bloomington: Indiana University Press, 1997], 39).

Myn herte me byddys euer more to love yowe
Truly ouer all erthely thing.
And yf thei be neuer so wroth, I tryst it schall be bettur in tyme
commyng.

(no. 415)

The letter appeals to modern readers' romantic sympathies, allowing us to imagine an age of courtly love that could include women as suitors. In fact, Margery's assumption of the lover's role seems to differ little from that of the aquiline suitors in Chaucer's *Parliament of Fowls,* and the imagined scene of her letter's reception seems to be as private as Criseyde imagines her bed closet to be in *Troilus.*[58] The poetry might be clumsy, but the use of rhyme indicates that the passage was conceived of as a literary tour de force.[59] More importantly, it appears to be an intimate expression of the poet's own feelings, and this idea is supported by the close to the letter. After her bit of passionate, literary bravado, Margery requests earnestly that "this bill be not seyn of non erthely creature safe only your-selfe."

Although it might appear from the contents of this letter that it must have been penned by the author herself, the letter's composition was not a secret "act of freedom in which spatial seclusion generates a metaphoric liberation," despite its seemingly private expression of love.[60] Rather, the process of writing this letter was clearly a cooperative, if not public, enterprise in terms of both the physical act of its composition and the sentiments expressed. First, although it is rarely noted, Margery did not produce the letter on her own. Rather, it was dictated to one of her father's clerks, Thomas Kela.[61] It is im-

[58] Margery's letter, like *The Parliament of Fowls,* is a Valentine's Day greeting; it is addressed to her "well-beloved Valentine." See Martin Camargo, *The Middle English Verse Love Epistle* (Tübingen: Max Niemeyer, 1991), 4.

[59] This is especially interesting because it announces itself as an explicitly textual event, that is, one in which she could redefine herself as an active agent through reference to well-known textual models, the love lyric and the letter. *Ars dictaminis* guidebooks outlined specific elements that various kinds of letters should include, such as a superscription, commendation, salutation, inquiries concerning health, and so on. For more on the *ars dictaminis,* see Davis, "Litera Troili and English Letters"; Giles Constable, *Letters and Letter-Collections* (Turnhout: Brepols, 1976); James J. Murphy, *Rhetoric in the Middle Ages* (Berkeley: University of California Press, 1974); and Martin Camargo, *Ars dictaminis, Ars dictandi* (Turnhout: Brepols, 1991).

[60] Stanbury, "Women's Letters and Private Space in Chaucer," 281.

[61] Davis observes that it is Kela's hand in the identification of no. 415 (*Paston Letters* 1:662).

possible to tell whether Kela merely transcribed Margery's dictation, if he collaborated with her, or if he composed the text at Margery's (possibly vague) request that he write something convincing to John. This uncertainty concerning the author–scribe relationship is, of course, always present when we are faced with texts that have been dictated by one person to another. Despite recent claims for the remarkable, strategic control that writers who dictated their texts (such as Margery Kempe) exerted over their writing, there is no failsafe method for proving which words were those of the author and which those of the scribe.[62] Nevertheless, what we do know is that the seeming absence of the scribe in this letter is so overwhelming that thc only traces of his presence appear to be in his handwriting. Although Margery Brews, the ostensible author, does not seem to modify her emotional register in the presence of Kela, and the tone of the poem, if not the actual facts of its composition, seems to suggest a direct, unmediated relationship between the lovers, it is important to note that Margery was neither spatially nor metaphorically liberated from her reliance on Kela.

Indeed, despite the striking "you and me against the world" rhetoric in Margery's poem, we know that even on a familial, emotional level, Margery was not acting against the world's advice. Rather, both her mother Dame Elizabeth and Kela encouraged her affair with John III and did everything in their power to make the match come off. Like her daughter, Dame Elizabeth took to letter-writing to take care of the situation: in a letter to John III, she remarks that John had made Margery "suche advokett for yowe that I may neuer hafe rest nyght ner day for callyng and cryeng vppon to brynge the saide mater to effecte" (no. 791). It should come as no surprise perhaps that Dame Elizabeth, like her daughter, depended on scribal assistance to pen her missives; her letter to John was dictated to no scribe other than Thomas Kela. And Kela himself seems to have become entangled in the mother–daughter strategy to persuade John to work out the details of the marriage. He assures John of Margery's affection—"I

[62] See, for example, Lynn Staley, *Margery Kempe's Dissenting Fictions* (University Park, Pa.: Pennsylvania State University Press, 1994). Although Staley remarks that scribes of course "left their marks upon the manuscripts they copied" (11), she casts this aside in favor of strong, authorial control in which the scribe is introduced as a writerly trope, especially in texts written by women. Staley argues that representations of scribal intervention in texts were "ways of employing the scribe as a figure of speech" that related to "the author's perception of the act of producing literature" (37).

knowe be the comynicacion that I hafe hade wyth" Margery that she "owyth yowe hyr good herte and love"—and suggests that John take up the economics of the match with Margery's father again if he really wants to win Margery's hand. He is also careful to present Dame Elizabeth's support for the match. Kela, for example, quotes Dame Elizabeth's sage advice about the matter: "it was a febill oke that was kut down at the first stroke," encouraging John not to give up on Margery because of a few financial setbacks (no. 792). The proverb appears in the letter Dame Elizabeth sent to John (written by Kela) just before Valentine's Day 1477.[63] Although we lack such clear evidence of particular, scribal influence and collaboration for Margaret Paston's literate practice as is available in relation to her daughter-in-law, it is apparent that she, no less than Margery, composed her letters in the immediate presence of various scribes, in the imaginative space occupied by the recipient of her letters, and, more abstractly, in view of the social field that determined what a wife was supposed to do.

Margaret Paston's position as John's wife in the 1440s was of course very different from Margery's role as female suitor in the Valentine letter. For this reason, although Margaret's letters were also influenced by the conditions that made letter-writing a shared rather than private experience, her response to the public nature of literate interactions differed from Margery's. Margery, on the one hand, attempted to obscure the collaborative nature of her letter-writing when she distinguished her emotional investment in the relationship with John from the financial difficulties that inflected their marriage negotiations. Margaret, on the other hand, having assumed the authority associated with her position as a gentleman's wife, increasingly relied on various types of textualized, external validation in her literate practice. Although she depended on scribal assistance for the

[63] *Paston Letters*, no. 791. In this same letter, Dame Elizabeth invites John to visit for Valentine's Day weekend. She writes that on this holiday "euery brydde chesyth hym a make." Given Dame Elizabeth's association between Valentine's Day and birds choosing mates, it is tempting to suggest (although impossible to prove) that she and Margery were reading Chaucer's *Parliament of Fowls*. We do know that John Paston II, John III's brother, owned a copy; see Bennett, *Pastons and Their England*, 113. On the combination of birds and Valentine's Day, see Nick Havely's introduction to the *Parliament*, in *Chaucer's Dream Poetry*, ed. Nick Havely and Helen Phillips (London: Longman, 1997), 226. If anyone was standing in the way of the match it was John and her own father; in the prose portion of the Valentine letter and another letter sent a few days later, Margery "lets" John "pleynly vndyrstond" that her father "wyll no more money parte wyth-all in that behalfe but an c li. and 1 marke, whech is ryght far fro the acomplyshment of yowr desyre" (no. 416).

composition of her letters, Margaret appears, unlike Margery, to have felt no need to disavow that assistance or to dismiss the importance of public opinion. On the contrary, Margaret's letters explicitly articulate public support for her actions. Rather than gaining assistance through letters of support from her scribe, Margaret herself recorded public opinion in her own letters and used it to enhance her social authority.

One of Margaret's strategies for textualizing public affirmation was to document public approval, such as John of Dam's response to her pregnancy; yet another was to differentiate in writing between such approval of herself and disapproval directed at others. She does this in a letter written in 1444, a few years after the birth of her oldest son. Conforming to an *ars dictaminis* model of composition, the letter respectfully addresses her husband and gives an account of affairs at home. It goes on to present the domestic details that Margaret has successfully managed and then, after a description of the errands completed for John, a request for new caps for the children (the ones John had sent were too small and too cheap), and greetings to her mother- and father-in-law, it states that "Heydonis wyffe had chyld on Sent Petyr Day." As the story unfolds, it becomes evident that Margaret has heard rumors about the fathering of the child, and the letter goes on to describe their neighbor Heydon's enraged response to the birth:

> I herde seyne that herre husbond wille nowt of here, nerre of here chyld that she had last nowdyre. I herd seyn that he seyd yf sche come in hesse precence to make here exkewce that he xuld kyt of here nose [cut off her nose] to makyn here to be know wat sche is, and yf here chyld come in hesse jpresence he seyd he wyld kyllen. He wolle nowt be intretit to haue here ayen in no wysse, os I herde seyn. (no. 127)

It may seem obvious that this letter contrasts Margaret's own domestic obedience with Heydon's wife's infidelity, but what is less apparent is Margaret's refusal to comment on the situation.[64] Employing a

[64] The same punishment is referred to in *The Revelations of St. Birgitta. Edited from the Fifteenth-Century Ms. in the Garrett Collection in the Library of Princeton University,* ed. William Patterson Cumming, EETS, o.s., 178 (London: Oxford University Press, 1929); a woman punished in the afterlife for her sensuality declares, "My nose is cutte of; for as amongest you it is wonte to be do vn-to thaym that tres-

common linguistic marker of gossip, "I herd seyn," repeatedly, Margaret reveals details about her neighbors without commenting on them. The diction is precise, legalistic, and shows a commitment to veracity. Assuming an objective, vaguely journalistic tone, Margaret writes about Heydon's threats but never offers her letter's recipient any information about her own view of the situation. If the reader senses that Margaret disapproved of Heydon's response, it is only because she or he finds the information conveyed appalling: Margaret never expresses an opinion about Heydon's wife's conduct or Heydon's rage, and it is impossible from the content of the letter to derive Margaret's understanding of the affair.

When writing is a pragmatic substitute for oral communication, it often fails to exploit the explicitly linguistic advantages of written texts and instead imitates spoken habits. Margaret, a writer who chose her medium only out of necessity, refrained in many of her letters written during the 1440's from differentiating between what is effective in spoken communication, which depends extensively on extra-linguistic cues, and the elaborations and specificities needed to make written texts accessible. In particular, she relied heavily on John's knowledge to supplement the words she dictated. The anecdote from the letter related above is a case in point: although the cuckold John Heydon was not just a neighbor but also one of the Pastons' greatest enemies, we get no sense of this from Margaret's letter.[65] Our insight into letters depends at least in part on piecing together such information even when it does not appear in the text itself. If we fail to do so, we misunderstand items such as Margaret's reference to Heydon in her next letter as one of John's "gode frendys" (no. 128). Because letters are written for a specific and generally very small audience, such omissions rarely pose problems for the intended recipient. John of course, unlike later readers, did not need his wife to

passen in suche a caas to thaire more schame, right so is the mark of my shame sett vpon me endelesly" (111).

[65] Helen Castor, "The Duchy of Lancaster and the Rule of East Anglia, 1399–1440: A Prologue to the Paston Letters," in *Crown, Government and People in the Fifteenth Century,* ed. Rowena E. Archer (Stroud: Sutton, 1995), draws attention to the political situation in which Heydon and another of the Pastons' enemies, Tuddenham, were participants. She suggests that the traditional view, espoused by Richmond, that the earl of Suffolk (and his associates including Heydon and Tuddenham) engaged in a " 'systematic and illegal exploitation' " of the earl's powers in East Anglia, is inaccurate. Rather, according to Castor, "the version of events portrayed in the [Paston] letters may have been profoundly coloured by the fact that it was the Pastons, and not the earl of Suffolk, whose claim to a prominent place in local landed society was of recent origin and uncertain provenance" (78).

offer commentary on his enemies in her writing. Instead, what Margaret supplied were written texts that referred to the outside world in language that differed little from conversation, and this "oral" quality of Margaret's letters has often been remarked upon.[66] Although the tendency to imitate speech found in Margaret's letters is quite different from the formal and explicitly textual impulse that organized documentary labor such as her husband's, Margaret's letters were much like John's documents in their reliance on quantities of evidence. Proof of her able handling of situations at home lay not in the form of her letters but in their contents, which needed no interpretation because, at least as far as Margaret was concerned, her anecdotes spoke for themselves.

What kind of understanding of written texts does a person have who writes by speaking and reads by listening? The answer must have at least as much to do with her sense of the ways that spoken language allows one to shape, reflect, and resist lived experience as it does with writing. Spoken language that functions pragmatically, which, for example, opens doors or make meals appear, is one obvious category of such oral communication.[67] Another, which was of paramount importance in late medieval England, was gossip. With its ability to transform social life, gossip was viewed, from moral and religious angles, as a particularly virulent social problem. Numerous late medieval guides to conduct, such as the *Book of the Knight of the Tower, The Good Wife Taught Her Daughter,* and *The Thews of Good Women* as well as more explicitly religious writing like *Jacob's Well,* denounced idle talk, especially among women. According to *The Good Wife,* for instance, once women started gossiping, rumors flew, and "a sclaundre" that is raised is "euell for to styll."[68] This sentiment accords with Patricia Meyer Spack's analysis of the "anxiety aroused by gossip," which she suggests "derives partly from its incalculable scope. One can never know quite where it goes, whom it reaches, how it changes in transmission, how and by whom it is understood."[69] In fact, although many of these writers worry about what

[66] Janel Mueller, *The Native Tongue and the Word* (Chicago: University of Chicago Press, 1984), 90–91, for example.

[67] See John R. Searle, *Speech Acts: An Essay in the Philosophy of Language* (Cambridge: Cambridge University Press, 1969); J. L. Austin, *How to Do Things with Words* (Cambridge: Harvard University Press, 1975).

[68] Tauno F. Mustanoja, "The Goodwife Taught Her Daughter," *Annales Academiae Scientiarum Fennicae,* ser. B, vol. 61 (1948): 204.

[69] Patricia Meyer Spacks, *Gossip* (New York: Knopf, 1985), 6. On gossip in the Middle Ages, see Chris Wickham, "Gossip and Resistance among the Medieval Peas-

the biblical book of James identifies as the tongue's ability to "defile" the body, they were ultimately as concerned, as the comments of both Spacks and the medieval author of *The Good Wife* indicate, with the ease with which one could transmit information orally.

If speaking gossip was easy, was it hard to write it? And did Margaret have a sense that the words she spoke when dictating were fluid and ephemeral speech, or did she think of the letters as fixing her words so that they were, as the Gawain-poet says of his poem, "stad and stoken / In stori stif and stronge, / With lel [true] letteres loken"?[70] It is worth noting in this context that the word "dictate" was not used until the early seventeenth century to distinguish between words one wrote oneself and those that one spoke for another to write down. Margaret and her friends and associates generally used the verb "writen" to describe their actions even when they had clearly employed a scribe, suggesting that despite the oral component of their writing, they distinguished between speaking and dictating. I bring this up because it helps us imagine what Margaret might have understood as the way that a written text functions and not in order to claim that there exists a distinct point of transition from orality to literacy in her life.[71] If writing was writing even when it was dictated, then it follows that the experience of composing a written text through an amanuensis, even when it included explicitly oral features, was shaped by the writer's sense of the difference between

---

antry," *Past and Present* 16 (1998): 3–24; Susan E. Phillips, "Gossip's Work: The Problems and Pleasures of Not-So-Idle Talk in Late Medieval England" (Ph.D. diss., Harvard University, 1999); I. M. W. Harvey, "Was There Popular Politics in Fifteenth-Century England," in *The McFarlane Legacy: Studies in Late Medieval Politics and Society,* ed. R. H. Britnell and A. J. Pollard (Stroud: Sutton, 1995), 155–74, mentions the seriousness of rumor (161). See also Colin Richmond, "Hand and Mouth: Information Gathering and Use in England in the Late Middle Ages," *Journal of Historical Sociology* 1 (1988): 233–52; and Charles Ross, "Rumour, Propaganda, and Popular Opinion during the Wars of the Roses," in *Patronage, Crown, and Provinces in Later Medieval England,* ed. R. A. Griffiths (Gloucester: Sutton, 1981), 15–32.

[70] *Sir Gawain and the Green Knight,* in *The Poems of the Pearl Manuscript,* ed. Malcolm Andrew and Ronald Waldron (Exeter: University of Exeter Press, 1996), ll. 33–35.

[71] Brian Stock states that "There is in fact no clear point of transition from a nonliterate to a literate society," in *The Implications of Literacy: Written Language and Models of Interpretation in the Eleventh and Twelfth Centuries* (Princeton: Princeton University Press, 1983), 9. Studies of the relationship between orality and literacy are numerous; for an excellent, recent overview, see Matthew Innes, "Memory, Orality and Literacy in an Early Medieval Society," *Past and Present* 158 (1998): 3–36.

speaking and writing. In Margaret's case, she came to value the relative permanency of written texts over spoken ones, translating the unofficial, oral nature of her information into the verifiable evidence that her husband's textual understanding demanded. The advantage of writing over speaking was that writing allowed her to document speech as evidence.

One of Margaret's primary techniques for turning idle talk into evidence was the use of direct quotation, a tactic that she also used to demonstrate public approval of her behavior in some of her early letters. Later in her marriage, Margaret came to employ direct quotation less in simple praise of her life and more to validate her understanding of situations. For example, in a 1449 letter written to John, she told him that Lord Moleyns had threatened to kidnap her if John refused to give up his claims to the estate at Gresham, where Margaret had been staying. To ground her report in reality rather than in exaggerated fear for her own safety, she notes that Lord Moleyns's men said that her kidnapping "xuld ben but a lytell hert-brennyng" to John (no. 132). In repeating the phrase, she distances herself from the affair, demonstrating that the kidnapping is a distinct possibility and not just an idle worry of her own. In a further attempt to establish her estimate of the dangers of the situation, she tells John that she "durst no lengere abyd there" because her "wele-willerys" had advised her that Lord Moleyn's men had said, "jf they myt gete me they xuld stele me and kepe me wyth-jnne the kastell, and than they seyd they wold that ye xuld feche me owth" (no. 132). Her careful explanation of her behavior through direct quotation of sources and her avoidance of public knowledge of her flight—"ther was non in the place wist that I xul com thens save the godewyf"—contribute to the letter's use of reported information to create order. If her behavior looked "feminine" and hasty, her letter demonstrates that it is, in fact, "masculine" and judicious.

The contrast between Margaret's use of direct quotation in the letter about Heydon's wife and in the kidnapping letter underscores a gradual shift in her textualization of evidence from unadorned transcription to evaluation. Expressing increased confidence in writing's ability to stabilize chaotic situations, Margaret wrote a letter in 1448 concerning an attack on James Gloys, the Paston's chaplain, by a neighbor, Wymondham, that conflates objectivity and interpretive accuracy. After offering an account of the confrontation between Gloys and the neighbor Wymondham that closely resembles the "do you bite your thumb at me, sir" episode between Shakespeare's Capulet and Montague servants, Margaret warns John to keep Gloys in London because "in god feyth he js sore hatyd both of Wymdam and sum of hys men, and of other that Wymdam tellyth to hys tale as hym lyst, for there as Wymdam tellyth hys tale he makyth hem belevyn that Jamys ys gylty and he no thing gylty" (no. 129). Unlike the earlier account of domestic scandal, that is, the story of Heydon's wife's infidelity, this letter draws an interpretive point about the domestic uproar: John must protect Gloys's person, and more importantly, he must look after Gloys's reputation, which is being destroyed by Wymondham's spurious gossip. This direct call for action was no doubt in large part due to Gloys's central position in the Paston household, and especially to his important advisory relationship to Margaret, but this makes it no less important to understanding Margaret's literate practice. In defending Gloys, Margaret contrasts her own objective, textual practices with the false tale-telling of her enemies. Distancing her written narrative from Wymondham's spoken distortions, she denounces his gossip and recategorizes her own written account as news. Wymondham, she asserts, goes about multiplying Gloys's enemies by raising slander against him, whereas she writes what *actually* happened.

Implicit in this criticism of Wymondham is a growing sense of written texts as distinctly different both in kind and in function from spoken communications. In highlighting the contrast between her written version of events and Wymondham's gossiping, Margaret's letter focuses attention on the relative stability and permanence of written texts over spoken accounts. By recategorizing her narrative as official news, Margaret both rejected the illegitimate reproduction of false tale-telling and embraced letter-writing as an explicitly textual event.[72] Writing over the course of a decade to John about affairs at home, she came to see her letters not merely as substitutes for face-to-face communication with her husband but as an entirely different means of communication. My point is not that Margaret finally became truly literate—this would argue for some sort of category of optimal literate understanding, and no such category exists in isolation from social context—but I am arguing rather that her sense of what letters were changed over time and through the conditions of both her writing and her involvement with written documents. By the mid-

[72] Bourdieu would see this as an attempt to textualize a type of "creative speech," a term which he uses to describe legal discourse, because it "bring[s] . . . into existence that which it utters" (*Language and Symbolic Power,* 42).

1440s, Margaret was not merely reporting on domestic life but also performing tasks for John like tracking down receipts, collecting rents, and searching through titles. Even if she could not read and was performing these duties through the assistance of one of the family's servants, Margaret experienced written texts as documents that recorded and fixed information for pragmatic purposes. She was not trained as a lawyer, but like her husband, she came to depend heavily on the documentary power of writing.

Margaret's preference for written texts over spoken evidence was based on her growing appreciation of the power of documents as physical objects that offered proof. In the kidnapping letter, for example, Margaret reports to John that she had a discussion with Moleyns's man, Barrow, about the family's claims to Gresham. In this discussion with Barrow, she asserted the superiority of the Pastons' evidence of their claim to the property over Moleyns's evidence:

> Barow told me that ther ware no better evydens in Inglond than the Lord Moleynys hathe of the maner of Gressam. I told hym I sopposyd that thei were seche evydens as Willyam Hasard seyd that yowr were: he seyd the sellys of hem were not yett kold. I seyd I sopposyd his Lordys evydens were seche. I seyd I wost wele, as for yowr evydens, there myt no man haue non better than ye haue, and I seyd the selys of hem were to hundred yere elder than he is. (no. 132)

Using citation to give her account of the exchange authority, Margaret illustrates the competition between the oral and the written in determining who has power over social arrangements. Although her own literate authority depended on an accurate representation of orality, her affinity for legal models of textuality resulted in the dismissal of Hasard's verbal assertions: Barrows "seyd" one thing, Margaret another, but the truth lay in the "evydens," that is, in the titles to the property. She describes an oral argument, but it is physical, documentary evidence whose age proves its validity that Margaret and Barrow competed over, and not merely spoken assertions. In fact, one must hope that the documentary evidence was more convincing than Margaret appears to have been in her argument with Barrow, in which her comeback to his claim that the seals on their documents were "not yet cold," that is, that they were newly made, was along the lines of "no, *yours.*" The point is not of course about her debating skills but rather about her faith in physical documentation: although it could be forged like the supposedly "hot" seals of the Pastons' documents or the "false forgyd euydens" that she needed to see William Worcester about in 1460, Margaret put a great deal of confidence in such proof.[73] Like her husband the lawyer, she understood that despite the efforts of forgers, documents could be less easily changed or distorted than could conversation. Documents, unlike speech, could be produced on subsequent occasions.

The discussion of evidence in the letter concerning Barrow is focused on documentation as a topical concern, but Margaret's attraction to writing on the basis of its ability to record the truth extended to her own literate strategies. In October 1465, John I's manor at Hellesdon, an acquisition from the Fastolf estate, was sacked by the duke of Suffolk's men on the grounds that the duke's forebears had owned the manor; there seems to have been no virtue and little belief in his claim at the time of the assault. Nevertheless, on its strength, Suffolk brought five hundred men, according to Margaret's estimate, to Norwich and attacked the manor. At the time, John I was in London, imprisoned in the Fleet, possibly as the result of a conspiracy spearheaded by the duke, on vague charges concerning "bondage." A week after the attack, Margaret composed a letter in which she reported on conditions at Hellesdon. With her husband in jail, Margaret was left to manage his affairs at home, and if there were anything like a "natural" topic for these letters, it would certainly include descriptions from an embattled wife to her imprisoned husband of the destruction of their home. But perhaps surprisingly, Margaret's letter begins not with a verbal snapshot of the devastation but with a seemingly mundane description of some lost receipts. She writes,

> I cannot send [John Rus, one of John Paston's agents,] the byllys that ye send to me. I toke them to Arblastere for to haue delyuerd to Ser Thomas, and he told me that he had lefte the seyd byllys at hom wyth Blaunch hys doghtere. I send to here for hem, and they cannot be founde. (no. 196)

The tone, one nearly of annoyance, shows a touching commitment to maintaining at least the façade of the everyday. Despite the fact that she goes on to describe the destruction left by the duke's men as so

[73] *Paston Letters,* no. 157. Clanchy describes the relationship in the earlier Middle Ages between symbolic objects and documentation (*From Memory to Written Record,* 253–66). See also Green, *A Crisis of Truth,* 251–82.

"fowle and orubelly [horrible]" that no one can believe it "but yf they sey [see] it" themselves, her opening remark suggests that it's business as usual outside of the Fleet.

Here, as in the letter to her son with which this chapter began, Margaret acknowledges her husband's interest in keeping his "writings" in order. But her investment in written records goes well beyond concern with their safekeeping: the letter itself functions as a kind of document for her husband, a written statement of the damages done by Suffolk's men. Dictating with unflinching precision the explicit infractions committed, she reckons the extent of destruction to their property:

> The Duck ys men rensackyd the church and bare a-way all the gode that was lefte there, both of ourys and of the tenauntys, and lefte not so moch but that they stode vppon the hey awtere and ransackyd the jmages and toke a-way such as thay myght fynd, and put a-way the parson owte of the church tyll thay had don, and ransackyd euery mans hous in the town v or vj tymys . . . and as for lede, bras, pewtere, yren, dorys, gatys, and othere stuffe of the hous, men of Coshay and Cavston haue it, and that thay myght not cary thay haue hewen it a-sondere in the most dysspytuose wyse. (no. 196)

Although the letter is marked by a sense of anger and loss, it is loss that is precisely expressed in terms of the physical damages done. Its tendency to itemize (lead, brass, pewter, iron, etc.) shows a carefulness and attention to the details of the crime that are linked to Margaret's belief in justice through legal institutions: several lines after the passage quoted above she writes, "Yf it myght be I wold som men of wyrshop myght be send from the Kyng to see how it ys both there and at the logge, ore than any snowys com, that thay may make report of the troth; ellys it shall not mo be seyn so playnly as it may now."[74] Memory, according to Margaret, is not enough: if right is to prevail, the truth needs to be seen and then documented.[75]

[74] The tendency to list points, indicated by the word "item" is a typical feature of John I's letters; Margaret adopts this custom in some of her later letters.

[75] She knew of what she spoke; a few years later, in 1469, Paston associates responsible for organizing Edward IV's journey through the region to the shrine at Walshingham arranged for the king and his entourage to follow a route past Hellesdon in order that he might see the damage done. The king said, according to John II's uncle, "He supposyd as well that it myght falle downe by the self as be plukyd downe, for if

Margaret's insistence that "men of wyrshop" make a report about the conditions at Hellesdon reminds us that she did not have a superstitious faith in the validity of written texts but rather understood that like any report, valid written texts depended on legitimate sources of information. A reader needed to have confidence in the writer's ability to record situations accurately, and he or she also needed to know that the writer was presenting information objectively. However, although Margaret may have felt such concerns about other people's writing, she herself seemed to have no such doubts about her own interpretive understanding. In fact, her confidence in her ability to read situations accurately and then fix their meaning in her letters goes so far that she claims her knowledge of events is more convincing than the evidence she is confronted with. For example, several months after the Gloys/Wymondham confrontation and shortly before the threatened kidnapping, she recounts a meeting with some of Lord Moleyns's men in a letter to John. Before the meeting, Moleyns's men had made threats against a number of public officials and against some Paston associates. The Paston employees to whom Margaret spoke denied having been threatened, but Margaret claims to know better. She asserts, "*I know veryly the contrary,* for of his own [Moleyn's] felaschep lay in awayt sondery dayis and nytys abowt Gunneldys, Purrys, and Bekkys plasys" (no. 131; italics added). Basing her knowledge on the authority of her own experience, Margaret assumed that when verbal evidence such as that of the Paston employees contradicted her understanding of the situation, that that evidence was inaccurate.[76] She simply rejected such claims, dismissing them and constructing her own allegedly superior documents. By weighing the evidence and rejecting claims inconsistent with her own interpretations, Margaret employed a legal model

it had be plukyd down he seyd that we myght haue put in ouyr byllys of it when hys jugys sat on the oyeer determyner in Norwyche" (*Paston Letters,* no. 333).

[76] The association between women and experience versus that between men and authority is famously important to Chaucer's Wife of Bath: "Experience, though noon auctoritee / Were in this world, is right ynogh for me" (*Riverside Chaucer,* ll. 1–2). Karma Lochrie notes that this distinction goes back to the "Aristotelian distinction between masculine and feminine realms of experience as corresponding to the spiritual and the physical" and goes on to observe that "Scholars are more likely to focus on the autobiographical (and hence mundane) when the subject is a woman. It is as though the Wife of Bath had set women's agenda for times to come by asserting her experience (and autobiography) over authority" (Lochrie, *Margery Kempe and the Translations of the Flesh* [Philadelphia: University of Pennsylvania Press, 1991], 226).

in her literate practice that is similar to the one her husband used to settle claims over land ownership and inheritance.

Despite clear signs that Margaret's later letters show a writer who understood herself as authorized to interpret the world, Margaret's interpretive authority continued to be constituted through her husband's authority even in the later years of her marriage, and her commitment to documentary evidence was inseparable from his. This was both because John was the primary recipient of her letters and because he shared her faith in the power of documents. Had John I retained control of the family's economic fortunes until Margaret's death, she would perhaps have continued to have written her interpretively self-possessed letters without having to confront her "mistaken" sense of textual authority. John appears to have been quite happy with her documentary capabilities—if anything, he wished she would write more frequently.[77] Yet Margaret's authority depended ultimately on her husband's willingness to accept the validity of her interpretations, and her understanding of literate authority was ultimately based on a misrecognition of her social position: she came to believe that her literate authority was a natural property of her person rather than "an effect of the network of social relations."[78] Once John I died and her son, John II, became the head of the family, the shifting of family authority forced Margaret to confront the male-dominated basis of her literate practice.

Although Margaret had come to experience her letter-writing as a strategic practice that allowed her to shape her audience's understanding of events, she did not see the use of written documentation as exclusive to her person. Rather, by the 1460s she was promoting letter-writing as a method that members of her family, especially her eldest son, John II, might adopt when they needed to prove their worth. This may appear to be another case of a mother behaving as mothers always do. After all, the most immediate cause for John II's need to prove his worth was his father's disapproval, and one of the most explicit passages concerning the effectiveness of writing comes from a letter Margaret wrote during a heated argument between John I and his son. John I, furious that his son was spending more money

[77] In *Paston Letters*, no. 76, for example, "I merveyll that I here no tidyngges from yow hough ye haue do at the assises"; John wanted more news.

[78] This sort of "misrecognition" is described in Slavoj Žižek, *The Sublime Object of Ideology* (London: Verso, 1989), 25.

than John I thought he should, had in 1463 forbidden his son the house until John II could remember "what tyme he hath lost and hough he hath leved in jdelnes," that is, when "he can do more thanne loke foorth and make a fase and a countenauns" (no. 72). Margaret, although sympathetic to her husband's anger over their son's improvident habits, sought to reconcile the two and advised her son to send a letter seeking his father's forgiveness. She wrote to John II,

> It was told me ye sent hym [John I] a letter to London. What the entent therof was I wot not, but thowge he toke it lyghtly I wold ye shuld not spare to write to hym ageyn as lowly as ye cane, besecheying hym to be your good fader, and send hym such tydyngs as bethe in the contré ther ye bethe in, and that ye be ware of your expence bettyr and ye have be before thys tyme. (no. 175)

What, one might ask, could be a more universal pattern of family behavior? A father who resents his son's failure to measure up, a mother who wishes her husband and son would get along, and a son who seems intent on going his own way—these are all the elements of a narrative of family relations that may seem timeless.

Yet to focus on what seems familiar to us about the Pastons keeps us from seeing what distinguishes this medieval family's strategies from those of families from other times, and at least one of these differences lies in the method that Margaret proposed for resolving the conflict. Although it may appear that her solution was simply that her son send his father a letter begging his pardon, what matters about this tactic is that it is underwritten by the sense that resolution depends on common understandings of written text's evidentiary capabilities. In other words, if it seems obvious that Margaret's advice would be for her son to reestablish the harmonious structure of filial relations, it was not natural that the means suggested for doing so would be through particular kinds of textualized stances. Her general advice to her disgraced son was to submit to his father's authority and to fulfill his father's expectations, but the method that she recommended for doing so was explicitly textual and "legal": John should imagine himself as a humble supplicant and offer written evidence of his virtuous behavior. So important to the family's identity was legality and its evidentiary demands that Margaret in effect suggests that her son write a letter of petition to his father that would establish the grounds for his "suit" and thus regain his father's good graces. Taking the hierarchical order of her husband and son's relationship as self-evident, Margaret proposed that John II present his written documents to his father, who would judiciously evaluate his son's humility and obedience in terms of the written evidence that John II's letter would provide.

Although John II followed his mother's advice to write to his father, he did not "reinsert" himself into his father's legal and textual interpretive community as his mother had recommended. Rather, John II's subsequent letters to his father show a writer who at least in part rejected the model of writing that his parents promoted. John II had, on the one hand, mastered the humble commendation. For example, he began a letter to John I written in 1464 in the following manner:

> Ryght worschypful syre, jn most lowly wyse I comaund me to yowre good faderhod, besechyng yow of yowre blyssyng. Mut it plese yowre faderhod to remembre and concydre the peyn and heuynesse that it hathe ben to me syn yowre departyng owt of thys contré, here abydyng tyl the tyme it please yow to schewe me grace, and tyl the tyme that by reporte my demenyng be to yowre plesyng. (no. 234)

Assuming the textualized position of submission that Margaret recommended, after the *ars dictaminis* tradition, John appears to have taken her letter-writing advice to heart. The opening form of address in its observance of convention seems to present a young man entering willingly into his father's interpretive field and ready to play the social/familial game according to the rules established by his father. Nor is this simply evidence of submission. Rather, in demonstrating linguistic competence, using the "legitimate language" of a son to a father, John's letter, like those of his mother, exhibits both an awareness of the social stakes involved in the exchange and his own sense of competence as a writer.[79] But while complying with standards that required persons in dependent economic and legal roles to address their superiors with humility, John II appears, on the other hand, to have rejected the necessity of transcribing episodes of obedience for approval. Replacing his mother's emphasis on past action with vague gestures toward the future, John II refrained from detailing his compliance with his father's standards for conduct. Instead of proving

[79] See Bourdieu, *Language and Symbolic Power*, 58.

that he had indeed sought to obey his father's commands, John offers his father promises concerning his behavior in the future: "Wherfor I besech yow of yowre faderly pyté to tendre the more thys symple wryghtyng, as I schal owt of dowght *her-afftere doo* that schal please yow to the vttermest of my powere and labore" (no. 234; italics added). Although it might be argued that this remark is simply an attempt not to antagonize his father further, the passage is telling in its appeal to his father's pity rather than his sense of justice. To ask for justice would mean John II felt his actions were in some way defensible; to ask only for fatherly pity meant that any account of his behavior would be sure to displease John I further.

John II appeals to his father's emotions in this letter, but his strategy is nevertheless explicitly textual and no less influenced by a sense of writing's power than was his mother's letter-writing. John did after all send his father a letter, as his mother had advised, and he attempted to use that letter to repair his relationship with his father. But although Margaret and John II both wrote letters to John that depended on the forms of obeisance, they differed in terms of their use of evidence. Margaret tried to teach John II to use his letters to offer written evidence of his good behavior so that his father might evaluate his actions and approve of them; John II, on the contrary, offered counterevidence to his father's judgments. Rather than composing letters that recorded his obedience through examples of proper filial conduct, John II made written excuses for his lassitude, remarking, for example, that his father should

> concydre that I may not nere haue noo mene to seke to yow as I awght to do sauyng vndre thys forme, whych I besech yow be not take to no dysplesure, ner am not of power to do any thynge in thys contré for worschyp or profyht of yow nere ease of yowre tenauntys whych myght and scholde be to yowre pleasing. (no. 234)

Fearing his father's further displeasure, John II asked him to consider the circumstances of the letter's composition: banished, John II asserts his only avenue for reconciliation is his letter. Although Margaret never refers to the limitations of writing, for John II this communication is merely a letter, that is, something that bears little relationship to things that might actually bring his father "worship or profit." As a consequence, John II, instead of "report[ing]" that his "demenyng" was to his father's "plesyng," insisted that his father was mistaken in believing that John II could do anything at all. Yet in refusing to offer the brand of written evidence his mother recommended and his father demanded, John II modified rather than rejected the legal structure that supported his parents' letter-writing. Margaret seems to have worked as her husband's legal aide, finding evidence that supported his claims and presenting it for his approval; John II, on the contrary, sought to make his own oppositional claims, and he set himself up increasingly as his father's (legal) opponent in his letters.

In terms of medieval family relations, the conflict between John I and John II is interesting because it shows a particular form that competition between male family members may take. But more importantly for my argument, it allows us to see one way that family dynamics and textual understandings were intertwined and mutually redefining in the later Middle Ages. John II did not discount written evidence, obviously, since the letters he received and wrote remain, as do those of his mother and father. He did, however, resist his father's paternal and evidentiary agendas. For John I, this resistance was a source of perpetual annoyance; he and John II fell out frequently during the last years of John I's life. Relatively few "personal" letters remain from John I, but in one of the few, written during his son's early adulthood, John I expresses intense disappointment. Angry that his son was wasting time and money, John I had a good deal to say about his son's lack of character and laziness: he remarked to Margaret that their son "only leuith, and euer hath as man disolut, with-owt any prouicion, ne that he besijth hym nothinge to vnderstand swhech materis as a man of lyuelode must nedis vnderstond."[80] John II's promises of future action in the letter quoted above must have only confirmed his father's certainty about John II's unfitness as a "man of livelihood."

As far as John I's own literate practice was concerned, his son's challenge had little effect on their relationship. John I, as an established lawyer, head of the Paston household and family, and promi-

[80] John's vigorous description of his son's laziness is worth noting. He wrote to Margaret, "as for yowre sone: I lete yow wete I wold he dede wel, but I vnderstand in hym no dispocicion of polecy ne of gouernans as man of the werld owt to do, but only leuith, and euer hath as man disolut, with-owt any prouicion, ne that he besijth hym nothinge to vnderstand swhech materis as a man of lyuelode must nedis vnderstond. Ne I vnderstond nothing of what dispocicion he porposith to be, but only I kan thynk he wold dwell ageyn in yowr hows and myn, and ther ete and drink and slepe" (*Paston Letters*, no. 73).

nent member of Norfolk society would have seen little reason to worry about John II's ambivalent attitude toward writing: it was just another of his son's failures to take life seriously. Margaret's literate practice, however, was greatly affected by John II's ideas about writing, although this only became apparent after John I's death in 1466. Just two letters from Margaret to John II are extant before 1466, the one discussed above in which she urged him to write to his father (and in which she also urged him to write to his grandmother) and another warning him in 1465 that Hellesdon, the Paston estate at which he was staying, was about to be attacked by the duke of Suffolk; both of these letters assume that their recipient will recognize the importance of written texts in the context of the family's economic and social aims. However, after John I's death and John II's assumption of authority as the male head of the family, John II became the primary recipient of Margaret's letters, and this new audience resisted the literate practice that Margaret had developed in relation to her husband throughout her marriage.

In October 1466, Margaret was still writing letters about attending to legal affairs and continued to use her letters as documents that presented evidence, but the conditions under which she composed the letters had changed dramatically in the course of the year. Central to the changes in the family after John I's death were revisions of economic responsibilities, and this affected Margaret's literate practice. When, before her husband's death, she thought of her economic responsibilities, she did so with the full understanding that his interests were hers: simply put, marriage to Margaret had brought her husband her family's Mautby estates, which John I was entitled to hold for life once he and Margaret produced an heir, and her financial concerns were managed by her husband as his own.[81] This state of affairs changed when her son John II assumed control of the family's estates upon his father's death. Not until their mother's death could Margaret's sons enjoy the same financial privileges from the Mautby estates that John I had controlled: John II, in other words, could not touch his mother's profitable holdings to support the Paston "cause" as his father had been able to, and yet as the new head of the family he continued, like his father, to require vast sums to maintain the family's real estate holdings.[82] Margaret, however, gained access to

[81] Richmond, *First Phase,* 133.

[82] And there was one further complication: John II's paternal grandmother Agnes Paston was still alive, and Agnes's husband William Paston had left her property for

the returns from the Mautby estates, which her husband had controlled, but lost her position as spousal partner to the family's head. As a result, once her son took charge of the Paston estates, Margaret became wary of his interest in "her" money.

If we read her letters to John II in light of the change in the family's configuration, it appears that the faith in written evidence which Margaret expresses, and, more broadly, her sense that reality could be fixed through textual transformation, collided with her son's newly achieved status as head of the family—by his investiture as the legal and economic representative of his branch of the Pastons.[83] For example, the subject of the letter quoted at the beginning of this chapter in which Margaret emphasized the importance of retaining written evidence shows how she came to respond in her letters to this economic challenge. Specifically, the letter is concerned with the institutional apparatus for effecting this transfer of family authority, John I's will, and in it Margaret broaches the change in their relationship. Offering advice to her son that is both general in its advocacy of safeguarding evidence and particular in its concern with keeping down the costs involved in the legal transaction, Margaret remarked that in proving the will John should "haue a lettere of mynystracyon to such as ye wyll, and mynestere the godys and take no charge" (no. 198). He should, in other words, obtain a written document, and this suggestion does not differ from advice Margaret would have given him while his father was alive. But although her position concerning documentation remains constant, a note of defensiveness creeps in at the end of the letter that draws attention to the rapidly growing distance between Margaret's stake in the family's legal ensnarements and that of her son.

Writing from Caister Castle, one of John II's newly inherited holdings that, like Hellesdon and Gresham, was coveted by enemies of the Pastons (and that would be besieged by the duke of Norfolk just three years later), Margaret closed her letter by noting that it was in John's interests, not her own, that she remain at the precariously held castle: "Wryten at Castere the moren next aftere Symon and Jude, where as I wold not be at thys tyme *but for youre sake,* so mot I they [prosper]" (no. 198; italics added). The difference between such a remark and her stoic request that her husband

---

life worth £100 a year—more money that "belonged to the family" but which John II could not receive his portion of until Agnes's death.

83 See Bourdieu, *Language and Symbolic Power,* 117–26, for a discussion of the notion of investiture.

send more "crossbows" when Gresham was besieged in 1449 indicates the extent to which her investment in her husband's holdings as opposed to those of her son differed, and it is especially in the Caister letter's pronouns that this difference is apparent.[84] In the first half of the letter, Margaret depends primarily on a series of "I-you" propositions such as "*I* wold *ye* shold" (italics added) to emphasize the distinctness of her and John II's economic interests. The use of this coupling to offer business advice—which is sprinkled throughout the letter but concentrated in its first fifteen lines—advertises Margaret's superior knowledge of legal affairs to her son; she combines a mother's long-suffering patience with an accountant's caution:

> I avyse you that ye in no wyse take no charge therof [of the will] tyll ye know more than ye doo yet, for . . . thay wyll lay the charge vppon you and me for moo thyngys then ys exprest in youre fadere ys wyll, the whych shud be to grete fro you or me to bere. (no. 198)

The message is clear: Margaret does not want John to rush to collect the inheritance because she is worried that it will cost her money. But it isn't the letter's only message. Another construction, "you-us," complicates what appears at first to be a straightforward separation of mother from son via pronominal distinction. Competing with "I-you" in the letter's third paragraph, "you-us" mingles Margaret's preoccupations with her son's: "yf *ye* canne gyte any more there as *ye* be, for els, by my feth, I feere els it will not be well wyth *ous*" (italics added). Left at Caister, Margaret's "you-us" shows an awareness, even if it is begrudging, of her new relationship to her son and his monetary decisions.

John II experienced the ways that institutional authority produced textual authority firsthand, and he could not have accepted his mother's claims for the supreme efficacy of documents, even if their economic agendas had remained synonymous. John II's increasingly divergent conception of the relationship between written documentation and institutional authority reshaped Margaret's literate practice after 1466, but it would be a mistake to focus too much on his or her personality, as John I himself might have done, as an explanation of

[84] Compare *Paston Letters,* nos. 130 (a letter written to her husband when Gresham was being attacked) and 198 (one written to her son concerning Caister).

this shift. Behaviors such as the putting on of "countenances" for particular situations that John I viewed as his son's personal failings, that is, situations he saw as signs of John II's lack of real seriousness and character, were part of the training John II received at court as a gentleman. John II, having lived in Edward IV's household and traveled with his retinue, witnessed the manner in which the Yorkist government made its decisions on the basis of royal favor rather than judicious consideration of evidence and was overwhelmed by the sense that institutional power must be unceasingly courted. John I had of course sent his son to court to establish important connections to aid him in his legal disputes, but the difference between father and son was as much about the difference between legal and courtier ideologies as it was about anything else. John II was knighted in 1463, and there seems to have been no question about his assumption of the title and its significance for the family. Nevertheless, John I had himself declined to be knighted in 1457, suggesting that although he clearly understood the value of court connections, he also saw disadvantages in such arrangements.[85] John II, growing up as part of a social class—and generation—that had little faith in the sense of the written record's impartiality, depended on the favor of influential friends to secure his fortunes. As a result, he had less faith in writing's ability to record the truth than his mother had, and this distrust in turn reshaped his relationship with his mother.[86]

As John's letters reveal his growing lack of trust in the ability of documents to affect social conditions, they resist both the performative and reflective capabilities of the written word that formed the basis of Margaret's literate practice. On August 21, 1469, Caister Castle, the site from which Margaret had written the October 29, 1466, letter to John II, was attacked by the duke of Norfolk's men after a springtime of threats. Although the siege, replete with crossbow shots and cannon fire, was still under way, Margaret wrote her son a letter on September 12 in which she demanded that he ask the lord of Clarence or the archbishop of York to send "writyng" to the duke of Norfolk that would "graunte them that be in the place here lyfes and ther goodes" (no. 204). John II's response, written three days later, repudiated her faith in the supreme power of written documentation. Dismissing his mother's suggestion concerning the letters, he tells her "as

[85] Bennett describes the refusal (*Pastons and Their England*, 13).

[86] Richmond describes John II's "strategic" participation in court culture with great feeling (*Fastolf's Will*, 33, 167).

fore to labore thois letteris and the rescu togedre, they ben ij sondry thyngys (as concerning both obtaining the letters and the rescue [of the estate] those are two separate things)" (no. 243). That is, the letters, according to John, have nothing to do with saving Caister. Rather, John suggests that the means of securing the estate is through the favor of friends. If the Pastons' friends help, "it may goodlely and wele be browt abut," but letters, as his mother proposed, "wolde nat advayle."[87] In fact, in the same letter John II goes on to question the validity of his mother's report. He writes, "Moodre, vppon Saterday last was Dawbeney and Bernay were on lyve and mery, and I suppose ther cam no man owt of the place to yow syn that tyme that cowde haue asserteyneyd to yow of there dethys" (no. 243). John's point is that his mother's information is wrong and her news mere speculation. Going even further in his repudiation of her written tactics, he insists that she is motivated by the desire to manipulate rather than inform him. He writes, "Moodre, I fele by yowre wryghtyng that ye deme in me I scholde not do my deuyre wyth-owt ye wrot to me som hevye tydyngys" (no. 243). Her letters are not, according to her son, the unmediated source of documentary truth that she proclaims them to be but merely a mother's poorly veiled attempt to control her son's behavior.[88]

The conflict between the two was irreconcilable. Predictably, Margaret responded by rebuking him for his "dysworschep": countering his opposition with a restatement of the power of the written word in general and of the veracity of her writing in particular, she insisted that she did not write "fabyls and ymagynacyons" but accurate reports of her son's affairs. Letting him know that she recognized and rejected his dismissal of her written authority, she refused to change her epistolary habits, adamantly stating that she had "wrytyn as yt haue be enformed me, and wulle do" (no. 205). Margaret's final letters refuse to give up the authority invested in her writing. Not surprisingly, the last two letters written to John II reject his challenges to

[87] John's remarks about friends and money are worth quoting: "the grettest deffaut erthly is mony, and som frendys and neyborys to helpe; wherffore I beseche yow to sende me comfort what money ye coude fynde the menys to get ore cheuysche vppon suerté sufficient ere vppon lyfflod to be jnmorgage ere yit solde, and what peple by lyklyod, yowre frendys and myn, kowde make vppon a schort warnyng, and to sende me worde in all the hast as it is nedffull" (*Paston Letters*, no. 243).

[88] Margaret's faith was not only in written documents; see *Paston Letters*, no. 199, in which she tells her son to reassure his allies that "thei may haue summe comfort that thei be no more discoraged, for if we lese our frendes it shall be hard in this troblelous werd to kete them ageyn."

her authority (and to her money). In response to John's inquiry concerning a debt owed, Margaret writes,

> I putte yow in certeyn that I wull neuyr pay hym peny of that duty that ys owyng to hym thow he sue me for yt, not of myn owyn pursse, for I wul not be compellyd to pay yowr dettys ayens my well; and thow I wuld, I may nat. (no. 227)

Margaret, in her letters to John II, did not seek assurance as she had in those to John I. Rather, her letters assert their own authority: "And take this for a full conclusyon in thys matere, for yt xall be noon othyr-wyse for me than I wryte here to yow" (no. 227). Margaret fully recognized the possibility that her son might not act according to her will, but she made it clear that she meant what she had written. Because her understanding of her literate authority was based on a misrecognition concerning her gendered and familial position, she had (mistakenly) come to believe that her literate authority was a natural property of her person. But however distasteful the recognition was, she became at least partially aware of the ways that her former authority as her husband's wife was diminished when her primary social and legal designation was based on her maternal position. Drawing on the military metaphors that so aptly described her situation, Margaret went from referring to herself in her final letter to her husband as the "captenesse" at Hellesdon in 1465 to conceding in 1466 that she could "not wele gide nor rewle sodyour" because "thei set not be a woman as thei shuld set be a man" (nos. 180 and 199, respectively). It is one of the very few acknowledgments that Margaret made of her gendered status, and it is unsurprising that it came after her son assumed control of the Paston estates.[89]

Although to conclude that Margaret (ultimately) recognized her lack of (essential) authority as a writer allows us to see something im-

[89] Sherry Ortner, "Rank and Gender," in *Making Gender: The Politics and Erotics of Culture* (Boston: Beacon Press, 1996), 59–115, is very helpful on the variety of relationships between gender and social rank. Particularly relevant to Margaret Paston's situation is Ortner's treatment of the "logic of hierarchical systems," which she argues "tends toward (even if it never reaches) gender equality" (107). Ortner notes that despite this tendency, "Within the 'strata,' " that is, the social gradations, "men are formally superior to women, have near-exclusive access to positions of social leadership, and dominate decision making on issues of importance to the unit as a whole" (107).

portant about her literate practice—that it depended on her familial relationships and that changes in those relationships necessarily affected her writing—such a conclusion is also deceptive. It is misleading in much the same way that the Gieses' insistence on the naturalness of Margaret's literate exchanges is misleading: it makes Margaret's letter-writing into one identifiable thing that we can account for fully—ultimately and essentially. This conclusion may make it seem that there is a very clear answer to the question "On what was Margaret Paston's literate practice based?" But the point of this chapter is, I hope, more complicated than this. As convinced as I am that Margaret began writing in relation to her familial situation, I am just as convinced that what matters about her literate practice for us, and perhaps for her, is that it shows us how writing could (rather than had to) change things. John II's experiences at court showed him the limits of written texts; but then he had advantages that his mother lacked, and in any case, even his rejection of her firm faith in the written word was transitory, momentary, and overstated. The narrative of Margaret's discovery of the limits of her power, as much as that describing her discovery of her authority as a writer, is just a way of making sense of the fact that an apparently "semi-literate" woman dictated many letters over the course of her lifetime without noticing the strangeness of her situation. But perhaps it would be better to call them situations, because my point is, finally, that we cannot, no more than Margaret did, choose one point, the ultimate point, to define her literate practice. By looking at the course of her life as a letter writer, however, we might be able to start to see how those changes came about through and in response to her writing.

CHAPTER 2

Margaret Beaufort's Literate Practice:
Service and Self-Inscription

By the early sixteenth century, facility with written texts was so common among certain social groups that observers remarked on the quality as well as the extent of women's literate abilities. For example, in Bishop John Fisher's "mornyng remembraunce," a sermon delivered in 1509, after the death of Margaret Beaufort, King Henry VII's mother, Fisher notes approvingly that Margaret had been "right studyous" in her reading of vernacular religious writings, even those that were "ryght derke," and that she had translated devotional works from French into English.[1] As historians such as Rowena Archer have observed, aristocratic women in the later Middle Ages often received some informal training in literate modes in order to manage their future husbands' estates.[2] Further, as Michael Clanchy explains, noblewomen's familial responsibilities extended to introducing their children to religious writing through books of hours, which were widely owned in late medieval England.[3] Given wide-

[1] *The Works of John Fisher,* ed. J. E. B. Mayor, EETS, e.s., 27 (London: Trübner, 1876), 292.

[2] Rowena Archer, " 'How ladies . . . who live on their manors ought to manage their households and estates': Women as Landholders and Administrators in the Later Middle Ages," in *Woman Is a Worthy Wight: Women in English Society c. 1200–1500,* ed. P. J. P. Goldberg (Stroud: Sutton, 1992), 149–81.

[3] Michael T. Clanchy, *From Memory to Written Record, England 1066–1307,* 2d ed. (Oxford: Blackwell, 1993), 112. Christopher de Hamel notes the popularity of books of hours among high-class medieval housewives (*A History of Illuminated Manuscripts* [London: Phaidon, 1994], 168). On education at home, see Sharon D. Michalove, "The Education of Aristocratic Women in Fifteenth-Century England,"

spread understandings of the written word's centrality to the functioning of aristocratic households, we might expect that in his sermon Fisher would reaffirm the fundamental traditionality of Margaret's reading and writing, and in fact he does this to a great extent. Her reading and writing, like everything that "she spake or dyde," "meruayllously became her," according to her confessor. The eulogy is primarily concerned with the manner in which Margaret kept "hospytalyte," and not with strictly intellectual pursuits; Fisher praises her reading as part of her devout "active life," the path of devotion recommended to noblewomen, and exactly appropriate to her situation and person.[4] Yet although most of Fisher's sermon is taken up with a comparison between Margaret Beaufort and the biblical Martha, who represented household care and community involvement in the later Middle Ages, Fisher's comments suggest that Margaret's sense of writing's significance encompassed more than its usefulness for managing business affairs and its expediency for transmitting basic, religious principles. Rather, Margaret was "studious"—a Middle English word that retained its original Latin meaning, "zealous" or "diligent"—an enthusiastic reader who tackled difficult texts. Her zest for learning was such, according to Fisher, that she had told him "[f]ul often" she regretted "that in her youthe she had not gyuen her to the vnderstondynge of latin."

Fisher's praise for Margaret Beaufort's scholarship appears, however, to be elliptical, that is, dependent on the omission of a qualifying phrase: Margaret was "right studious" for a woman, and she had learned as much as a woman might—no man without strong Latin skills would have been considered "right studious" at the close of the fifteenth century. There would of course have been no reason for Fisher, educated at Cambridge and later that university's chancellor, to have thought of Margaret's involvement with the written word in any other way. Yet, if we think about this expression of regret from Margaret's point of view, it is difficult not to take her complaint as a serious expression of scholarly disappointment. The past subjunctive tense of her expression of regret—"if only I had studied Latin in my youth"—suggests a desire on her part for a different past, that is, for a life history that might have allowed her to be a right studious scholar and not simply a right studious woman who had, according to Fisher,

---

in *Estrangement, Enterprise, and Education in Fifteenth-Century England,* ed. Sharon D. Michalove and A. Compton Reeves (Stroud: Sutton, 1998), 117–39.

[4] *Works of John Fisher,* 292.

just "a lytell perceyuynge" of Latin, enough that she could read the rubrics in her ordinal and follow mass.[5]

This chapter is about the ways in which Margaret Beaufort responded to an aristocratic/familial dynamic in which women acquired literate skills as part of a broadly patriarchal system. That system promoted women's involvement with the written word as service—directed toward the household's maintenance and in support of family, faith, and community—and was bolstered by single-sex divisions in aristocratic households. Although encouraging the development of literate practices that furthered the family's economic and social aims, such divisions simultaneously offered women relative autonomy over their use of written texts. I argue that Margaret Beaufort's literate practice depended first on the "traditional" sense that writing was pragmatically useful for managing familial and household affairs, and second on an understanding of the written word as allowing for self-inscription, that is, imaginative insertion of one's own person and interests into the words of the text. Margaret's education appears to have been informal, but she nevertheless learned from the women in her family, in particular from her mother, Margaret Beauchamp, and her mother-in-law, Anne Stafford, what it was that women might do with written texts. After her son's accession, Margaret turned increasingly to the print trade to "serve" a reading public, an extension of her familial role that was fostered by her involvement in London's monastic/lay devotional community.

In their important biography of Margaret Beaufort, Michael Jones and Malcolm Underwood refer to evidence from the Westminster Abbey Muniments that sheds some light on the literate concerns of Margaret Beaufort's mother, Margaret Beauchamp. According to Jones and Underwood, the documents show that after renegotiating payments on a ransom owed her by "the captive count of Angoulême," the elder Margaret "order[ed] a comprehensive survey of the evidences and meticulously check[ed] the financial calculation" herself.[6] The ransom appears later in this chapter in relation to the

[5] On women and Latin education in the thirteenth century, see Clanchy, *From Memory to Written Record*, 198–200.

[6] Michael Jones and Malcolm Underwood, *The King's Mother: Lady Margaret Beaufort, Countess of Richmond and Derby* (Cambridge: Cambridge University Press, 1992), 138. They refer to Westminster Abbey Muniments, 12181, fol. 52. There is an extensive body of literature on Margaret Beaufort. Jones and Underwood's book is the best and most recent; I refer to it as the primary source of information about

younger Margaret's mixing together of finances and family, but for the moment I ignore this aspect and focus attention on Margaret Beauchamp's sense of writing's usefulness and, more importantly, on her ability to exploit its utilitarian value. If a scholar such as Richard Green were to consider the description of the elder Margaret's fact-checking, he might use it as evidence that the transition in England from "trouthe" to "truth," from trust placed in a person's integrity to trust in documents' external facticity, was complete.[7] There is no doubt that Margaret Beauchamp considered the documents more reliable than the count's person and, furthermore, more reliable perhaps than the persons of her servants who were to calculate the payments. But what is most telling about her review of the accounts, at least in terms of my argument, is that Margaret felt she could and should take care of the evaluation of the evidence herself. She thought of herself, in other words, as both able to work with financial receipts and legal documents and as responsible for doing so. This may seem unremarkable, but it is important because it demonstrates the level of autonomy that noblewomen had over such transactions: Margaret Beauchamp depended neither on the authority of a male family member nor on that of a trusted servant to oversee the renegotiation of the ransom payments.[8]

Margaret Beauchamp was clearly a "strong-willed and determined landowner," as Jones and Underwood point out, but her confidence in her literate self-sufficiency was not simply characteristic of her personality (*KM* 138). Rather, she, like many women of her social class, had come to rely on written texts and her ability to work with them

Margaret's life and cite it in the text as *KM* from this point on except where otherwise noted. Other important biographies include Charles Henry Cooper, *Memoir of Margaret Countess of Richmond and Derby* (Cambridge: Bell, 1874); Caroline Halsted, *Life of Margaret Beaufort, Countess of Richmond and Derby* (London: London, Smith, Elder, 1839); and E. M. G. Routh, *A Memoir of Lady Margaret Beaufort, Countess of Richmond and Derby, Mother of Henry VII* (London: Oxford University Press, 1924). On Margaret's books, see W. E. Axon, "The Lady Margaret as a Lover of Literature," *The Library,* n.s., 8 (1907): 34–41; and Susan Powell, "Lady Margaret Beaufort and Her Books," *The Library,* 6th ser., 20 (1998): 197–240. Both essays are indispensable.

7 Richard Firth Green, *A Crisis of Truth: Literature and Law in Ricardian England* (Philadelphia: University of Pennsylvania Press, 1999).

8 See Archer, "Women as Landholders," 157. Archer refers to a set of thirteenth-century rules in the possession of the widowed countess of Lincoln that suggests the landholder take matters into her own hand: " 'If plaintiffs come to you about injuries done them or demands made on them, you yourself ought to study your rolls concerning that manor' " (157).

because aristocratic family life encouraged women to do so out of necessity. Aristocratic women's financial and economic responsibilities were generally greater than those of gentle women such as Margaret Paston, and for this reason their training in literate modes was superior, but the familial dynamic was quite similar: absent husbands depended on wives to manage their affairs. This was especially true for Margaret Beauchamp, whose second and third husbands, John Beaufort, Margaret Beaufort's father, and Lionel Lord Welles, were both involved in military campaigns that kept them out of the country for years at a time. Soon after his marriage to Margaret's mother, John Beaufort left for France, where he had earlier spent seventeen years in captivity, "the longest period endured by an English aristocrat during the entire Hundred Years War" (*KM* 28). The expedition was financially disastrous and resulted in John's expulsion from the English court; it is often assumed that his death, which came very shortly after his return to England in 1444, was a suicide (*KM* 35). Similarly, although Margaret Beauchamp's third husband, Lord Welles, lived at Maxey with his wife and all of her children for several years, he left for Calais in the early 1450s to fight alongside his stepdaughter's uncle, Edmund Beaufort. Finally, while Margaret Beauchamp was "between" husbands, she lived as a widow—for five years after her first husband, Oliver St. John, died, for three years after John Beaufort died, and for more than twenty years after Lord Welles's death in 1461—and during those periods she was fully responsible for her financial affairs.

It would be very interesting to know how aristocratic girls acquired the knowledge and skills that allowed them to manage large estates, but such evidence is almost completely lacking.[9] They were not, like their brothers, sent off "at age six to be given separate masculine training, the 'initiation rite' which would integrate them into male/Latinate culture," as Ralph Hanna has observed.[10] It seems

[9] For a few examples in which writers were concerned explicitly with education, see Clanchy, *From Memory to Written Record,* 197–200 (on Walter of Bibbesworth); Susan Groag Bell, "Medieval Women Book Owners: Arbiters of Lay Piety and Ambassadors of Culture," *Signs* 7 (1982): 754–58 (on Vincent of Beauvais and Francesco di Barberino); and June Hall McCash, "The Cultural Patronage of Medieval Women: An Overview," in *The Cultural Patronage of Medieval Women,* ed. June Hall McCash (Athens: University of Georgia Press, 1996), 22–23.

[10] Ralph Hanna, "Some Norfolk Women and Their Books, ca. 1390–1440," in *Cultural Patronage of Medieval Women,* 289. Hanna cites Walter J. Ong, "Latin Language Study as a Renaissance Puberty Rite," *Studies in Philology* 56 (1959): 103–24; and Nicholas Orme, *From Childhood to Chivalry: The Education of the English*

likely that girls' training was left to female relatives, especially mothers and older sisters. Margaret Beaufort would have had five half-siblings, three of them sisters, when she was born in 1443.[11] Presumably Margaret learned from her half-sisters and her mother: as Rowena Archer suggests, "the expertise acquired through parental example" is "the least traceable but probably the most important single preparation" that aristocratic girls had in learning to manage their own and their husbands' estates.[12] All of Margaret Beauchamp's daughters would have seen her supervising the household and taking charge of financial affairs in the absence of her husbands. The girls learned at the very least that as noblewomen, they too would marry and shoulder similar responsibilities.

Although it is unclear how girls acquired the specific practical skills used to keep accounts, we know that at least some aristocratic mothers taught their children basic language skills by giving them religious books, especially books of hours. The advice, summed up by Christine de Pizan in *Le trésor de la cité des dames,* that mothers should provide their daughters with devotional books when they were at the age to begin reading, was widespread in the later Middle Ages.[13] Susan Groag Bell points out, for example, that Isabeau of Bavaria gave her six-year-old daughter a book of hours and in 1403 gave another daughter an "alphabet psalter."[14] Books of hours were especially popular as teaching aids because they were relatively simple and because they were designed to be used repeatedly throughout the day. Also called primers, the books of hours introduced the new reader to basic

---

Kings and Aristocracy, 1066–1530 (New York: Methuen, 1984), 16–28, as the sources for this information. See also Elizabeth J. Gardner, "The English Nobility and Monastic Education, c. 1100–1500," in *The Cloister and the World: Essays in Medieval History in Honour of Barbara Harvey,* ed. John Blair and Brian Golding (Oxford: Clarendon Press, 1996), 80–94.

[11] The youngest of the St. John sisters, Elizabeth, married in 1450, five years before Margaret herself was married, and, having grown up together, Elizabeth may have been particularly close to young Margaret; Jones and Underwood note the special care that Margaret took of the St. John family when her son became king (*King's Mother,* 112–14).

[12] Archer, "Women as Landholders," 152.

[13] Cited in Bell, "Medieval Women Book Owners," 756. Christine de Pizan had written in the same book that women should be ready to manage their husbands' estates as "wise and sound administrators" when their husbands had to "travel and go off to the wars"; she saw the study of devotional books as the way to acquire literate skills that would allow women to manage their affairs. Archer translates the passage ("Women as Landholders," 151).

[14] Bell, "Medieval Women Book Owners," 756–57.

religious texts, including the Hours of the Virgin, the Penitential Psalms, the Litany of Saints, and the Office of the Dead.[15] A calendar of saints' days and feasts usually came at the front of the book, another basic, devotional aid, and this was often followed by excerpts from the Gospels. As introductory books, the primers taught readers to associate religious devotion with the written word and everyday life. If textual skills (reading, counting, writing) were learned in this way, then aristocratic girls were likely to conceive of literate ability as both spiritually and practically necessary.

Although we do not know how girls learned to read, it is possible to reconstruct how they might have been taught to think about reading by looking at the books their mothers' owned. We might consider the Beaufort Hours, a primer owned by Margaret Beauchamp and inherited by her daughter upon the elder Margaret's death, in this way. If we imagine the Beaufort Hours as a young girl's introduction to written texts, the first thing we might notice is the way that this primer actively encouraged even the reader who could not make sense of the Latin devotions to use books. The Beaufort Hours (London BL Royal 2 A Xviii) is composed of two sections. The first half, which has traditionally been thought to have belonged to John Beaufort, is made up of Latin prayers and is accompanied by thirteen full-page miniatures; among these is an Annunciation considered a masterpiece of fifteenth-century illumination.[16] The second half is a book of hours that Margaret Beauchamp commissioned from a workshop in London, probably in the early 1440s.[17] Although less esteemed by art historians, it also includes miniatures that a beginning reader might enjoy as she learned to work with books.

As well as attracting readers who were not yet able to read, the illuminations depicted scenes in which women were reading and

15 See Anne F. Sutton and Livia Visser-Fuchs, *The Hours of Richard III* (Stroud: Sutton, 1996), 3.

16 See Kathleen Scott, *Later Gothic Manuscripts, 1390–1490. A Survey of Manuscripts Illuminated in the British Isles* (London: Harvey Miller, 1996), 2:127–32. This part of the Hours is now believed to have been part of a psalter that is in Rennes, Bibliothèque Municipale 22 (Scott, *Later Gothic Manuscripts,* 2:128).

17 Jones and Underwood discuss this idea, based on Nicholas Rogers's unpublished thesis (*King's Mother,* 32). It had previously been thought that Margaret Beauchamp commissioned the book of hours from a London artist named William Abell; Scott does not think this is the case (*Later Gothic Manuscripts,* 2:130). On Abell, see Jonathan Alexander, "William Abell 'Lymnour' and Fifteenth-Century English Illumination," in *Kunsthistorische Forschungen: Otto Pächt zu seinem 70. Geburtstag,* ed. A. Rosenauer and G. Weber (Salzburg: Residenz Verlag, 1972), 166–72.

taught young girls to think of themselves as readers. First, some of the illuminations feature saints reading, including Saint Anne, Saint Barbara, and the Virgin, and these images modeled pious literate practice for girls such as Margaret Beaufort, proffering the female saints' sanctity as the justification for religious study. Second, the illustrations incorporate the lay reader into the book's devotional world by portraying scenes in which the patron herself was a reader. In the famous Annunciation, for example, the male and female patrons kneel at benches on which rest open books. Their hands are held together in prayer, and they look upward at the Virgin, whose book is open before her. The illumination draws attention to the Virgin's status as "Liebhaberin von Büchern," as Klaus Schreiner has called her, and makes explicit the connection between the Virgin's reading and that of the person looking at the book of hours.[18] Even a girl just beginning to read would see the connection established among the three books and their readers: the Virgin has just been reading, and the patrons follow her example; finally, the reader of the book of hours will do so herself.

Although the first half of the Beaufort Hours includes pictures that could have influenced Margaret Beauchamp's daughters' ideas about books, it is her half of the Hours, the primer she commissioned from London, that addresses the book's reader as *the* reader in the most personal manner. It does this by including images of Margaret herself in its illustrations. One of the historiated initials in the second half of the book, the illumination painted inside the first letter of a section of text, shows a woman, probably Margaret Beauchamp, in fifteenth-century clothing kneeling with an open book before her and a scroll in her hands. Directly above this initial is another Annunciation in which a book lies open behind the Virgin, who, following the scene's conventional representation, seems to have been interrupted in her reading.[19] As in the example described in the previous paragraph, the contemporary woman's appearance as a reader who looks at the Virgin, who also holds a book, reinforces associations between the two women and their actions. The page's arrangement invites the actual reader, the book's owner Margaret Beauchamp, to imagine herself as the reader represented in contemporary dress, thus establishing visual symmetry between the actual reader, the represented reader, and the Virgin. When Margaret Beauchamp's daughters looked at this

[18] Klaus Schreiner, "Konnte Maria Lesen? Von der Magd des Herrn zur Symbolgestalt mittelalterlicher Frauenbildung," *Merkur* 44 (1990): 83.

[19] Scott, *Later Gothic Manuscripts*, 2:128, 1: color plate 6.

page, they would have been seeing their mother inside of her own book. In fact, "Margaret" appears in another illustration, a quarter-page miniature. In the miniature, the woman wears exactly the same clothes as does the one in the Annunciation and kneels before her guardian angel. Scrolls extend from both figures: the woman's scroll reads "Sub umbra alarum tuarum protege me," and the angel answers her request for protection, "dominus custodiat te ab omni malo."[20] Patrons were often included in illustrations, and although it might have been for the owner's own pleasure, such representations probably had a didactic function, allowing mothers to teach their daughters to read not only by living example or by pointing at the examples of women saints but also by identifying themselves with specific pictures in their books.

For older girls who had acquired greater familiarity with the fundamentals of medieval religion, the pictures in the books of hours functioned as interpretive aids. Primers like Margaret Beauchamp's often included illustrated psalters, for example, and the illuminations prompted the reader to respond to the text of the psalms, among the most important religious works for late medieval believers, in particular ways. When Margaret and her daughters read Psalm 1 (*Beatus vir*), for instance, they also "read" the historiated initial with which the passage began. The text of the psalm concerns study of God's law, and it was among the best known of the psalms, almost always illustrated in pictoral cycles, and popular because it promised spiritual rewards. Given the psalm's emphasis on meditation and study, it might come as a surprise, then, that the historiated initial that accompanies the text encloses a Tree of Jesse, a traditional image that depicts the Virgin's descent from Jesse and features her ancestors as branches. If the purpose of the primer was to model spiritual study, why choose to illustrate a passage expressly concerned with meditation on God's law with an image that draws attention to genealogy? The answer seems to lie in late medieval ideas about women's devotional reading and familial responsibility. In this particular Jesse Tree, the Virgin and Christ child appear at the top of the image in the most prominent position. Like many of the miniatures in the Hours, including the tableau in which a mother and father look on from the city gates as their daughter is rescued by Saint George (fol. 5v) or those of Saint Christopher caring for the Christ child (fols. 11v and 25), the picture filters the scriptures for the female reader through a domestic lens.

The initial that accompanied Psalm 1 taught girls who read the

[20] Ibid., 2:127, 1:162 (black-and-white plate).

book that meditation on God's law was domestic and familial, and the reading that the initial proposed of the psalm appears to have been designed specifically with female readers in mind. Kathleen Scott's table of illustrations covering psalters from 1400 to 1500 shows that in most cases, Psalm 1's illustration represented David, often playing his harp or praying, and not a Tree of Jesse.[21] Possibly the Jesse Tree seemed a more appropriate choice for a female audience than was the "masculine" image of David as poet, musician, and anointed king; if this is true, then the second and third verses of the psalm have particular, gendered resonance. Blessed is the woman, then, whose delight is in "the law of the Lord" and who meditates on that law "day and night." When she does so, she shall be "like a tree planted by rivers of water," bringing forth her "fruit in her time." The righteous woman's "leaf shall not wither," and all things that she does shall "flourish."[22] The illumination and written text work together to confirm the significance of devotional reading to a successful life: the girl who learns to read will prosper, bear fruit, and sit at the "top" of a noble line with her offspring.

When a reader processed written texts in this way, she imagined books as speaking directly to her. In Margaret Beauchamp's book, the text of Psalm 1 and the illumination worked together, at least for the reader who had a "little perceiving" of Latin, to draw the reader visually and linguistically into the meaning of the psalm. In this way, the biblical verses are directed specifically at the reader's experiences as an aristocratic woman, and they speak explicitly to her hopes for a blessed life. In the Beaufort Hours, this direction is visual, but often the primary evidence for arguing that a book "speaks" individually to the reader is the addition of prayers or personal inscriptions by later owners of a manuscript. We know, for instance, that in Richard III's Hours, which had belonged to someone else before Richard took possession, certain prayers that had personal significance for Richard, such as the Collect of Saint Ninian, were added.[23] Sometimes alter-

[21] Ibid., 2:378–79. In 2:375, Scott explains that the psalms illustrated in the cycles are Psalm 1 (*Beatus vir*), Psalm 26 (*Dominus illuminatio mea*), Psalm 38 (*Dixit custodiam vias meas*), Psalm 52 (*Dixit insipiens*), Psalm 68 (*Salvum me fac*), Psalm 80 (*Exultate Deo*), Psalm 97 (*Cantate Deo*), and Psalm 109 (*Dixit Dominus*). In volume 2, table 3, "Pictorial Subjects of Selected English Books of Hours c. 1390–c. 1480," shows that the Jesse Tree was used in two other psalters she includes in her survey.

[22] ". . . lege Domini voluntas eius et in lege eius meditabitur die ac nocte et erit tamquam lignum quod plantatum est secus decursus aquarum quod fructum suum dabit in tempore suo et folium eius non defluet et omnia quaecumque faciet prosperabuntur" (Psalm 1).

[23] Sutton and Visser-Fuchs, *Hours of Richard III*, 41–44.

ations of the words of the original text reveal the extent to which devotional books were personalized. A good example of this is the Wingfield Hours, a psalter owned by Anne Stafford, who became Margaret Beaufort's mother-in-law after Margaret's marriage to Sir Henry Stafford in 1458.[24] The Wingfield Hours "reads" to and for its owner by naming her as God's servant. For instance, a line from one prayer reads "O domine Ihesu Christe parce michi famule tue Anne," identifying Anne Stafford specifically as the person speaking/reading. Similarly, all adjectives modifying the supplicant in the second half of the manuscript are feminine.[25] Just as the illuminations in the Beaufort Hours particularize the reader's experience of the text, the psalter identifies Anne as *the* reader and not just *a* reader of the Wingfield Hours. Naming the reader, the psalter insists that she take on the identity that it creates for her and in turn offers itself as her means of communicating her desires.

In tracing the influence that Margaret Beaufort's mother may have had on her involvement with written texts, I have been suggesting that aristocratic women's literate practice involved imaginative acts of inscription in which the book spoke to and for the reader. We need not assume this meant the reader was passive: her imaginative response to the written and visual texts involved a creative, positive action on her part, an attempt to process and evaluate evidence and apply it to her own situation. However, readerly inscription could also transform the written text itself through the addition of writing that supplemented the original. Margaret Beauchamp, for example, literally wrote herself and her family into the pages of her book: when she commissioned her half of the Hours, she had ten blank pages attached at the back so she could add annotations; these pages are now filled with dates and details concerning her family, including the

[24] Carol Meale observes that the psalter was wrongly thought to have been owned by Anne's husband, Humphrey duke of Buckingham, because its borders were lined with Stafford family heraldic badges. See Meale, " 'Alle the bokes that I haue of latyn, englisch, and frensch': Laywomen and Their Books in Late Medieval England," in *Women and Literature in Britain, 1150–1500*, ed. Carol M. Meale (1993; reprint, Cambridge: Cambridge University Press, 1996), 136. I should add that in numbering Margaret Beaufort's husbands, I have excluded Margaret's first marriage to John de la Pole, which occurred when she was six years old. Jones and Underwood suggest that Margaret herself did not recognize its validity, referring in 1472 to Edmund Tudor as her "fyrst husband" in her will. See Jones and Underwood, *King's Mother*, 37 n. 4.

[25] M. R. James, *A Descriptive Catalogue of the Fifty Manuscripts from the Collection of Henry Yates Thompson* (Cambridge: Cambridge University Press, 1898), 132. On the same page, James cites another passage that reads "ut avertas iram tuam a me famula tua Anna."

birth dates of her daughter Margaret Beaufort and grandson Henry Tudor, the obit for John Beaufort, references to her ancestors, and historical dates such as the death of Catherine Valois, Henry V's wife.[26] The Beaufort Hours was no longer the text that Margaret Beauchamp commissioned or the book thought to have been passed down through her husband's family but an emended text, one in which the owner responded to and reshaped the original by linking her imaginative insertion into her book with the social world that she inhabited. Specifically, the written additions allowed the reader to incorporate her family history into the book, and by writing it down (or having it written down for her) it became part of the record that constituted who the reader and her family were, what was significant in their lives, and how they understood themselves in relationship to their world. Margaret Beauchamp, for example, had entered her daughter's birth date as the first entry in the Hours's calendar; when the younger Margaret looked at her mother's book, she would have understood that she, like her mother, now "appeared" in the book, that her birth had reshaped the content of the book because her mother thought it was an important event. She was, literally, an addition to the text whose presence exemplified her mother's help in perpetuating the Beaufort family and honoring its ancestral claims. The inscriptive impulse was in this way part of the familial dynamic that underwrote medieval women's literate practice, encouraging readers to think about themselves and their families as part of a written record; while it served patriarchal ends, it also gave women license to "document" themselves and their lives in potentially liberating ways.

Aristocratic girls' education did not end after they left home, and Margaret Beaufort continued to learn about writing from the women who became part of her family when she married. In particular, it seems to have been Anne Stafford, Margaret Beaufort's mother-in-law, who, after Margaret's own mother, had the greatest influence on Margaret's literate practice. Anne Stafford introduced the younger Margaret to reading as a communal, household practice. Although Margaret Beauchamp continued to play an important role in her daughter's life, after Margaret Beaufort married her second husband,

[26] Printed in Frederick Madden, "Genealogical and Historical Notes from Ancient Calendars, & c," in *Collectanea Topographica et Genealogica* (London: John Bowyer Nichols and Son, 1834), 1:277–80. See also Edith Rickert, "The So-Called Beaufort Hours and York Psalter," *Burlington Magazine* 104 (1962): 238. Rickert notes that Margaret Beauchamp herself "may be represented as a kneeling votive figure in two miniatures (fols. 26 and 34) at the beginning of the hours" (238).

Henry Stafford, she became part of a female family circle that revolved around her mother-in-law.

Anne's first husband, Humphrey Stafford, duke of Buckingham, was one of the wealthiest men in England, and after he died in 1460, Anne remained unmarried until 1467. Anne administered her own financial matters with care; she was, for example, "severe" in using "the law, against tenants and servants alike" (*KM* 143). Carole Rawcliffe notes that after Duke Humphrey's death, Anne executed her financial affairs much more successfully than her husband had, spending a great deal less and generating an enormous cash surplus, and she was directly involved in the supervision of her daughter-in-law's household as well.[27] But while she clearly managed her estate quite capably, Anne also had literate interests that extended beyond her supervision of financial arrangements. Like Margaret Beaufort, Anne descended from the Beaufort line—she was Joan Beaufort and Ralph Neville, earl of Westmoreland's daughter—and like her mother, she is associated with book collecting.[28] In addition to the Wingfield Hours mentioned previously, Anne's books, listed in her will, included "a boke of English of Legenda Sanctorum, a boke of ffrensh called Lukan, an other boke of ffrensh of the pistell and Gaspelles and a prymmer with claspes of silver and gilt covered with purpull velvett."[29] These books became Margaret's upon Anne's death in 1480.

Although book collecting sounds like a solitary pursuit, Anne Stafford's involvement with books was communal, and her promotion of morally significant writing counted among her household duties. On the one hand, her activities followed what has become a recognizable pattern of women's participation in literate culture: she, her daughter Anne Vere, and Margaret Beaufort formed a small, reading community in which the three women exchanged books and, presumably, conversation about their reading. We have records of this kind of activity as early as 1469, when, as Jones and Underwood mention, unnamed books that Anne Stafford had lent to Margaret were returned from Woking in Surrey, Margaret and her husband's home, to

[27] Carole Rawcliffe, *The Staffords, Earls of Stafford and Dukes of Buckingham, 1394–1521* (Cambridge: Cambridge University Press, 1978), 123–24.

[28] Rawcliffe suggests that Anne Stafford was "something of a bibliophile" (ibid., 95).

[29] Ibid., 96. This passage from Anne Stafford's will is widely cited in work on Margaret Beaufort. See, for example, Axon, "Lady Margaret as a Lover of Literature," 34–41; Jones and Underwood, *King's Mother,* 173; Cooper, *Memoir of Margaret Countess of Richmond and Derby,* 17.

Anne's house in London; it seems likely that Anne started sharing her books with Margaret by 1467, when Margaret and Stafford moved from her estate at Bourne in Lincolnshire, which was close to Margaret's own mother's home at Maxey, to Surrey (*KM* 143, 137–42). Evidence of Anne Vere's participation in this reading circle is less clear, but we know that she bequeathed her copy of Christine de Pizan's *Epistle to Othea* to Margaret in 1472.[30] Since Anne Vere died a year after her brother's death, it was probably a personal bequest, made because she knew and liked her sister-in-law, as well as a familial gesture of respect for her brother's widow.[31] Anne perhaps assumed that Margaret would like the book, and this group of readers, tied together by family relations, social class, and physical proximity, seems to have enjoyed the mutual support that Felicity Riddy has described as a key component of such small "textual communities."[32]

Anne Stafford, on the other hand, appears to have been involved in a much broader reading community than that made up of her intimate, female relations. The best evidence of this is contained in the preface to a religious poem titled *The Nightingale.*[33] *The Nightingale,* dated to the mid-1440s and dedicated to Anne, opens by addressing its patron, "the ryght hyghe and myghty pryncesse, The Duchess of Bokyngham," who it is hoped will "of hure noble grace / Amonge hyre bokys" find a place for this "lityll quayere." This information explains that Anne is a great reader who owns many books, but it

[30] Powell, "Lady Margaret and Her Books," 205.

[31] On the basis of last testaments, Anne Stafford's sister Cecily might also be included in this "textual community." See Karen Jambeck, "Patterns of Women's Literary Patronage: England, 1200–ca. 1475," in *Cultural Patronage of Medieval Women,* 240. Jambeck's source for this information is John Gough Nichols and John Bruce, eds., *Wills from Doctors' Commons* (Westminster: Nichols for the Camden Society, 1863), 2–3.

[32] Felicity Riddy, " 'Women talking about the things of God': A Late Medieval Sub-Culture," in *Women and Literature in Britain, 1150–1500,* 109. Rather than assuming that such small groups of readers were drawn together by their reading preferences, it seems to me especially important to note that those interests were formed in relation to other people and the books with which they were familiar: Margaret Beaufort, in other words, came to read the *Epistle* because her sister-in-law owned it and not because Anne knew Margaret would like it. This does not mean that it entered her repertoire against her will or that it did not influence her taste in books, but that the conditions under which she became familiar with it were at least partially dependent on her social (specifically familial) affiliations.

[33] *Lydgate's Minor Poems: The Two Nightingale Poems,* ed. Otto Glauning, EETS, e.s., 80 (London: Kegan Paul Trench, 1900), 1–15. Critics no longer believe that *The Nightingale* was written by Lydgate.

does not indicate anything about her "reading community." In fact, its evocation of a library of collected books among which the duchess herself will find a spot for this book implies that her reading is an independent activity. However, the dedication goes on to suggest that Anne's reading is communal and public: Anne will, according to the poet, "command[]" "hryre peple" to listen to the poem when she "call[s] [them] vn-to hyr high presence" (ll. 9–10). It is possible that the poet alludes to the familial reading circle mentioned above, but it is hard to imagine that the poet would call the audience Anne's "people" if all he meant was that the duchess would read the poem for her daughter and daughter-in-law. At the very least, *The Nightingale* poet's imagined audience seems to be large enough to be "called" together and to include members who are socially attached to Anne, probably members of her household. In fact, the audience he alludes to sounds much more like the traditional picture of readers as "a courtly audience of leisured aristocrats, male and female, that used to be extrapolated from the *Troilus* frontispiece" than it does like the now commonplace idea that women belonged to intimate, familial reading communities.[34]

Although the audience evoked in *The Nightingale* appears to be aristocratic, the poem itself is religious and not chivalric. This does not keep the poet from drawing upon chivalric conventions. Described as a group of "galantus," that is, fashionable people, the imagined audience is decidedly courtly and familiar with aristocratic tastes. This is revealed especially by their alleged interest in romance. The poet suggests that his readers would be attracted to a poem concerning "the amerouse sentensce / of the nyghtyngale" (ll. 12–13). The nightingale was the "bird of *fin amor,*" the symbol of "terrestrial, worldly love" in medieval literature, and the poet invokes an audience familiar with the intricacies of romance and subtleties of the love lyric.[35] However, although the poet conjures up a sophisticated, courtly audience, he offers that audience a poem that uses the conventions of romance for a religious purpose. Rather than a love story, the poet offers Anne and her companions a religious allegory in

[34] Riddy refers to Roberta Gilchrist's unpublished dissertation in which Gilchrist discusses religious *familiae* and the " 'increasingly domestic personality of nunneries' " (Riddy, " 'Women talking about the things of God,' " 109). See Gilchrist's later work, *Gender and Material Culture: The Archaeology of Religious Women* (London: Routledge, 1994).

[35] *Rossignol: An Edition and Translation,* ed. J. L. Baird and John R. Kane (Kent, Ohio: Kent State University Press, 1978), 36.

which the nightingale is "Crist hym-self ande euery cristen-man."[36] It is interesting that *The Nightingale*'s substitution of religious rhetoric for romance coincides with what Anne F. Sutton and Livia Visser-Fuchs have described as a "drop both in the status and the fashionableness of romances" in the middle of the fifteenth century.[37] In this case, the result is a literary text that incorporates elements of traditional, secular writing, such as the sleepless narrator whose heart is troubled, with serious attempts to understand the deep, spiritual significance of life's complexities. If the poet has understood his audience, it suggests that Anne Stafford and "hyre peple" were looking in written texts to find answers to religious and moral questions. Intimating that people like Anne desire more from their reading than entertainment, the poet deftly reminds his audience who they are (elite readers who have grown beyond their taste for romance) and suggests they listen to his poem.

The Nightingale appeals to its audience by bringing together romance discourse and devotional intensity, going so far as to employ liturgical terms—matins, lauds, prime, terce—to frame the poem in the same way that books of hours did. Sutton and Visser-Fuchs's discussion is useful in this context because they remind us that religious enthusiasm was not incompatible with courtly habits. Their argument is not with the popularity of romance—they agree with the traditional view that romances were widely read in the fifteenth century—but rather with the commonplace notion that the genre's stature as court literature remained unchanged during the later Middle Ages.[38] Rather than dismissing romance out of hand, *The Nightingale*'s author shows his readers that their knowledge of love can lead to deeper spiritual understanding. In this way, he asserts that

[36] *Nightingale*, l. 115. *The Nightingale* is based on a Latin poem, *Philomena praevia*, by John Pecham. Along with Pecham's poem, John of Hoveden's *Philomena* (which was translated into Anglo-Norman) is associated with devotions to the Holy Name (important later in this chapter). On the tradition associating the nightingale and the singing of God's praises, see the Baird and Kane edition of *Rossignol*, esp. 1–16. They note (important in relation to devotion to the Holy Name) that the nightingale is a favorite image in Richard Rolle's poetry (28).

[37] Anne F. Sutton and Livia Visser-Fuchs, *Richard III's Books: Ideals and Reality in the Life and Library of a Medieval Prince* (Stroud: Sutton, 1997), 213. They single out the twenty years between 1465 and 1485 as especially important in this context.

[38] Ibid. Sutton and Visser-Fuchs argue that this traditional view is based on two related assumptions: "that Caxton printed a great number of such texts *and* that he was very much influenced by the taste of the Burgundian court. Both can be rejected" (240).

literature is educational and poets (and the people who make poetry available) are teachers. The really sophisticated reader, according to the poet, will want to study the most edifying literature: he modestly offers his own poem as suitable material. Anne's role in all of this, it appears, was to help her companions understand that religious writing (such as *The Nightingale*) was more profitable than romance. The poem suggests then that she habitually gathered an audience, an extension of a familial or household circle, in order to elevate its literary taste.

More generally, *The Nightingale*'s dedication implies that aristocratic women such as Anne Stafford thought of themselves as public teachers who could (and should) use their social authority to "speak" the poet's message. In dedicating *The Nightingale* to Anne, the poet presents his patron, a woman authorized to gather together a large group of "hyre peple," with a "script" that she can follow. His poem, he proposes, will become the lesson she teaches, his words will be her words, and she will educate the public that already benefits from her social and economic influence. It is possible to imagine the poet's proposal as merely self-interested, that is, a calculated attempt to win a larger audience for his writing. Yet even if this poet thought of Anne Stafford's household as a medieval salon, Anne's role in the poem's transmission could also enhance her own social standing. By providing a large audience with instructive literature, the aristocratic woman, if she had the right poet and the proper amount of economic and social clout, might be thought of as Othea in the translation of Christine de Pizan's book, a teacher of prudence and wisdom.[39] Anne Stafford certainly had the requisite political power: Jones and Underwood point out, for example, that she "had been chosen by the anxious aldermen of London to lead a delegation to treat with the Lan-

[39] The English translation of the *Epistle,* a book in which the female Othea stands as a model of prudence and wisdom, was first dedicated to Anne Stafford's husband, Humphrey duke of Buckingham. Interestingly, however, the translation is, as Carol Meale notes, later rededicated to an unnamed "high priestess," and it is likely that the new dedicatee was Anne Stafford. Other possibilities are Anne Vere or Anne Beauchamp. See also A. I. Doyle, Appendix B, in *The Epistle of Othea, Translated from the French Text of Christine de Pisan by Stephen Scrope,* ed. Curt F. Bühler, EETS, o.s., 264 (London: Oxford University Press, 1970), 125–27. Karen Jambeck cites Diane Bornstein's description of the *Epistle*'s exploration of women's roles "as teachers and arbiters of culture" ("Patterns of Women's Literary Patronage," 232). See Bornstein, "Self-Consciousness and Self Concepts in the Work of Christine de Pizan," in *Ideals for Women in the Works of Christine de Pizan* (Detroit: Michigan Consortium for Medieval and Early Modern Studies, 1981), 19.

castrian army in February 1461, 'with other wytty men with her.' "[40] If scholarly speculation is correct and she was the unnamed "high priestess" to whom the English translation of Christine's *Epistle* was rededicated (having first been dedicated to Anne's husband), her status as a woman with moral superiority may also have been widely recognized in late medieval England. In any case, the model of aristocratic women's engagement with written texts proposed in *The Nightingale* is public, instructive, and socially influential.

My claim, that Margaret Beaufort "studied" her mother-in-law's literate practice and came to think of herself as obliged to provide readers with written texts, is of course speculative. However, it is supported by the similarity between the dedication to Anne in *The Nightingale* and the first printer's dedication to Margaret Beaufort. In Caxton's translation of the French romance *Blanchardyn and Eglantine,* he writes that his patron, Margaret, is an aristocratic woman whose public teaching will fortify her people. Caxton dedicates *Blanchardyn and Eglantine* to "the kyngis moder of excellent bounte," the "right noble puyssaunt & excellent pryncesse."[41] As George Keiser has suggested in relation to similar dedications, calling attention to such sponsorship "must have been professionally, economically and personally very satisfying" for Caxton.[42] The dedication in *Blanchardyn* reads like an advertisement. Caxton explains first that the illustrious Margaret had asked him to translate and print the book and then suggests that the study of *Blanchardyn and Eglantine* will transform the reader into a member of the royal elite, like his patron.[43] According to the printer, chivalric romances such as *Blanchardyn and Eglantine* teach readers proper social behavior: men who

[40] Jones and Underwood, *King's Mother,* 142–43. The quotation is from *An English Chronicle of the Reigns of Richard II, Henry IV, Henry V, and Henry VI,* ed. J. S. Davies, Camden Society, o.s., 64 (1856), 109.

[41] *Caxton's Blanchardyn and Eglantine c. 1489,* ed. Leon Kellner, EETS, e.s., 58 (London: Trübner, 1890), 1.

[42] George Keiser, "The Mystics and the Early English Printers: The Economics of Devotionalism," in *The Medieval Mystical Tradition,* ed. Marion Glasscoe (Cambridge: D. S. Brewer, 1987), 11. See also A. S. G. Edwards and Carol M. Meale, "The Marketing of Printed Books in Late Medieval England," *The Library,* 6th ser., 15 (1993): 95–124.

[43] George Painter, as Keiser notes, suggests that "when Caxton printed *Blanchardin and Eglantine* . . . for Lady Margaret, he was seeking her help in regaining royal favour after the accession of Henry VII" (Keiser, "Mystics and the Early English Printers," 11). See George D. Painter, *William Caxton: A Biography* (New York: Putnam, 1977), 166–69. See also M. J. C. Lowry, "Caxton, St. Winifred and the Lady Margaret Beaufort," *The Library,* 6th ser., 5 (1983): 116.

read of "valiaunt actes of armes" will learn to perform such deeds if they wish to "stande in grace" with their ladies; women will learn to wait faithfully for their men. Caxton was no doubt interested in the status of romance in the late fifteenth century and promoted its prestigious associations to secure sales. But although the dedication helped Caxton sell books to clients eager to emulate the royal mother, it also announces Margaret's concern with the education of England's people. Like the good mother of conduct literature, Margaret, the king's mother, is shown to care for readers by providing them with morally uplifting and socially useful books. In this way, Margaret, like her mother-in-law, provides literary "nourishment" as a form of community service. Anne and Margaret are the "high priestess" and "excellent princess," respectively, whose commitment to literate culture shows their dedication to their public.

The point about the literate practice that Anne Stafford and Margaret Beaufort shared is not simply that it enhanced their public images (or those of their protégés). Rather, it is that women such as Margaret and Anne helped to create the sense that women's participation in literary pursuits was a socially prestigious act of public service. Reading was not automatically equated with piety, nor was involvement in the production of printed books necessarily "active life in God's service."[44] And although it is certainly true, as we can see from Fisher's funeral sermon, for example, that women who avidly studied devotional writing accrued prestige during the fifteenth century, aristocratic women could only have had partial understandings of the effect that literate actions would have had and not complete awareness of what literary patronage and reading meant or were coming to signify. In this regard, George Ballard's observation that Margaret Beaufort's level of education and literary enthusiasm was "according to the custom of that age, not very extraordinary" is useful and interesting.[45] For more than forty years, from the time Margaret was born until Caxton printed *Blanchardyn and Eglantine,* her literary endeavors were unremarkable. She learned to read, probably from a book of hours, and to write, and occasionally borrowed some of her mother-in-law and sister-in-law's books. Yet in the last twenty or so years of her life she was instrumental in the printing of dozens of texts, pro-

[44] Powell, "Lady Margaret and Her Books," 199.

[45] George Ballard, *Memoirs of British Ladies, Who Have Been Celebrated for Their Writings or Skill in the Learned Languages, Arts and Sciences* (1752; reprint, Detroit, Mich.: Wayne State University Press, 1985), 63.

duced two English-language translations, and was directly responsible for the expansion of England's universities. Although it is true that Margaret's scholarly attainments were limited, she saw the opportunities afforded by print, which had arrived in England only thirteen years before she commissioned the printing of *Blanchardyn,* and came to have a substantial impact on medieval literary and devotional culture.

Before discussing Margaret's involvement in the print trade, it is necessary to consider the explicitly familial nature of her literate practice in relation to her son Henry because, as will become clear, it was her public role as the king's mother that made possible her extraordinary role in the distribution of written texts after 1485. In particular, Margaret and Henry's exchange of letters indicates how important her sense of writing as self-inscription would become. Traditionally, scholars have looked at Margaret Beaufort's letters to her son as expressions of natural, maternal affection. As recently as 1994, Anne Crawford wrote, "The devotion between Henry and his mother was extraordinary. They had barely seen each other since he was a small child and their relationship had been sustained solely by letter."[46] It might, however, be more accurate to say that the relationship was at least in part produced by the letters. After Henry was two years old, he lived apart from his mother, first in Wales among the Tudors, his wardship having been granted by Edward IV to William Lord Herbert, and later, when he was fourteen years old, in exile in France with his uncle, Jaspar Tudor, an enemy of Edward's (*KM* 41–42, 58). Jones and Underwood mention several visits between Henry and his mother during these years, and they explain that in addition to these occasional visits, Margaret "maintained contact with her son through messages delivered by her servants" (*KM* 42). From the beginning, Henry and his mother communicated through writing, and their relationship was mediated by the written word. Margaret, moreover, availed herself of documentary tactics to secure her son's future. For example, she drew up wills that safeguarded Henry's inheritance against her husbands' interests: as Jones and Underwood note, a record produced in the presence of Edward IV, Margaret, and Margaret's third husband, Thomas Lord Stanley, guaranteed "the grace and favour of the king's highness" toward Henry and included Stanley's commitment to respect the conditions arranged for the settlement of Margaret's west-country holdings prior to his marriage to her (*KM* 60).

[46] Anne Crawford, *Letters of the Queens of England* (Stroud: Sutton, 1994), 145.

Margaret's use of the written word was largely instrumental, that is, aimed at securing Henry's financial rights through the courts and law; she was highly sensitive to the ways in which institutional writing shaped her familial identity and created the social space in which she lived. One might even argue that she "inherited" this sense from her great-grandparents. Margaret's grandfather, John Beaufort, earl of Somerset, and his siblings were "bastards," the offspring of John of Gaunt and his mistress Katherine Swynford. After marrying Katherine in 1396, their father saw to it that the children were retroactively legitimized by virtue of a papal bull and an act of Parliament.[47] In this case, institutional documentation allowed the family to recategorize itself as legitimately part of the royal line. Margaret herself employed similar tactics to affirm her social identity. For example, having for years signed legal papers as "M. Richmond," the traditional form employed in sign manuals, Margaret changed her signature to "Margaret R." after Henry's accession in 1485. The new signature echoed Henry's "H. R.," Henrici Rex, and affirmed her royal authority. In addition, she amended her personal seal to include the Tudor crown and the caption "et mater Henrici septimi regis Anglie et Hibernie," linking her identity with Henry's by means of an implement used in verifying documents.[48]

Margaret Beaufort's reinvention of her signature and seal are examples of women's growing awareness of the power of written documentation, a subject central to the previous chapter. Her newly formed markers show Margaret textualizing her relationship to the king in order to provide evidence of her royal authority. Given the uncertainty that had surrounded Henry's fate, the advantages of royal

[47] The four Beaufort children were legitimized through both papal bull and act of Parliament; Gaunt and Swynford's desire for the children's retroactive legitimacy had more to do with economics and status than morality, however: the church's legitimization did not make the children heirs to titles and property but the secular authority's did. See W. H. Bliss, *Calendar of Papal Registers, 1364–1404* (London: His Majesty's Stationery Office, 1902), 4:545; John Strachey, *Rotuli Parliamentorum, 1278–1503* (London: 1832), 3:343. The documents made it possible, eventually, for Henry Tudor to become king even though Henry Bolingbroke, the Beauforts' half brother, had used his royal, documentary discretion to insert the clause "excepta dignitate regali" into the act of legitimation in 1407.

[48] Jones and Underwood, *King's Mother,* 86. A. F. Pollard, ed., *The Reign of Henry VII from Contemporary Sources* (London: Longmans, Green, 1913), 1:217–18: "Margaret had no technical right to this royal signature." But see also Retha Warnicke (who sees no reason to think the signature makes royal claims), "The Lady Margaret, Countess of Richmond: A Noblewoman of Independent Wealth and Status," *Fifteenth-Century Studies* 9 (1984): 225, 243 n. 14.

support, both in terms of social status and institutional backing, were obvious to Margaret, and in fact she took advantage of his documentary authority from the time that he became king until his death. Henry's mother, like his great-great-grandfather, was part of the king's family, and Margaret's familial status, like John of Gaunt's, allowed her to secure necessary documentation. For example, in 1485, shortly after ascending the throne, Henry had his mother declared "femme sole" by act of Parliament while her third husband was still alive. This proclamation had the transformative power that the act of legitimation did for the Beauforts, instantaneously changing her legal and economic status through the power of institutional documents. It allowed her to control her own property and to represent her own interests in court, a situation that was highly unusual in late medieval England if a woman's husband was still alive.[49] The written act had obvious consequences for Stanley's ability to influence his wife and to determine the course of their affairs. The vow of chastity that Stanley allowed Margaret to take in 1499 (renewed in 1504) might be seen as the religious confirmation of Margaret's determination to separate her affairs from those of her husband (*KM* 187–88). Royal authority was more useful than aristocratic power, and the act of Parliament and vow of chastity cemented Margaret's relationship with her son.

In the previous chapter, I considered the ways in which Margaret Paston's familial situation led her to use written texts as evidence; conversely, although writing's evidentiary function was also important for Margaret Beaufort, her success in employing documentary writing often had as much to do with her personal relationship with Henry as it did with cultural understandings of writing as "proof." One of the observable patterns of Margaret's relationship with Henry is a shift in political and social influence from mother to son. Before Henry was king, his mother looked out for his personal and financial interests; once he became king, her authority as his mother was tempered by her inferiority as subject. This is noticeable, for example, in Henry's decision to use Margaret's house in Surrey as a royal palace. Margaret disliked the arrangement but had little choice in the matter until Henry was dead (Margaret made sure to recover the house "within weeks of her son's death").[50] However, although Margaret and her son possessed varying degrees of social power and Henry might choose to exert his authority over his mother when it suited

[49] Halsted, *Life of Margaret Beaufort*, 166.
[50] Jones and Underwood, *King's Mother*, 83.

his purposes, he and his mother both wrote letters in which they emphasized their mutual dependence on one another. Margaret, for example, habitually wrote letters to Henry in which she refers to her son as "your bounteous goodness," "my good king," "your grace" or "your majesty" and apologizes for causing him "any displeasure," commending herself to him, as she suggests in one letter, "yn as humble maner as y can thynke."[51] At the same time, however, she dwells heavily on her maternal relationship to Henry. In a letter from 1501 dated "St. Anne's day," Margaret reminds Henry of this day's significance, writing that upon this day "I did bring into this world my good and gracious prince, king, and only beloved son."[52] Contriving to combine possessiveness and humility, she defers in her letters to her king and at the same time claims originary authority over her son.[53] Similarly, Henry's letters to his mother acknowledge the "debt" he owes his mother. Henry, for example, begins a letter concerning the Orléans ransom, mentioned earlier in relation to his grandmother, with a request for his mother's "dayly and continuall blessings."[54] Asking for a parent's blessing was a conventional fifteenth-century address from a child, but his letter enlarges on this convention by expressing the obligation he feels toward his mother "not onely" in relation to the ransom payments, to which she granted him title and interest, "but in all other thyngs" which would please her and bring her honor. He wishes to "plese" his mother as much as her "herte can desire" because, as he writes, "I knowe welle that I am as much bounden so to doe as any creture lyvyng, for the grete and singular moderly love and affection that hit hath plesed you at all tymes to ber towards me."

In Margaret's and Henry's letters, financial obligation figures as an allegory in which mother and son can renegotiate their emotional bonds. Henry's remarks cited in the paragraph above "read" her willingness to cede her right to the ransom payments as love; his mother, in turn, interprets her financial strategies for her son, declaring that everything which is hers is in fact his. She explains to Henry, if "y fortune to gete thys or eny parte therof," that she would consider

[51] Henry Ellis, *Original Letters Illustrative of English History* (London: Harding, Triphook, and Lepard, 1824), 1:46.

[52] Pollard, *Reign of Henry VII from Contemporary Sources,* 1:220.

[53] Margaret's letters follow the formal characteristics that Norman Davis has found typical of fifteenth-century letters; see Davis, "The Litera Troili and English Letters," *Review of English Studies* 16 (1965): 236.

[54] Ellis, *Original Letters,* 1:43.

none of the profits her own but rather "yt shalbe yours." Margaret is, like Henry, anxious to demonstrate that her ambitions concerning the ransom payments are actually expressions of love and of a shared understanding: she goes on to write that she wishes Henry would comprehend her meaning "as veryly as y thynke yt."[55] In writing about this financial obligation, Henry and his mother create and sustain their emotional relationship. This is not to say that they were not eager to make a profit on the payments. As Jones and Underwood remark with some dismay, this "constantly recurring theme" of their letters "carries all the hallmarks of the avarice that was to taint both their reputations" (*KM* 82). Margaret and Henry certainly wanted the money, of course, but the letters are also, like those they sent to Orléans, "negotiations." In corresponding about the ransom payments, Margaret and Henry found a way to rewrite and reinterpret an aspect of the Tudor/Beaufort family narrative for one another, "emending" their texts as Henry's grandmother, by adding her own information, "emended" her book of hours.

Margaret may have considered her early involvement in the distribution of printed books as a personal emendation as well. Her first association with the production of written texts, Caxton's translation and printing of *Blanchardyn and Eglantine,* involved an act of familial reinterpretation similar to her reading and response to Henry's letters. This is not, however, the way that her early interactions with the printers are usually described. Instead, scholars generally consider her patronage of Caxton in the 1480s to be politically motivated. For example, Jones and Underwood, taking up George Painter's line of reasoning, speculate that Margaret purchased a French copy of *Blanchardyn and Eglantine* sometime close to 1483 because "the action of the romance mirrored some of the political events of the time," specifically negotiations in 1483 to arrange a marriage between Henry Tudor and Elizabeth of York, daughter of Queen Elizabeth Woodville—who had sought sanctuary from Richard III at Westminster Abbey.[56] Caxton printed the English translation, at Margaret's re-

[55] Ibid., 1:44, 47.

[56] The parallel is between the hero Blanchardyn and Henry Tudor: both lived in self-imposed exile until aided by foreign forces. This reading equates Eglantine, Blanchardyn's beloved, with Elizabeth of York; the evil king Alymodes with Elizabeth's uncle, Richard III; and the foreign aid of the Saracens with Henry's support by the Welsh. See Painter, *William Caxton,* 166; and Jones and Underwood, *King's Mother,* 182. Painter bases his account on the questionable assumption that Caxton "must have" first sold a copy of the romance "to Margaret Beaufort through her envoy Lewis, who came to negotiate with Elizabeth Woodville in the sanctuary of the

quest, in 1489, four years after Henry acceded. From the point of view of scholars such as Painter, Margaret was attracted to the book because it told a story similar to her own situation, and once Henry was king, she intentionally and strategically planned the book's translation and printing as an attempt to shape public attitudes toward her son's right to rule. There is no doubt that this kind of publicity was necessary: the sense that Richard III lacked public support was, for example, one of the reasons that Margaret and other nobles attempted to free the princes in the tower (*KM* 62). Yet it seems to me that there were far more effective ways of doing this than printing a romance that roughly resembled Henry's courtship of Elizabeth. Margaret might have had a genealogical roll published, or perhaps have one displayed as John duke of Bedford did to promote Henry VI's kingship in 1423. She could have commissioned a prophecy and used it as Edward IV's supporters used the *Prophecy of the Eagle* to justify his accession in 1461.[57] Or she might have turned away from written texts and staged a pageant or had her badge, or Henry's, emblazoned on city walls.[58] Both the limited production of printed books in 1489 and the allegorical nature of the romance's impact suggest that the skilled politician would have turned elsewhere for propaganda.

Rather, I argue that *Blanchardyn and Eglantine* appealed to Margaret specifically because she could find herself, or at least her son, in the words on the page. In the same way that readers of books of hours inserted themselves into the written prayers imaginatively or, when their names were written in, scribally, Margaret read the romance because it represented an idealized version of her experience of the world. The romance narrative appealed to Margaret because it described life in a way, even if it was fictional, that seemed true and desirable and not simply because it reflected specific details of her experience or reinforced political strategies. The most obvious truth for Margaret would have been the way that *Blanchardyn and Eglantine* explored the dangers of political factionalism but then affirmed the ultimate safety and success of its hero. Early in the narrative Blan-

---

Abbey, so near his shop" in 1483. Or, alternately, that Margaret herself, having been called to Westminster in 1483 by Richard for the coronation, "may well have visited her in person and even have met her ally the Printer" (166). There is no evidence that 1483 is the year in which Margaret purchased the romance.

[57] Sutton and Visser-Fuchs, *Richard III's Books*, 138, 188. The genealogical roll was displayed at Notre-Dame in Paris and included a picture and a poem.

[58] Jones and Underwood note that after the death of Richard duke of York in 1460, "nervous Londoners daubed the Beaufort portcullis badge onto the walls and doors of their houses" (*King's Mother*, 43).

chardyn, Parzival-like, leaves his royal home without knowledge of chivalric arts. Although he is disguised as a mere soldier, the other characters comment repeatedly on the nobility that seems to shine through his common clothing. Even the impervious Eglantine, from whom he steals a kiss, refrains from putting him to death because she intuits his underlying superiority. Blanchardyn, like Henry, inhabits a world in which his destiny as the "successoure legytyme" is, retrospectively, obvious. He is "naturelly inclyned" to speak truthfully and "appeteth and desyreth" all things noblemen value; he learns chivalric arts just as "the goode byrde affeyteth hirself," that is, instinctively, and succeeds in restoring order to the kingdom.[59]

My observation about Margaret's reading is not, however, that she thought of the romance as a simple reflection of historical circumstances. It might have done this for another reader, but for Margaret *Blanchardyn and Eglantine* provided an opportunity to reimagine political outcomes. Margaret had certainly already considered the possibility that Henry could become king when she purchased the book, or perhaps more to the point, she readily recognized that however disputed the family's lineage was, Edward IV was uncomfortable with what could have been considered a Tudor claim to the throne.[60] It was not until 1483, however, that such a possibility seemed even remotely likely. Edward IV died unexpectedly in April of that year; his brother Richard almost immediately declared Edward's sons illegitimate and seized the throne. Richard III's failure to win popular favor became apparent quickly. Margaret and others hatched a plot to rescue the princes from the tower; the rescue failed, and soon thereafter the princes were believed to be dead. At this point, the Woodvilles, including Elizabeth, Edward IV's queen, and Margaret, entered into an alliance whose result was the planned marriage of Henry Tudor and Elizabeth of York, Elizabeth Woodville's daughter, and a series of rebellions. Henry would not accede the throne for two more years; in the meantime, Richard III's forces put down the uprisings. Margaret's punishment for her participation was both forfeit of her estates and titles and something like house arrest: her husband, Thomas Lord Stanley, who had remained loyal to Richard, was to keep her apart from her household servants and relations (*KM* 61–65).

[59] Old French *afaiter:* 1. fashion or shape 2. educate, rule, direct toward a goal.

[60] Jones and Underwood cite Bernard André's *Memorials of King Henry VII* on this subject; André observes that Margaret had warned Henry in 1476 not to return to England if Edward offered him one of his daughters in marriage. See André, "Vita Henrici Septimi," in *Memorials of King Henry VII,* ed. James Gairdner (London: Longman, Brown, Green, Longman, Roberts, 1858), 23; Jones and Underwood, *King's Mother,* 61.

Political plotting is one thing and reading another. I suspect that Margaret's reading of *Blanchardyn and Eglantine* was, at least by the time it was printed in English, commemorative: she herself came to read the romance as a text in which she could already see (and perhaps believed she had always already seen) Henry's accession of 1485.[61] Before the victory at Bosworth Field, the romance narrative probably appealed to Margaret because it seemed to promote both the status quo, the order of her world with a satisfying romance resolution, and, paradoxically, a utopian vision of unity among conflicting forces. Without threatening her ordinary understanding of social relations, *Blanchardyn and Eglantine* allowed Margaret to respond to its narrative as disruptive of and complicit with institutional order. In this romance, enemies are united in opposition to institutional power: even the Saracens, who were generally synonymous with evil in late medieval literature, are represented positively, coming to Blanchardyn's aid when he needs it most in his struggle against wicked King Alymodes. Nor is this disruption limited to questions concerning sovereignty and military power. Hereditary authority, the privilege of "birth," is questioned repeatedly by the romance's depiction of Blanchardyn's *learned* chivalric prowess. Although Blanchardyn's nobility is established from the outset—he is the "successoure legytyme" of the king and queen of Friesland—he is represented as having acquired all the talents associated with nobility through education. He was "take for to be endoctryned in lytterature and in goode maners / to a clerck, the which wythin short tyme made hym expert and able in many and dyuers sciences, that is to wyte, in gramayre, logyke and philosophie."[62] While the other characters remark frequently on the nobility that seems to emanate from the disguised Blanchardyn, what finally constitutes nobility in the romance is proper education of a worthy individual.[63]

This reading accounts for Margaret's renewed interest in the ro-

[61] This way of thinking about books is very much like Augustine's theory of signs. See Talal Asad, *Genealogies of Religion: Discipline and Reasons of Power in Christianity and Islam* (Baltimore: Johns Hopkins University Press, 1993), 154 n. 28, in which he summarizes Augustine's theory as presented in *De doctrina christiana.* On Augustine as a reader see Brian Stock, *Augustine the Reader: Meditation, Self-Knowledge, and the Ethics of Interpretation* (Cambridge: Harvard University Press, 1996).

[62] *Caxton's Blanchardyn and Eglantine,* 12.

[63] Sutton and Visser-Fuchs allude to "the debate about the nature of true nobility" that raged in the Middle Ages and note that Buonaccorso da Montemagno's *Controversia de vera nobilitate* was printed in English for the first time in 1480 (*Richard III's Books,* 134).

mance after her son's accession, but it does little to explain why we should not think of her commission to Caxton as purely propagandistic. Margaret did, after all, choose to have this particular book translated and published, and since she read French fluently and already owned a copy in that language, it was not a personal desire to own the book in "rude and comyn" English that motivated the request. I would argue, however, that although her decision was of course directed at a reading public, that decision was not simply politically motivated. Rather, it appears to have been driven by a sense of obligation, a kind of noblesse oblige, to those readers, whoever Margaret imagined them to be, of the English version of the romance, and we can see this sense of obligation in Caxton's association of the translation with chivalric education. In Caxton's dedication, Margaret appears to address readers, much as Anne Stafford does in the dedication in *The Nightingale,* who want to read books because those books have the ability to transform the readers' lives. By associating Margaret's natural relationship with Henry with her command that the book be translated "into our *maternal* and englysh tonge" (italics added), Caxton indicates that Margaret's command is prompted by solicitude: like the good mother of conduct literature, Margaret offers the translation to readers because it will teach them as the French text had taught her. We might, cynically, consider this as merely a marketing ploy. Patrons responsible for the production of translations in the later Middle Ages were regularly praised for their civic-mindedness. In Christine de Pizan's life of Charles V, for example, she declares that although Charles " 'knew Latin well and needed no one to expound it to him,' " he had translations written " 'out of the great love he felt for his successors.' "[64] It is possible that Charles's actions were politically motivated, and even if we cannot separate Christine's statement about his intentions—her description of his "love"—from his political ambitions, her comment nevertheless offers a useful way to think about medieval translation and patronage.

Rather than imagining that translation and printing were displays of virtue, tactics, or strategies, which we can read as manipulations of public understanding, we might instead think seriously about what it would mean to consider this kind of patronage as an expression of love, as Christine calls it. If, as I suggested in relation to Margaret

[64] Cited in Richard Firth Green, *Poets and Princepleasers: Literature and the English Court in the Late Middle Ages* (Toronto: University of Toronto Press, 1980), 151.

Beauchamp's and Anne Stafford's books of hours, certain late medieval readers turned increasingly to written texts to gain greater understanding of their spiritual lives, then it might be useful to think of lay reading as approximating reading in monastic communities. Love of God, the foundation of monastic disciplinary programs, involved the learning of virtue, which the orders cultivated through their written rules and the textual traditions associated with the rules. In monastic orders, the abbot was responsible for teaching the rule and upholding its conditions. This placed him in a position of authority over the other monks, although his superiority was derived from the rule and not from his person. Abbot and monks were joined together by their common desire to fulfill the terms of the rule, and "Virtuous obedience thus presupposes and results in 'a common will' " that structures monastic life.[65] Reading for a text's moral sense meant that regardless of personal circumstance, readers benefited from their reading because it was a way of understanding and responding to truth. If this was in fact the case even for secular readers, then providing copies of printed texts united patron, readers, and their common desire for understanding in a manner that presupposes no hidden, political meaning (although such acts may, of course, have resulted in heightened political status for the patron). Instead, patronage appears closer to the fulfillment of spiritual obligations described in a book of prayers Margaret commissioned from Caxton in 1491 in which the supplicant asks that she and her fellow believers "may doo our duete and homage eche wyth othe[r] and for other."[66] Having the romance printed was a way to fulfill the public teaching role modeled in the dedication to the *Nightingale,* which involved a specific sense of obligation to pass on the "lust" for learning, as the *Nightingale* poet calls it, to others.[67]

Although in the examples above Margaret relied heavily on writing and printed texts, her dependence on the written word differed from the increasingly common understanding of texts as evidentiary docu-

[65] Asad, *Geneaologies of Religion,* 159. See also Jacques Leclerq, *The Love of Learning and the Desire for God: A Study of Monastic Culture,* 2d ed. (New York: Fordham University Press, 1977).

[66] *STC* 20195, fol. 18.

[67] It is quite possible, as George Painter suggests, that Caxton sought out Margaret (and not the reverse) to promote his printed books, but this depends on Caxton's sense that an aristocratic woman would want to have her name associated with the print trade. Even if it were true, it only tells us about Caxton's entrepreneurial program and not about Margaret's literate practice. See Painter, *William Caxton,* 166.

ments. She did, as I noted earlier, keep a close watch on her financial records; like her mother, if accounts did not tally up she made sure to root out the source of the discrepancy.[68] However, both her correspondence with Henry and her promotion of Caxton's romance take part in a different notion of the function of writing. In both instances, Margaret imagines the written word as revealing (or potentially revealing) "hidden" truth. Instead of using written texts to reflect objective, external conditions, the purpose of writing in her letters to Henry and in her distribution of *Blanchardyn and Eglantine* is to unify individuals and groups of individuals. In reading his mother's letters, Henry is to recognize that his mother's inner thoughts concern her unconditional love for him and not her finances—and Henry is to understand her as if he could read her mind.[69] Similarly, readers of the romance are expected to understand the book's allegory as a representation of what is best and most advantageous for all, and not as self-interested propaganda produced by the Tudors: Caxton's dedication helps the reader see that it would be "natural" for the king's mother, and by association, the nation's mother, to provide her children with an exemplary book, just as an aristocratic mother might give her biological children a book from which they should learn.

Although Caxton's dedication highlights an important aspect of Margaret's literate practice, her desire to provide readers with printed books was also shaped by her participation in London's devotional culture after she moved to the city with her third husband. Relocation was among the least controllable and the most common changes in an aristocratic woman's life following remarriage. After Margaret's marriage to Stanley, the king's household steward, she divided her time among Stanley's residences in Lancashire and North Wales, her house at Woking, and, most centrally, court in London; after her son acceded, she spent most of her time at her own houses, Coldharbour and Collyweston.[70] Although the households in Surrey and Lin-

[68] Jones and Underwood, for example, mention an episode in which her feodary at Collyweston, Richard Galee, concealed sums of money from her. Margaret discovered the crime and on several occasions sent one of her representatives to Collyweston to investigate the fraud (*King's Mother,* 133).

[69] Ellis, *Original Letters,* 1:47.

[70] Jones and Underwood list Margaret's estates in Appendix 2, *King's Mother,* 262–67. In Appendix 1, they offer Margaret's itinerary for 1498–99 to show how closely her movements paralleled those of her son. The nearly three months she spent at Collyweston was the longest time she stayed in one place that year (260–61).

colnshire were relatively isolated, once Margaret married Stanley her home was for a great part of the year the center of political activity, Edward IV's court.

It might then seem that she would have become part of a literary community located at court, given that the king and queen were known to own books. For example, although Edward was less well known for his literary interests than was his younger brother Richard, he collected many books ranging "from a small Latin formulary to English translations of Cicero printed by Caxton and Guillaume Caoursin's *Siege of Rhodes,* and from St. Augustine's *City of God* to tracts on alchemy and Lorenzo Traversagni's *Triumphus justitiae.*"[71] Similarly, Elizabeth Woodville, like her husband, also owned a number of books, among which may have been Lydgate's *Life of Our Lady,* which is dedicated to an unnamed queen "ffor to comffort and to passe tyme in redyng."[72] Yet despite clear evidence of royal interest in books, there is no indication that Edward or Elizabeth shared their enthusiasm with Margaret as part of an aristocratic, household community.[73]

Rather, although the royal household was the focus of political life, London's religious institutions, especially Syon Abbey and the Carthusian monasteries, the London Charterhouse and the one at Sheen, increasingly shaped the literate culture of late medieval England.[74] Scholars have recently become very interested in Syon

[71] Sutton and Visser-Fuchs, *Richard III's Books,* 31–33. They state that Edward owned at least forty-five books; his collection included Christine de Pizan's *Epistle to Othea,* which Margaret, as I noted above, also owned.

[72] Ibid., 36. See also Sutton and Visser-Fuchs, " 'A most benevolent queen': Elizabeth Woodville's Reputation, Her Piety and Her Books" *The Ricardian* 11 (1994–96): 214–45.

[73] Elizabeth Woodville shared an interest in Caxton with Margaret; Elizabeth (the Woodville family more generally) patronized Caxton's production of printed books early in his career in England. On Caxton's relationship with Elizabeth Woodville, see Painter, *William Caxton,* 121–30. See also Theresa D. Kemp, "The Knight of the Tower and the Queen in Sanctuary: Elizabeth Woodville's Use of Meaningful Silence and Absence," *New Medieval Literatures* 4 (2001): 171–88. On Cecily, see C. A. J. Armstrong, "The Piety of Cicely, Duchess of York," in *England, France, and Burgundy in the Fifteenth Century* (London: Hambledon, 1983), 135–56.

[74] For example, Susan Powell remarks that "it is well documented that Syon Abbey . . . exploited the resources of the printing presses in the dissemination of devotional material, much of it produced in-house" ("Syon, Caxton, and the *Festial,*" *Birgittiana* 2 [1996]: 187). See also J. T. Rhodes, "Syon Abbey and Its Religious Publications in the Sixteenth Century," *Journal of Ecclesiastical History* 44 (1993): 11–25; Ann M. Hutchison, "Devotional Reading in the Monastery and in the Late Medieval Household," in *De Cella in Seculum: Religious and Secular Life and Devotion in Late Medieval England,* ed. Michael G. Sargent (Cambridge: D. S. Brewer, 1989);

Abbey's role in the promotion of devotional reading, but it was the London Charterhouse, on account of its location, that seems to have had the most immediate and recognizable impact on Margaret's literate practice. The Carthusians were an ascetic order, but although Carthusian tradition held that monasteries were to be founded in remote areas in imitation of the desert fathers, the London Charterhouse, established in 1370, was "metropolitan."[75] The London Charterhouse was in the city, unlike Sheen and Syon (Sheen has been described as "three hours' rowing time upstream from London bridge," and Syon was directly across the river), and its location made it a vital part of the city's identity. Built on a cemetery in which innumerable plague victims had been buried, it was visited regularly by lay believers who considered the contemplative order's monastery part of London: the city's inhabitants wandered within its walls, laid claims to "ownership" of individual cells through benefactions, requested burial on its grounds, and left personal belongings to the house.[76] Margaret and her husband, like many lay believers, participated actively in the city's religious and political life, and in 1478, they were admitted to confraternity with the Carthusians.[77]

Margaret had been affiliated with religious institutions before. For

Veronica Lawrence, "The Role of the Monasteries of Syon and Sheen in the Production, Ownership and Circulation of Mystical Literature in the Late Middle Ages," in *The Mystical Tradition and the Carthusians,* ed. James Hogg (Salzburg: Institut für Anglistik und Amerikanistik, 1996), 101–15.

75 Lawrence, "Role of the Monasteries of Syon and Sheen," 102. She takes this information from Rhodes, "Syon Abbey and Its Religious Publications," 11; on the urban nature of the London Charterhouse, see Roger Lovatt, "The Library of John Blacman and Contemporary Carthusian Spirituality," *Journal of Ecclesiastical History* 43 (1992): 216.

76 Concerning the relationship between lay spirituality and the London Charterhouse, see Vincent Gillespie, "Cura Pastoralis in Deserto," in *De Cella in Seculum,* 161–81; Joseph A. Gribbin, " 'Ex Oblatione Fidelium'—The Liturgy of the London Charterhouse and the Laity,' " in *The Mystical Tradition and the Carthusians,* ed. James Hogg (Salzburg: Institut für Anglistik und Amerikanistik, 1996), 83–104; and Lovatt, "Library of John Blacman." Lovatt and Gribbin both suggest that the monastery's "evangelical" function was recommended by one of its founders, Bishop Northburgh, and also that the physical arrangement of the church's chapels, cells, and altars as well as the urban character of the city itself shaped monastic attention to lay spirituality.

77 Drawing on traditional ideas of Margaret's piety and of women's religious interest more generally, Jones and Underwood suggest that it was Margaret's idea to join the fraternity and not her husband's (*King's Mother,* 147, 180–81). It seems likely, given the admission of multiple members of Stanley's family, that he also had close ties to the Carthusians.

example, in 1465 she and her mother were admitted to confraternity with Crowland Abbey. Similarly, in the same year she secured Henry's admission to the confraternity of the Order of the Holy Trinity (*KM* 47). These earlier associations seem to have been largely pragmatic; Crowland Abbey's lands bordered those of Margaret's mother, making relations with the foundation materially significant, and affiliation with the Order of the Holy Trinity, a society concerned with redeeming Christians held captive by Turks, was presumably an effort to secure allies to ensure her son's safety. In contrast, her involvement with the Carthusians, although it may have been motivated initially by the order's prestige in London, depended on the convergence between her growing sense of the centrality of writing and the order's mission to speak "to the Christian world through the books which they wrote, copied, and transmitted."[78] Margaret, having already developed both an interest in written texts as interactive and a sense of responsibility toward other readers, responded to the Carthusian brand of affective spirituality by becoming involved in the reproduction of devotional writings.

Although the Carthusians are contemplatives, set apart from secular life for the purposes of meditation, the London Charterhouse was intimately engaged with pastoral care. Its concern with lay spirituality was so great that the monastery even incorporated devotions popular with lay believers, such as veneration of the Blessed Virgin, into its liturgical celebration. Joseph Gribbin has detailed the particular liturgical innovations that were made by the London Carthusians, and he notes, for example, that the English Carthusians were in disobedience of the general chapter's instructions concerning the canonical office of the Virgin. The London house was saying the office on Saturdays when it was supposed to be saying ferial offices (on those days that were not major festivals or saints' days), and the general chapter expressed its displeasure with the English Carthusians' failure to follow procedures.[79] Popular with lay believers through association with books of hours—the Hours of the Virgin formed the core of the primers by the thirteenth century—the office continued to be said by the London house on Saturdays, despite the general chapter's

[78] Michael G. Sargent, "The Transmission by the English Carthusians of Some Late Medieval Spiritual Writings," *Journal of Ecclesiastical History* 27 (1976): 225.

[79] See H. Leith Spencer, for a useful summary of liturgical calendars and a description of "feriae" (Spencer, *English Preaching in the Late Middle Ages* [Oxford: Oxford University Press, 1993], 20–33).

rebuke.[80] In their answer to the general chapter's charges, the London house argued that when they complied with the chapter's order, lay believers were injured and "the devotion of the faithful daily waxes cold."[81]

The London Charterhouse's Saturday celebration of the canonical office of the Virgin is indicative of its general sensitivity to the religious needs of the city. In fact, its responsiveness was so great that lay spirituality shaped Carthusian devotional life. In particular, the London Carthusians modified their spiritual practice to accommodate the linguistic difficulties of lay believers who were eager for spiritual nourishment but unable to follow Latin expertly. The office was popular with lay audiences because it was relatively uncomplicated and because it was familiar.[82] Because the Hours did not change according to the day of celebration, they were relatively easy to follow and could be recognized even if the listener had little grasp of the Latin in which they were performed.[83] Although the monks themselves were learned, their support of lay believers' enthusiasm for masses that may have been only partially understood is fully in keeping with the order's emphasis on experiential knowledge. As John Van Engen suggests, Carthusian writers insist that "what needed to be transcended was the intellective faculty, the need to reason a person's way into the being of God."[84] Believers who could not understand the Latin completely could nevertheless "hear" God speak if they "listened" with their hearts, and celebration of masses that encouraged this kind of devoted attention were an important part of the order's mission.

[80] Roger S. Wieck, *Painted Prayers: The Book of Hours in Medieval and Renaissance Art* (New York: George Braziller, 1997), 9–10.

[81] Gribbin, " 'Ex Oblatione Fidelium,' " 91. Gribbin cites his own archival work, which is presented in his published thesis, *Aspects of Carthusian Liturgical Practice in Later Medieval England* (Salzburg: Institut für Anglistik und Amerikanistik, 1995).

[82] The fact that worshippers wished to hear the office suggests that they knew (and at least to a certain extent understood) the celebration, which was of course in Latin. On lay believers' attraction to specific masses, see Eamon Duffy, *The Stripping of the Altars: Traditional Religion in England c. 1400–1580* (New Haven: Yale University Press, 1992), 373–74.

[83] Wieck, *Painted Prayers*, 10: "the Hours of the Virgin remained basically the same every day. The only variable was the three Psalms that constitute the nocturn of the first Hour, Matins (these Psalms changed depending on the day of the week . . .). The contents of the remaining Hours, Lauds through Compline, did not change."

[84] John Van Engen, "Preface," in *Carthusian Spirituality: The Writings of Hugh of Balma and Guigo de Ponte*, trans. Dennis D. Martin (New York: Paulist Press, 1997), xix.

Participation in London's active religious culture, and especially attention to Carthusian ideas about devotion, shaped Margaret's subsequent involvement with the print trade and her service to a reading community. Her second commission from Caxton was a printed book of prayers in Latin and English. Unlike her previous request, an English translation of a French romance, this one was not intended to make undecipherable texts available to readers. Instead, this book's mixture of Latin and English suggests that Margaret's commission depended on a widespread distinction between what the Carthusians referred to as the "substance of truth" and the "froth of words." In 1491, Margaret and her daughter-in-law Elizabeth, with whom Margaret seems to have shared literary interests much as she had with her mother-in-law Anne Stafford, commanded Caxton to print a prayer book that began with the *Fifteen Oes* in Middle English and included many other prayers, some in Latin, some in English.[85]

The language of the prayers is significant because the use of both Latin and English suggests that the readers' response to the texts was not dependent on intellectual understanding. This is not to say that the selections were chosen randomly. Rather, although it is not possible to categorize the prayers according to monastic source (they are not all, for example, Bridgettine or Carthusian), it is possible to identify the "theme" of the collection. Specifically, despite the difference in languages used, it appears that every prayer in the book is concerned with physical and spiritual protection. For example, in a prayer beginning "Most dere lorde and sauyour sweet Jhesu," the supplicant requests that Jesus stand as a "shelde and protection ayenst al myne enymes bodely and gostely."[86] Jesus as Son is not the only source of protection: the collection includes prayers seeking the help of guardian angels; prayers that Saint Roche and the tau cross would defend against the plague; prayers for the Holy Trinity to safeguard the believer from the same evil that put Daniel in the fiery furnace; prayers that Jesus' Holy Name keep one from damnation. Even the

[85] When the prayer book is discussed, it is generally described as Bridgettine because the *Fifteen Oes,* the first text in the book, was thought to have been written by Saint Bridget. The extent of Margaret's association with Syon Abbey remains unclear. See Edwards and Meale, "Marketing of Printed Books," 115. On the *Fifteen Oes,* see Rebecca Krug, "The Fifteen Oes," in *Cultures of Piety: Medieval English Devotional Literature in Translation,* ed. Anne Clark Bartlett and Thomas H. Bestul (Ithaca, N.Y.: Cornell University Press, 1999), 107–17, 212–16. Caxton's edition is *STC* 20195 (Duff 150) 1491.

[86] STC 20195, sig. b ii.

Fifteen Oes, which might appear to be a meditation on the Passion, are protective: a very well known legend associated with the *Oes* asserted that repetition of the verses would drastically reduce one's time and suffering in purgatory. As one prayer from the collection puts it, these selections were to be used in defense against enemies "visibilus et invisibilis." This notion suggests that the repetition of written words, even uncomprehending repetition, was believed to safeguard the reader against negative consequences because it brought holy forces to one's aid. The use of Latin and English in the collection indicates that Margaret saw the act of speaking/reading the prayers as at least as significant as the linguistic meaning of the selections.

One could of course hardly make a definitive argument about Margaret's interest in Latin based on Caxton's collection. It is possible, for instance, to argue that Margaret and her daughter-in-law had little influence over the selection of prayers that comprised Caxton's edition. Perhaps Caxton himself decided to include the Latin prayers without Margaret's knowledge. Maybe he simply forgot to translate all the later prayers, having placed the Middle English *Oes* at the front of the book. However, another collection associated with Margaret, Westminster Abbey MS 39, allows us to draw some firmer conclusions about her interest in the Latin prayers. According to Ker, this manuscript was written in England and very likely was commissioned by Margaret for her husband, Thomas Stanley. Margaret's arms appear on the first folio; the Stanley jamb occurs nine times in the manuscript's decoration.[87] Its contents are remarkably similar to those of Caxton's collection. Like the printed book with the *Fifteen Oes* and other prayers, Westminster 39 includes prayers in Latin and in English; it also, like the *Fifteen Oes* book, is divided up by titles describing the subsequent prayers, such as "Oracio de passione cristi," "A devout prayer," and "Ad sanctam trinitatem," and by liturgical tags, for example, "Oremus," "in nomine patri," "sed libera nos a malo," and "Non nobis domine non nobis." Most significantly, there is great similarity between the contents of Westminster 39 and Caxton's printed book of prayers. The manuscript includes prayers to the Holy Cross, on the Passion, and to Jesus' Name, for example; more particularly, Westminster 39 and the printed book share a number of identical texts, including many of the same psalms and several

[87] N. R. Ker, *Medieval Manuscripts in British Libraries* (London: Oxford University Press, 1969), 411–15.

of the same prayers, such as "Infirmitatem nostram," "Deus propicius esto michi," and "Domine Jhesu christe fili die vivi deus omnipotens rex." Additional support for my contention comes from another collection of English and Latin prayers Margaret is thought to have owned, Fitzwilliam Museum MS 261, which is made up of tracts and prayers believed to protect against the plague, such as "Per hoc signum tau T a pestilencia," which appears, with slight changes, in Caxton's printed book.[88]

Given the similarities among these prayer collections, in terms of the common concern with protection that extended even to the inclusion of identical prayers, it appears that even if Margaret could not read Latin expertly, she could distinguish at least enough to recognize prayers that offered readers aid against harm. In other words, she could read Latin well enough to suit her purposes, and these purposes must not have included word-for-word comprehension of linguistic meaning. This is not to argue that readers were never concerned with the meaning of the words: the presence of Middle English translations for some of the poems, including the *Fifteen Oes,* indicates that Margaret, for example, wished to comprehend the exact sense of the prayers' words or at least thought the readers of Caxton's edition should be able to do so. But the incorporation of Latin prayers in several books Margaret is associated with, including the printed collection, suggests that for Margaret, as Eamon Duffy argues in relation to the "reading" of Latin-language primers by those without knowledge of Latin, "Virtue inhered in these passages quite apart from actual comprehension of their message."[89] Saying the verses in Latin seems to have had an importance quite apart from their precise meaning. Yet the "virtue" of the Latin prayers, at least in Margaret's case, was clearly not utterly divorced from the content of the prayers. If it had been, she would not have needed to or would not have been able to select poems that were believed to hold protective power. Rather than being unconcerned with meaning, Margaret's reading of the Latin prayers was apparently both content based and linguistically inexact. She recognized the prayers as protective but was also unable to make sense of each word of the text. This kind of reading, in its validation of the prayers' power apart from precise linguistic meaning, must

[88] See Francis Wormald and Phyllis M. Giles, *A Descriptive Catalogue of the Additional Illuminated Manuscripts in the Fitzwilliam Museum* (Cambridge: Cambridge University Press, 1982), 1:194–96.

[89] Duffy, *Stripping of the Altars,* 217.

have been similar to Carthusian belief in the ability to "grasp the divine apart from a parallel cognitive preparation."[90]

One avenue, then, that lay religious enthusiasm followed in the later Middle Ages was "ritualistic" interaction with writing. By means of verbal repetition, the actual reader inscribed herself in the prayers and claimed the promised protection, even when she was uncertain of their precise semantic meaning. This differed from another path, which we might also associate with Margaret's prayer collections, in which heightened concern with the linguistic meaning of the written text and increased interest in vernacular writings shaped literate interactions. In this case, either the reader's interest in the content of the text grows, which is not surprising, given that language is after all communicative, and she becomes increasingly curious about meaning, or she comes to believe that readers unable to understand Latin should have the opportunity to read the texts' contents with full, linguistic comprehension. She therefore makes vernacular texts available as an act of charity. Although it might seem that the ritualistic and linguistically comprehensive modes of reading would rarely attract the same reader, in Margaret Beaufort's case this was certainly the situation, as we have seen by considering the prayer collections discussed above. In her associations with the London printers, Margaret helped produce both Latin and English books, her interest primarily in production rather than language.

Beginning in the early 1490s, Margaret became involved in the printing and distribution of Latin and vernacular texts meant for both lay believers and clerical institutions. Although a great number of the texts she sponsored were explicitly designed for institutional, religious use, her role in the distribution of English-language writings is perhaps most familiar to scholars. For example, it is well known that in 1494 she and her daughter-in-law presented one of their ladies, Mary Roos, with a copy of Hilton's *Scale of Perfection and Mixed Life.*[91] Scholars often include this fact in discussions of reading communities because the book is inscribed by Elizabeth and Margaret to their friend: " 'I pray you pray for me / Elsyabeth ye quene' " and " 'Mastres Rosse y truste yn youre prayers / the whiche y pray yow y may be partener / of. Margaret R the kynges / modyr.' "[92] Margaret

[90] Van Engen, "Preface," xix.

[91] Lovatt, "Library of John Blacman," 218–19.

[92] Cited in Riddy, " 'Women talking about things of God,' " 109. The inscriptions are reproduced in P. J. Croft, *Lady Margaret Beaufort, Countess of Richmond: Descriptions of Two Unique Volumes Associated with One of the First Patrons of Printing in England* (London: Quaritch, 1958).

and Elizabeth had in fact commissioned de Worde's first printing of the book; as Michael Sargent has demonstrated, lay readers of Hilton at the close of the Middle Ages were numerous in the London area—the response to the *Scale* was enthusiastic.[93] However, although printing allowed Margaret to provide more books to a wider range of people, this did not mean she gave up buying books for herself or quit giving personal manuscripts to individuals—Westminster 39 and Fitzwilliam 261 were, for example, private collections intended for personal use—but the printing and distribution of printed texts gained increasing importance for Margaret in the years after her son became king. So, for example, in addition to the Hilton edition, she also had the *Fifteen Oes* collection printed in the 1490s as well as a Sarum book of hours (which was in Latin but designed for a lay audience), and early in the sixteenth century, de Worde printed a number of books, including the *Parliament of Devils, Nicodemus Gospel,* and a *Life of St. Ursula* in Margaret's name. All of these involvements would be considered "pastoral" had Margaret been a member of the religious establishment. In fact, similarities between her sense of responsibility toward secular readers and the London Carthusians' efforts to make devotional literature available to those in the secular world indicate both how influential the London house was and how receptive an aristocratic woman's literate education might make her to such a mission.

If Margaret's involvement with the print trade appears to be a straightforward act of piety, in which she made English writings available to lay readers, her commissioning of Latin liturgical texts complicates this idea.[94] For example, her commissioning of the production of the Latin office and proper of the mass for the feast of the Holy Name, which Pynson is believed to have printed for her in 1493, shows one of the ways that her patronage influenced clerical culture as well as lay devotion.[95] Often her role in the distribution of these writings is used to show how membership in a "tight-knit spiritual

[93] Michael G. Sargent, "Walter Hilton's *Scale of Perfection:* The London Manuscript Group Reconsidered," *Medium Aevum* 52 (1983): 204–8. See also H. M. Gardner, "The Text of the Scale of Perfection," *Medium Aevum* 22 (1936): 11–30.

[94] Powell makes a similar claim about Margaret and the print trade: "The importance she attached to the written word is demonstrated by her own reading and translation and promotion of printed texts. In her association with printers, in particular, she may be seen to have facilitated the Bridgettine and Carthusian 'outreach' " ("Lady Margaret and Her Books," 221).

[95] Powell argues persuasively for Margaret's responsibility for its printing (ibid., 209–11).

aristocracy" shaped late medieval devotional culture. For example, Eamon Duffy has asserted that "From its beginnings in England the cult of the Holy Name had aristocratic backing, and it achieved status as a feast in the 1480s under the patronage of Lady Margaret Beaufort, whose domestic clergy composed the Office."[96] Working backward from the time in 1494 that a papal bull sanctioned observance of the feast by Margaret, among others, Duffy provides his readers with a narrative in which Margaret worked diligently for almost twenty years to have one of her favorite devotions legitimized. However, although Duffy's speculations about the author of the office, Henry Hornby, are supported by scholars such as Pfaff, he seems to exaggerate the constancy and duration of Margaret's own enthusiasm for this devotion. Rather, it appears that her interest grew rapidly in the few years between the time that the *Fifteen Oes* collection came out and the printing of the office and proper of the feast in 1493, even if Hornby himself was interested earlier. This is suggested by the fact that although the 1491 printed book includes prayers that call on the Holy Name, they do so in a fairly limited fashion. For example, in the version of the prayer "Sanctifica quesum domine" printed in the *Fifteen Oes* collection, Jesus is never even named, but in the version printed in the York *Horae* early in the sixteenth century, Jesus' name is repeated and terms such as "pastor bone" that were associated with the devotion were also included.[97]

Although it may seem obvious that an office of the Catholic Church should be written in Latin, why would Margaret choose to have it distributed and printed in Latin if she was interested in promoting the relatively new devotion among the laity? As Denis Reveney observes, interest in the Holy Name did not spread widely in England until vernacular writers began to include discussions of the devotion in their works, and Margaret's own attraction to the Holy Name probably came at least in part through vernacular reading.[98]

[96] Duffy, *Stripping of the Altars,* 115, 284.

[97] *Horae Eboracenses: The Prymer or Hours of the Blessed Virgin Mary according to the Use of the Illustrious Church of York,* ed. C. Wordsworth, Surtees Society 132 (1920), 85; *Fifteen Oes* and other prayers, fol. 33. The edition of the *Scale of Perfection* that Wynkyn de Worde printed for Margaret Beaufort in 1494 included a passage concerning the Holy Name that appears in only certain of the *Scale* texts. On Hilton's *Scale* and the Holy Name passages, see Sargent, "Walter Hilton's *Scale of Perfection,*" esp. 195–97.

[98] Until the last quarter of the fifteenth century, the devotion was associated primarily with monastic practice. Denis Reveney discusses a Carthusian manuscript, British Library Additional 37049, which includes passages concerning the Holy Name that are heavily marked with the "Jesus monogram," IHC, indicating that the

Yet rather than producing a vernacular text that would assist lay readers, Margaret, in her promotion of the feast, distributed a Latin text that even she could not fully comprehend.[99] Although it may be that the Latin had the ritualistic appeal mentioned above, it is hard to imagine how this appeal would be effective in promoting an unfamiliar feast. The most likely answer to the question is that instead of an audience of lay readers, Margaret imagined a clerical audience for the printed office and proper. In providing clerical readers with the office, she mediated between "God's words" and the print trade. Like the Carthusians, in her involvement with book reproduction she made His words available to readers, and her desire to serve the clerical community may also explain her probable support of Caxton's 1491 printing of thc *Festial* and *Quattor Sermons.*[100]

Despite her influence on clerical culture, Margaret's relationship with the Church rested on a clearly marked division between her authority as a laywoman and that of the religious officials with whom she consulted. This is not to say that the Church remained aloof to worldly affairs or that clergymen did not respect social standing; however, at least in terms of spiritual status, Margaret was always disadvantaged in contrast with members of the religious community. Books such as Hilton's *Scale* and *Mixed Life* were attractive to lay believers precisely because they recognized this divide and responded by offering a middle path designated explicitly for people lacking a religious vocation. But that middle way, for all that vernacular writings did to encourage lay spiritual progress, continued to be understood as inferior to a "truly" spiritual life, one that demanded an individual and institutional commitment to the Church. Given this valuation, one might assume, as scholars such as Powell do, that Margaret's reading and patronage represented her attempt to approximate a "truly" religious life. This kind of argument is supported by the well-known sixteenth-century likenesses of Margaret dressed in widow's clothes, wearing as a headdress "a gabled coif and a wimple" that make her look a great deal like a nun, reminding viewers of the vow of chastity that she took in 1499 and of her provision that rooms be

reader of the manuscript understood the linguistic meaning of the passage even if the purpose of that attention to meaning was to promote an affective response (Reveney, " 'The Name Poured Out': Margins, Illuminations and Miniatures as Evidence for the Practice of Devotions to the Name of Jesus in Late Medieval England," in *The Mystical Tradition and the Carthusians,* ed. James Hogg (Salzburg: Institut für Anglistik und Amerikanistik, 1996), 139–40.

99 Ibid., 129–31.

100 See Powell, "Syon, Caxton, and the *Festial,*" 187–208.

set aside for her female friends and family members so they could remain with her over extended periods of time, like the "familiae" of religious communities.[101] In addition, in his funeral sermon Fisher describes her rigorous schedule of early rising and prayer, and there seems little question, even given her extensive secular involvements as detailed by Jones and Underwood, that Margaret modeled her daily life increasingly on a spiritual pattern.

However, rather than withdrawing from the world to devote herself completely to a religious life as if she were an anchoress, Margaret surrounded herself with men who were engaged in clerical and scholarly study.[102] The most famous of them was Bishop John Fisher, who became her confessor at the turn of the century. Many more were involved in her spiritual and secular affairs, the best known of whom included Henry Hornby, dean of her chapel by 1499 and supposed author of the office of the Holy Name, and Hugh Aston, her receiver general, who succeeded Fisher to Lythe rectory in 1504. She offered financial support to numerous others at institutions, including Eton, Cambridge and Oxford, and the London Charterhouse, as well as abroad, especially in France. These scholars in turn advised her and pursued her legal concerns as they conducted their studies. Margaret clearly had the necessary financial resources and secular authority to establish scholarly foundations, to commission printed books, and to support individual scholars, but she also relied on scholars and churchmen because they were knowledgeable in ways she was not.[103]

These scholars were trained to use writing in ways that were unfamiliar to Margaret but that attracted her attention after 1500. Specifically, about the time that Fisher became her confessor, Margaret began translating vernacular, devotional writing from French into English. Earlier, she had asked the printers to translate works for her. In 1504, however, she took upon herself the task of translating the fourth book of the *Imitation of Christ,* and in 1506 she translated the *Mirroure of Golde for the Synfull Soule;* Fisher's sermon suggests that she may have been responsible for other translations as well.

Translation and the correction of written texts were central to the

[101] Jones and Underwood, *King's Mother,* 294. Margaret kept rooms at Collyweston for the noblewomen of her family and acquaintances (*King's Mother,* 160–64).

[102] On Margaret's support of scholars, see Malcolm G. Underwood, "The Lady Margaret and Her Cambridge Connections," *Sixteenth Century Journal* 13 (1982): 67–82.

[103] Jones and Underwood offer a list of Margaret's "Officers, Servants and Scholars" for 1499–1509 (*King's Mother,* 268–87).

work of many religious men, who treated them both as an act of love toward others and as a personal, penitential experience. Vincent Gillespie notes that William Darker, a professed monk at Sheen, for example, whom Margaret may have known, copied *Speculum Christiani* at the end of the fifteenth or beginning of the sixteenth century "in remissionem peccatorum suorum." Darker's remark is especially interesting in relation to transcription and translation because it implies that the act of copying somehow "rewrites" sin, replacing the accumulated record of transgression with the devotional text-object. Writing was so intimately linked to the writer's own spiritual life that, as Hilton notes in the *Scale of Perfection,* a book Margaret had commissioned from de Worde, the author's purpose in composing devotional treatises was essentially double: to encourage others to pursue the spiritual life and to "stir" oneself out of "negligence"—to "do better than" the writer herself has done before.[104] Finally, Margaret's confessor, Fisher, in his sermon on Psalm 32 (*Beati quorum*), the second Penitential Psalm, employs a similar image in explaining the need of satisfaction. In this sermon, which was printed at Margaret's command, Fisher suggests that sin marks the believer's soul as if it were a pen and explains that "satysfaccion doth rase & expell it so clene away that no sygne can euer after be spyed of it."[105] A letter from Henry VII to his mother indicates that Margaret may in fact have long associated the personal effort of writing with genuine devotion: Henry concludes his letter with the anxious request that his mother "not be displeased" that he has failed to write the letter "with myne owne hand" on account of his failing eyesight.[106] Such attitudes toward writing have obvious affinities with the "ritualistic"

[104] *The Scale of Perfection by Walter Hilton . . . Modernised from the First Printed Edition of Wynkyn de Worde* (London: London, Burns, Oates and Washbourne, 1927), 172.

[105] *Works of John Fisher,* 31.

[106] Ellis, *Original Letters,* 1:44. The previous letter in Ellis's collection concludes, "Wrytyn wyt the hand of your humble douter" (1:43). On handwriting (as opposed to dictation) in the Middle Ages, see David Ganz, " 'Mind in Character': Ancient and Medieval Ideas about the Status of the Autograph as an Expression of Personality," in *Of the Making of Books: Medieval Manuscripts, Their Scribes and Readers,* ed. P. R. Robinson and Rivkah Kim (Aldershot, U.K.: Scolar, 1997), 280–99. Interestingly, at least some of Margaret's own letters to Henry were dictated. There is an echo of the importance of writing in one's own hand in *Blanchardyn and Eglantine:* Blanchardyn writes to his beloved, "ye shal vnderstande by mouthe ferthere of myn astate / And by couse ye shall gyue credence and feyth to this, myn owne hande wrytyng" (*Caxton's Blanchardyn and Eglantine,* 134).

reading of Latin that I proposed earlier in that they value the personal and spiritual qualities of the written word as well as its linguistic, communicative efficacy. Given these understandings of the relationship between writing and devotion, Margaret's translations may have been first personal, spiritual exercises before they were texts that she proceeded to have printed and distributed, and the labor of writing might have been as important as the content of the text.

But even if these translations were in part spiritual exercises, Margaret appears to have chosen the particular texts to be translated for specific reasons. The *Imitation of Christ,* for example, is a "self-inscriptive" text. Formally, it is a dialogue between Christ and the sinner/narrator, who reflects on a collection of Christ's words from the Gospels that are associated with the eucharist. In this dialogue, the sinner interrogates herself as she speaks to Christ. For example, she asks Jesus a long series of direct questions, such as "Who am I that thou wylte gyue thus thyne owne selfe to? How dare I, so symple and poore a synner, be bolde to appere before the?"[107] The narrator's is not the only first-person perspective in the *Imitation,* however, because Jesus also "speaks" directly to the reader/translator. He says to her, for instance, "What aske I of the more, but that thou study to resygne they selfe vnto me enterely?" (270). In fact, the *Imitation* fashions an elaborate identification between the reader's first-person questioning and Christ's narration, mingling their identities explicitly. This is, of course, what the eucharist itself is: Christ proclaims, "who so eteth my flesshe / and drynketh my blode, he shall dwell in me and I in hym" (259), and despite the fact that Jesus had "no nede of any maner of thynge" (263), the chapter repeats over and over that the Christian can say to God, "thou arte in me & I with the" (276). But the commingled identity is not only one of mutual spiritual presence but of shared words. The reader/translator proclaims that "these wordes beforesayd be thy wordes. Albeit they haue not ben sayd in one self tyme, nor wrytten in one selfe place . . . they be thy wordes / and thou hast proferred them. And they be now myn" (259). Similarly, the *Mirroure of Golde,* a book largely concerned with the world's vanity and the reader's preparation for death, imagines the process of spiritual understanding in terms of inscription. The treatise explains, for ex-

[107] *The Imitation of Christ,* ed. John K. Ingram, EETS, e.s., 63 (London: Kegan Paul, Trench, Trübner, 1893), 262. This edition employs Margaret Beaufort's translation of the fourth book. References to the *Imitation* are cited in parentheses within the text.

ample, that God's law, like the king's, is to be internalized, and when it is not, a "tree" grows in one's "consciens" on which "the synner is hanged and his good dedes" are thereupon "forfeted and ascrybed."[108]

Although both books include ideas about writing that were familiar to Margaret and other readers of her social milieu, the treatises themselves were largely unknown to English lay readers until Margaret's translations were printed. In the late fifteenth century, neither book had the widespread currency associated with vernacular texts such as the *Scale.* The *Imitation,* as Lovatt has shown, "had remained virtually inaccessible to those English readers who could not understand Latin" until 1502.[109] This would quickly change in relation to the *Imitation,* as Lovatt points out: Thomas More writes in his *Confutation of Tyndale's Answer,* for example, that readers should occupy themselves with nourishing books such as "the folowing of Christ and the devoute contemplative booke of Scala perfectionis."[110] But at the time that Margaret translated the *Imitation,* it was not among the vernacular works promoted by London's monastic houses for lay consumption. Similarly, Jacobus de Gruitroede's *Speculum aureum animae peccatricis,* which Margaret translated from a 1503 French edition, was unavailable to English-language readers until her version was finished three years later. How, then, did Margaret come into contact with these works?

The answer seems to be that Margaret learned about them from an elite group of university-trained clerics. Sargent, whose comment is representative, cites Lovatt's description of "an exclusive and tightly knit spiritual aristocracy" and explains that this "included some of the Carthusians, some of the Bridgettines, and the circle, religious and literary, that grouped itself around Lady Margaret Beaufort, bishop John Fisher and later Sir Thomas More."[111] This group appears to have distanced itself from the more ascetic monastic orders' traditional separation from university men. By the late fifteenth century, the Carthusians, for example, admitted increasing numbers of men

[108] *Mirroure of Golde for the Synfull Soule, STC* 6894.5 1506[?], chap. 2.

[109] Roger Lovatt, "The *Imitation of Christ* in Late Medieval England," *Transactions of the Royal Historical Society* 18 (1968): 97–121, quotation at 100. Similarly, Virginia Bainbridge observes that "The ideas represented by *The Imitation of Christ* did not take root" until after the reformation; see Bainbridge, "Women and the Transmission of Religious Culture: Benefactresses of Three Bridgettine Convents c. 1400–1600," *Birgittiana* 3 (1997): 61.

[110] Lovatt, "*Imitation of Christ* in Late Medieval England," 97.

[111] Sargent, "Transmission of Medieval Spiritual Writings," 239–40.

with university training.[112] As a result, these academics brought a renewed interest in Latin, continental literature to the London devotional community. This highly learned group was, as Sargent notes, always a very small number even among the Carthusians, and the transmission of Latin texts such as the original versions of the *Imitation* and the *Mirroure* made up only a slight portion of the order's literary work. Nevertheless, this small group of university-trained men, who gained ever-greater distinction in the order, shared many of Margaret's literate concerns.[113]

But perhaps "shared" is the wrong word. Despite the common assumption, by Duffy, Jones and Underwood, and Sargent, that Margaret was at the center of this elite community, her centrality must have been largely economic, social, and personal, not intellectual. She was a wealthy, influential woman responsible for shaping English literary, religious, and academic culture, but it is very unlikely that she herself dictated the tastes of her university-trained associates. If, as Fisher states, her Latin was poor, she was likely to have been responding to her clerical friends' reading suggestions and the books that they lent her. For example, we know that a monk from the London Charterhouse had given her some unspecified books in 1507 and also that she had supported a scholar at the London house, Richard Moyne, early in the sixteenth century; it is possible that the books were from Moyne.[114] We might assume that Margaret associated with the most advanced scholars because her social position was homologous with theirs: as the king's mother, she was considered the most distinguished lady in England, more venerable than the queen herself by virtue of her maternal authority, just as learned clerics such as Fisher were revered as the wisest fathers, men who cared for a whole nation of lay children. Certainly these levels of superiority appear to have attracted Margaret to these highly trained scholars, and the scholars in turn attended to Margaret because her social distinction made her eligible for their notice. However, although Margaret associated with scholars, she was not one herself, and this made a great

[112] Lovatt, "Library of John Blacman," 222–25.

[113] Lovatt points out that during the sixteenth century, priors of the English Charterhouses were overwhelmingly university men: "At some point during this period the priors of as many as eight of the nine English Charterhouses were men with a university education, and several houses had two graduate priors" ("Library of John Blacman," 224).

[114] Malcolm G. Underwood, "Politics and Piety in the Household of Lady Margaret Beaufort," *Journal of Ecclesiastical History* 38 (1987): 48.

difference in her literate practice. Even as the king's mother, as a woman with incredible wealth and resources, Margaret was excluded from the literate culture in which More and Fisher moved so effortlessly, and the most striking reminder of this exclusion, for Margaret and for the clerics she associated with, must have been her limited knowledge of Latin. It is surprising how easily modern scholars have ignored this barrier to knowledge in relation to Margaret Beaufort, especially because it has become so central to our thinking about heterodox groups such as the Lollards. But the fact remains: Margaret had only a partial understanding of Latin, and this put her in a distinctly different intellectual group from that of her clerical friends and associates. She relied on English translations throughout her life, for example, paying to have some made in 1508.[115] Although there is no question that she cultivated a brand of devotional study that appealed to a very select group of scholars—her purchase of other works associated with this continental strain, including a translation of Suso's *Horologium Sapyencie,* and the commissioning of the *Life of St. Ursula* confirm this—her reliance on translations, even when she translated herself, meant that she was always removed from the devotional and literary culture that she is so often described as supervising. Scholars such as Fisher had no such restrictions, and they valued Latin to such a degree (Fisher, for example, made spoken Latin compulsory for scholars at Christ's College in Cambridge—Margaret had founded the school in 1506) that Margaret's regret over her failure to study the language thoroughly must have been very sharp.[116]

Scholars often equate Margaret Beaufort's literate habits (her reading, translation, patronage of printers) with piety. Although a few critics, including Horace Walpole and Shakespeare, have viewed her motives with cynicism, commentary on Margaret's character, and often by extension on her bookish interests, is usually reverential. Susan Powell, for example, recently claimed that "the whole" of Margaret's "involvement with the book trade may be seen as the active life in God's service."[117] Powell is so committed to the reading-as-piety the-

[115] Powell, "Lady Margaret and Her Books," 201 n. 17: "SJC D91.19, p. 89 (26 May 1508): 'Item yevyn in rewarde to Master Carter [John Carter, one of her chaplains] for translatyng of ceryn bokys out of Latyn into Englysshe by Mr. Chauncellour [Henry Hornby].' xxs."

[116] Maria Dowling, *Fisher of Men: A Life of John Fisher, 1469–1535* (London: Macmillan, 1999), 13.

[117] Powell, "Lady Margaret Beaufort and Her Books," 199.

sis that she suppresses any suggestion that Margaret's interests were more or less than strictly devotional. For instance, although some evidence remains, as Powell conscientiously notes, that Margaret may have commissioned a romance, *Kynge Rycharde Coeur du Lyon,* in 1509, the year she died, Powell insists that Margaret surely showed "little inclination for light reading" at this point in her life and resurrects the serious, saintly description found in Fisher's sermon. Similarly, she remarks that although Margaret owned a copy of *The Canterbury Tales* and bought another copy in 1508 "it would be unwise to be misled into visions of her chuckling over her own copy" (however, she does concede that Margaret was "not incapable of lightheartedness"). In Powell's analysis, Margaret was an "active patron of learning" who provided secular and religious readers with important devotional writings which she herself first studied and then ordered printed and distributed.[118] According to Powell (and Fisher), Margaret read because she was devout and she was devout because she read; any indication that her reading or patronage did not conform to rigid, if unspecified, notions of spirituality and public service is insignificant.

Rather than describing Margaret Beaufort's literate practice as pious, this chapter concerned itself with the reflexive nature of Margaret Beaufort's social affiliations and her engagement with written texts. While I agree with Powell that Margaret ultimately accrued social and political prestige in relation to her involvement in literate culture (and that this involvement was largely religious at the end of Margaret's life), I think we can see that she did so only in retrospect. This is important because rather than taking the equation between piety and literate practice as a given, Margaret herself, and medieval women more generally, *contributed* to the idea that reading and providing books were spiritually and intellectually edifying actions. Margaret Beaufort's literate practice was like Margaret Paston's dynamic, changing over the course of her life: the meanings that she must have attached to it were, like those Margaret Paston came to embrace, intrinsic to the practices that shaped and in turn were reshaped by her literate investments. Although I have argued that Margaret Beaufort's literary inclinations changed over time, my point in this chapter has not been to reinforce the evolutionary model that underwrites Powell's essay—a model that finds Margaret renouncing the romances of her youth for old age's ascetic tracts. Instead, I have been interested in how various social, familial, and intellectual affiliations

[118] Ibid., 206, 239, 207, 239.

constituted Margaret's literate practice and were in turn influenced by her participation in literate culture. In particular, I argued that Margaret Beaufort grew up among people who assumed that involvement with specific kinds of writing was a shared part of women's domestic life and then demonstrated that this understanding of the communal and personal importance of written texts, which depended on a more general sense that social life was "legible," became inextricably entwined in both Margaret's familial relationships and institutional arrangements.

CHAPTER 3

Children of God:
Women Lollards at Norwich

In a now famous description of Lollard literacy, the chronicler Henry Knighton observed that "women who know how to read" are like "swine" trampling the "pearl of the gospel" underfoot.[1] Worried about an earthly existence in which ignorant men and women were reading the Gospel and spreading the good news, he perhaps wondered, as another late-fourteenth-century writer did, if God were signaling the end of the world by allowing the uninitiated to meddle with His word.[2] Knighton was certainly not the only writer to feel that lay readers were Philistines defiling the sacred. In the fifteenth century, for example, the Franciscan Thomas Palmer suggested that lay believers might read certain vernacular texts for their spiritual edification but not biblical writings, which were "difficillima et obscura," "secreta," and "arcana."[3] Intellectual barbarism was a quality shared by laymen and lay-

[1] Quoted in Margaret Aston, "Lollard Women Priests?" in *Lollards and Reformers: Images and Literacy in Late Medieval Religion* (London: Hambledon, 1984), 49–50; Knighton's observation appears in many discussions of Lollard women and reading. See, for example, Rita Copeland, "Why Women Can't Read," in *Representing Women: Law, Literature, and Feminism,* ed. Susan Sage Heinzelman and Zipporah Batshaw Wiseman (Durham, N.C.: Duke University Press, 1994), 268. The original reference was to lay readers, both men and women.

[2] Aston, "Lollard Women Priests?" 50; Aston cites G. R. Owst, *Preaching in Medieval England* (Cambridge: Cambridge University Press, 1926), 5–6, 135.

[3] Thomas Palmer, "De translatione sacrae scripturae in linguam Anglicanum," in Margaret Deanesly, *The Lollard Bible and Other Medieval Biblical Versions* (Cambridge: Cambridge University Press, 1920), 418–31. On Palmer, see Ralph Hanna III's influential essay, "The Difficulty of Ricardian Prose Translation: The Case of the Lollards," *MLQ* 50 (1990): 319–40. See also Ralph Hanna III, " 'Vae octuplex,' Lollard Socio-Textual Ideology, and Ricardian-Lancastrian Prose Translation," in *Criticism*

women according to sensitive souls like Knighton, but in clerical writers' estimates, laywomen who read were even worse than laymen who did. As Bishop Reginald Pecock wailed, women who poked their noses into Bibles became "coppid up" with pride in their learning and foolishly believed they were wiser than priests. Thomas Netter wrote in his *Doctrinale antiquitatum fidei catholicae ecclesiae* that all of this study of the scriptures by the Lollards led women to perch atop "stools" and read and teach the scriptures "in a congregation of men."[4] Although writers like Netter made it seem that there was a woman reader on every corner, in their clerical hysteria these writers greatly exaggerated the extent of Lollard women's ability to read or write, as Shannon McSheffrey has recently shown.[5] Indeed, the extent to which women were involved in Lollardy, literacy aside, may have been exaggerated if the court records tell us anything: in the Norwich heresy trials of 1428–31, only nine of the sixty defendants were women.[6]

McSheffrey's book makes it clear that this clerical exaggeration has become the medievalists' overestimation of Lollard women's ability to read and write. Scholars who imagine that women easily acquired highly developed literate skills are, according to McSheffrey, quite mistaken. Indulging a desire, one that is opposed to that of Netter and Pecock but which has strangely similar consequences for our understanding of Lollard literacy, to show that women were empowered by their participation in Lollard communities, these scholars make assumptions about women's wide-ranging literate practice and involvement in heretical movements without attending to the limitations that the patriarchal family placed on women. Because I think McSheffrey is right in emphasizing those limitations, it may seem that this chapter on Lollard women's literacy is superfluous. Perhaps by composing yet another discussion of Lollard literacy I am only contributing to this problem of exaggerating women's social power

---

and Dissent in the Middle Ages, ed. Rita Copeland (Cambridge: Cambridge University Press, 1996), 244–63.

4 Reginald Pecock, *The Repressor of Overmuch Blaming of the Clergy*, ed. Churchill Babington (London: Green, Longman and Roberts, 1860), 1:123. Netter is cited by Aston in "Lollard Women Priests?" 65.

5 Shannon McSheffrey, *Gender and Heresy: Women, Men, and the Lollard Movement, 1420–1530* (Philadelphia: University of Pennsylvania Press, 1996), 58–61; McSheffrey, "Literacy and the Gender Gap in the Late Middle Ages: Women and Reading in Lollard Communities," in *Women, the Book, and the Godly*, ed. Lesley Smith and Jane H. M. Taylor (Cambridge: D. S. Brewer, 1995), 157–70.

6 *Heresy Trials in the Diocese of Norwich, 1428–1431*, ed. Norman P. Tanner, Camden Society, ser. 4, vol. 20 (London: Office of the Royal Historical Society, 1977).

and in doing so intensifying the effect that Lollard studies have had on the study of medieval religion, which has been, according to Eamon Duffy, to help make it seem that "the English religious landscape of the Late Middle Ages was peopled largely by Lollards, witches, and leisured, aristocratic ladies."[7] Whatever the risks are of writing about women associated with the sect, this chapter is important because it considers not how many women were able to read and write but rather why written texts mattered to Lollard women and what they did with them. Although fewer Lollard women may have been literate, able to read and write, than some studies suggest, it is nevertheless true that women in such religious communities were involved with the written word. Like their male counterparts, Lollard women were enthusiastic supporters of Lollard learning. This chapter examines the nature of that enthusiasm.

What it has been supposed that Lollard women were doing was reading to learn about things that the Church withheld from them, and there is a very good reason that scholars have assumed this: it was the conclusion drawn by members of the religious establishment six hundred years ago. As Ralph Hanna points out in a brief but important essay, religious leaders such as Arundel were troubled by translation into the vernacular because they believed that "English texts . . . open the way to non-clerically supervised interpretation."[8] Having access to vernacular writing made it possible for untrained readers—those who had no knowledge of Latin—to study scripture. The works of medieval clerical writers, including writers such as Bishop Pecock, who themselves wrote in English, exhibit professional anxiety about vernacular translation of scripture and especially about its ability to make previously protected, sacred knowledge available to readers who were without adequate intellectual training. Writers such as Pecock assumed that lay readers wanted vernacular translations of scripture because they were considered to be like the fruit from the Tree of the Knowledge of Good and Evil in Eden, revelatory, intellectually empowering, and destructive. However, although clerical writers held the view that the Bible's desirability lay in its ability to convey hidden knowledge, this idea reflects only what clerical writers

[7] Eamon Duffy, *The Stripping of the Altars: Traditional Religion in England, 1400–1580* (New Haven: Yale University Press, 1992), 2.

[8] Hanna, "Ricardian Prose Translation," 335. Hanna makes the statement in relation to the difference he describes between the Lollard Margery Baxter's "reading" and that of a friar who figures in the transcript of her heresy trial.

thought about Lollard reading and not what the Lollards themselves were concerned with when they demanded vernacular texts.[9] Because the idea accords closely with academics' own use of written texts—as sources of information, as "proof" for arguments, as data—this model, which imagines reading as the process of uncovering hidden knowledge, has implicitly shaped studies of Lollard "hermeneutics." Less consideration has been given to what Lollard readers were themselves looking for, even in discussions of Lollard literacy, because we have assumed that we know, without question, why someone would want a translation of a text. It might appear that the eagerness for vernacular books, and especially for vernacular translations of scripture, recorded, for example, in the transcripts from the Norwich heresy trials of the 1420s and 1430s, must surely have been motivated by a desire for knowledge. Why else, one might ask, would they have wanted English-language translations? But such a question assumes that intellectual understanding is the only basis for wanting a book in one's own language, and it is in fact merely the most obvious reason.

In contrast, in describing the literate practice of women Lollards at Norwich circa 1430, this chapter shows how demands for vernacular texts emerged from the sense that engagement with the written word constituted spiritual identity. I argue that Lollard reading was certainly about learning, but that learning was spiritually formative and not strictly rationative. Some of the women indicted at the Norwich heresy trial could read and possibly write; others such as Margery Baxter were presumably illiterate in the modern sense of the word. Regardless of their literate ability, however, what they all had in common was a sense of the importance of written texts and of "study," even if they were unable to read for themselves. The question that this chapter poses is why these women valued writing so highly if they were not concerned primarily, as I will suggest, with acquiring information. I try to answer this question by looking at the three women associated with the Norwich conventicles for whom we have the most evidence: Joan White, wife of the famous itinerant Lollard preacher William White; Hawisia Moon, wife of Thomas Moon, who together with her husband invited Lollards into their home for

[9] On differences between clerical and lay learning, see Hanna, " 'Vae octuplex,' " 244–46; Nicholas Watson, "Censorship and Cultural Change in Late-Medieval England: Vernacular Theology, the Oxford Translation Debate, and Arundel's Constitutions of 1409," *Speculum* 70 (1995): 839–46; Copeland, "Why Women Can't Read," 259–62; and Anne Hudson, "Lollardy: The English Heresy?" in *Lollards and Their Books* (London: Hambledon, 1985), 155–57.

schooling; and Margery Baxter, a disciple of Joan White's husband and probably the best-known Lollard to modern scholars.

Brian Stock has suggested that heretical groups in the earlier Middle Ages were sometimes united by their participation in "textual communities."[10] In these communities, Stock argues, an individual's reading of written texts informed the group's religious understanding. We might think of the Lollards at Norwich as such a textual community, with Oxford-trained William White, the sometime priest and itinerant Lollard evangelist, as the individual at the center of the group.[11] According to the Protestant apologist John Foxe, White's ministry involved his continual labor "to the glory and praise of the Spouse of Christ, by reading, writing, and preaching," and he and his wife Joan lived in Hawisia and Thomas Moon's home and ran a Lollard school, or conventicle, prior to White's burning at the stake for heresy.[12] Margery Baxter was also affiliated with White's ministry, participating in his conventicles and, although illiterate, apparently zealously concerned with protecting White and his books from the authorities. Margery's response to White's sanctity, recorded in her own trial for heresy, suggests that she was deeply influenced by his ministry, so much so that she calls him a "sacred doctor" and "saint" to whom, she explains, she prays daily.[13] Although it is true that Lollards generally denounced the veneration of saints, what is more important about Margery's statement than its "inconsistency" with what has come to be taken as Lollard dogma is what it reveals about White. He was clearly a figure who inspired devotion, a leader who Stock would refer to as "charismatic," someone whose "power to motivate groups" appears to have been based not only in his learning but "derived from his oratory, gestures, and physical presence."[14]

[10] Brian Stock, *The Implications of Literacy: Written Language and Models of Interpretation in the Eleventh and Twelfth Centuries* (Princeton: Princeton University Press, 1983).

[11] On regionalism and Lollardy, see John Fines, "Heresy Trials in the Diocese of Coventry and Lichfield, 1511–12," *Journal of Ecclesiastical History* 14 (1963): 160–74; J. A. F. Thomson, *The Later Lollards, 1414–1520* (London: Oxford University Press, 1965); Richard G. Davies, "Lollardy and Locality," *Transactions of the Royal Historical Society*, 6th ser., 1 (1991): 191–212; and Derek Plumb, "A Gathered Church? Lollards and Their Society," in *The World of Rural Dissenters, 1520–1725*, ed. Margaret Spufford (Cambridge: Cambridge University Press, 1995), 132–63.

[12] *The Acts and Monuments of John Foxe*, ed. George Townsend (New York: AMS, 1965), 3:591.

[13] *Heresy Trials*, 47. Cited in the text from this point on as *T*.

[14] Stock, *Implications of Literacy*, 90.

Although there is little question that William White was a colorful and compelling teacher, his influence over the Norwich community was produced largely through his personal interactions with members of the sect. It was, in other words, his close relationship with members of the community and not merely his personality that shaped the community and its investment in written texts.[15] The most obvious example of this influence was his wife Joan's assumption of his teaching ministry after his death. According to Foxe, Joan took over William's ministry, "following her husband's footsteps according to her power, teaching and sowing abroad the same doctrine, confirmed many men in God's truth; wherefore she suffered much trouble and punishment."[16] Foxe wrote his *Acts and Monuments* in support of the Protestant cause and for this reason emphasized the "weak confounding the strong" aspect of Joan's ministry: times, according to Foxe, were so desperate that in those days even a woman was required to speak out in support of the truth. Like widows who took over their husbands' businesses, Joan on William's death ran the schools, staying with the Moons, and suffered persecution at the bishop's hands just as her husband had done.

We do not know enough about the Whites to make specific claims about how Joan learned to teach or what exactly her role in the conventicles was, but we do know that her ministry was closely associated with that of her husband. William White had been trained at Oxford, preached extensively, and was used to the public culture of clerical life even if he did turn aside from the established Church and its teachings. Joan, however, appears to have had no training whatsoever except that which she gained through her husband and the conventicles. In fact, as McSheffrey observes, although Foxe mentions Joan's ministry, she figures in the Norwich trials merely as William's wife, or, as McSheffrey puts it, "only as the instrument by which [William] defied the Church's doctrine of clerical celibacy" and not in the public role described by Foxe.[17] McSheffrey's point, the thesis of *Gender and Heresy*, is that Lollard communities were dominated by men, and her argument makes her understandably cautious about accepting Foxe's report without corroboration. Hudson and Aston, how-

15 See Margaret Aston, "William White's Lollard Followers," in *Lollards and Reformers*, 71–100; she considers White the source of ideas about Lollardy in this community.

16 *Acts and Monuments of John Foxe*, 3:591.

17 McSheffrey, *Gender and Heresy*, 57.

ever, have shown that Foxe appears to be a reliable source, and on these grounds we might want to think about the association between Joan's relationship with William and her public teaching role as presented by Foxe.[18]

Evidence from the heresy trials suggests that the Norwich community was particularly concerned with married life and its relationship to spirituality.[19] As Edmund Archer, a member of the community from Loddon in southeast Norfolk, stated in his abjuration from August 1430, "chastite of monkes, chanons, freres, nonnes, prestes and of ony other persones is not commendable ne meritorie, but it is more commendable and more plesyng unto God al such persones to be wedded and bringe forth frute of hare bodyes" (*T* 166). William Bate, who abjured on the same day as Edmund, rejected his former belief that the "common lyf of wedlock" was "more meritorie than is to lyve continent and chast" (*T* 160). So did John Skylan, whose trial took place during the same week as those of Edmund and William.[20] The similarity among the abjurations may point to a common source, as Aston suggests, in William White's teaching, or it may reflect the importance of the idea and its presence as a topic of conversation in the community, as Hudson argues. In either case, it is clear that the Norwich community understood marriage as a state more pleasing to God than that of clerical celibacy. We now associate such ideas about domestic life with Protestantism, and I think it is easy to underestimate, in retrospect, the revulsion that the clerical audience surely felt when confronted with Lollard assertions about procreation. Archer, Bate, and Skylan were not taking a Pauline stance and claim-

[18] Aston argues that Foxe is a fairly reliable source: "Our ability to assess Foxe's dependability is helped by his having transcribed some passages that we still have (e.g., notably, the case of Margery Baxter) as well as others that we do not have. Foxe certainly edited his material, but comparison of his text with the Latin version leaves one with some respect for his over-all accuracy and detail, and surely encourages serious consideration of his additional matter" ("William White's Followers," 74). See also Anne Hudson, *The Premature Reformation: Wycliffite Texts and Lollard History* (Oxford: Clarendon Press, 1988): "it would seem that Foxe is generally reliable to a fairly high degree" (40). Hudson provides a brief list of works that consider Foxe's reliability (40 n. 186).

[19] Claire Cross argues that women were involved in the text-centered activities of Lollardy because the movement was a "family sect." See Cross, " 'Great Reasoners in Scripture': The Activities of Women Lollards, 1380–1530," in *Medieval Women,* ed. Derek Baker (Oxford: Basil Blackwell, 1978), 359–80. Similarly, Hudson has noted that Lollardy had a "household basis" (*Premature Reformation,* 156).

[20] *Heresy Trials,* 148. McSheffrey cites Archer's abjuration (*Gender and Heresy,* 83).

ing that it was better to marry than to burn. Rather, they were *celebrating* conjugal sexuality and procreation as superior to celibacy and doing so on the basis of conjugal sex's spiritual benefits. Although the Norwich group's affirmation of family life is in keeping with what Reformation historians have observed about later Protestant sects, the emphasis in the Norwich abjurations is on conjugal relations as a necessary part of the life of those on the highest spiritual plane and not simply on domestic arrangements.[21]

Joan White's relationship to her husband was, like Margaret Paston's marriage to John, the circumstance that influenced her literate practice most directly. It certainly seems unlikely that Joan would have become a preacher, or at least have been reputed to teach publicly, if she had not been married to William. There is little evidence that women actually thought of themselves as preachers, and Joan's ministry would seem to have been at the most a substitute and not a replacement for her husband's—as Foxe says, she only taught "according to her power," no doubt in Foxe's mind a lesser power than that of her husband. Joan stayed on with the Moons after William's death, and she seems to have begun teaching only because there was no one else to take her husband's place. We might then settle for Joan's relationship to William to "explain" how she became involved in her ministry. It is perhaps as if she were a shopkeeper's wife who assumed control of the business after her husband died. The problem with this analysis is that it draws a false comparison between commercial and spiritual/educational enterprises. It is possible to inherit a shop; it is not possible to inherit knowledge or the ability to teach. Yet even if we choose to imagine that knowledge and skills could be passed on (and no doubt Joan did learn a great deal from her husband while he was alive), this conclusion still ignores a very important aspect of the situation: the ideological significance of marriage in the Lollard community. If we want to understand how Joan became a teacher, we need to begin by considering why it was so important for William, a former priest, to live as a married man. If we consider why White, or his friend the former chaplain Thomas Pert, insisted on marrying, we begin to see the limitations of this answer for understanding Lollard couples' spiritual and marital lives.

Among the most important of these limitations is the way this argument ignores the specific connotations that celibacy would have

[21] McSheffrey provides a very useful bibliography of work on the Protestant family (*Gender and Heresy,* 196 n. 3).

had for the Whites. McSheffrey, for example, although careful to observe that medieval Catholicism led "believers to think that God favored the chaste nun or priest over the married person," forgets what significance celibacy would have held for medieval believers, even for those who ultimately rejected its social claims. Instead, she assumes that the Norwich Lollards thought it was "natural" to marry and reproduce.[22] McSheffrey's is clearly a modern conception of sexual activity—as biologically driven and necessary. In the Middle Ages, however, even if it struck clerically trained men such as White and Pert as "natural" to reproduce, they would not have valued reproduction for its naturalness. Celibacy had come to be understood as a higher way to live in the world precisely because it was a rejection of the physical and fleshly, that is, a rejection of what was natural. The Norwich community esteemed marriage greatly, but they did not do so because it seemed inevitable that human beings would engage in sexual activity. In fact, the Norwich group's celebration of conjugal sex differed from positions espoused in earlier Lollard writings that were much closer to assuming that sex was instinctual. Wyclif's view, for example, expressed in the *Trialogus,* was, as Hudson points out, that "sacerdotal celibacy" was not required of priests because it was too difficult for them to remain chaste. Enforced celibacy encouraged sin, and Wyclif allowed clerical marriage for that reason.[23] This Pauline view is taken up even more strongly in the *Twelve Conclusions of the Lollards,* composed in 1395 and posted for Parliament to view, in which women's "uow[s] of continence" are said to lead to the "most horrible synne possible," the slaying of children before christening, abortion, and the destruction of "kynde," and men's pledges of sexual continence are described as promoting sodomy.[24]

Although Joan and William White clearly considered marriage a more perfect state than celibacy, a "positive good" as McSheffrey calls it, their valuation was based on the way that conjugal love brought men and women together in Christ and not on the naturalness of marriage.[25] William White, as Netter observed, had himself

[22] Ibid., 85; McSheffrey argues that "Lollards in the diocese of Norwich . . . rejected celibacy not because it inevitably led to fornication, but because it was unnatural not to marry and have children" (83).

[23] Hudson, *Premature Reformation,* 357.

[24] *Twelve Conclusions of the Lollards, Rogeri Dymmok: Liber Contra XII Errores et Hereses Lollardorum,* ed. Rev. H. S. Cronin (London: Kegan Paul, Trench, Trübner, 1921), 303, 297.

[25] Hudson discusses White's denial of his marriage (*Premature Reformation,* 357–58); possibly White believed it was appropriate to lie to the authorities: if it was

written several books advocating clerical marriage, none of which is extant, but we can gather something of the group's ideas from the abjurations recorded between 1428 and 1430. Richard Knobbyng of Beccles affirmed, for example, that "oonly consent of love in Jhu' Crist be tuex man and woman of Christes beleve is sufficient for the sacrament of matrimoyne, withoute contract made be wordis or solennizacion in Chirche" (*T* 115). Nearly identical statements concerning conjugal love in Christ and wordless consent without institutional verification are made by others who came before the court on the same day, April 18, 1430, including Baldwin Cowper and John Eldon, both from Beccles, who also aver that "oonly consent of love in Jhu' Crist"(*T* 126, 135) is required to sanctify marriage. It is possible that the consistency of these abjurations lies in the circumstances of the trial (they were made on the same day) and was produced by the authorities in charge of the proceedings. Nevertheless, that regularity suggests this position on marriage was believed to be central to the heretical practice at Norwich.

This idea of marriage was not sacramental—marriage was not a sign of divine love but part of it—but preferable, according to those accused, to celibacy because it joined man and woman in Christ. In contrast with the views espoused by Wyclif, then, the point of marriage for Joan and the other Norwich Lollards was not to stave off sin but to experience God's love more completely. As a result, marriage was linked in the Norwich community with spiritual education.

Two factors help us understand the significance of the Whites' conjugal relationship and its influence on Joan's participation in the Lollard schools. The first, which I have described above, is the Norwich group's view on marriage as it pertained to all believers. The second is the exemplary role that preachers played in Lollard communities. The Norwich defendants believed that marriage was directed toward a heightened spiritual life, that the union of a man and woman called forth God's love, and that it was a private and unmediated arrangement. As a consequence, the Norwich group understood clerical marriage as essential because believers, but especially religious leaders, should lead the most complete spiritual lives. There was a "democratic" impulse behind this understanding, a commitment to the priesthood of all believers (as Hawisia Moon stated in her abjuration, every believer was a "very pope" and therefore capable of speaking directly to God), and an understanding that marriage was equally avail-

"not leful to swere in ony caas," as one defendant put it, it could make little difference what one said (see *Heresy Trials,* 112).

able to all men and women. But the Norwich group also maintained that their preachers should be, in contrast with the orthodox clergy and their "vicious living" (as Hawisia called it), models that other members of the community could follow. In her deposition Margery Baxter declared, for instance, that William White was such an exemplar, calling him the "sanctissimum et doctissimum doctorem legis divine" (*T* 45). Suggesting that she and the other members of the community would carry on his teaching just as she had carried his books from Yarmouth and hidden them in Martham (*T* 41), Margery's deposition shows the impact that an exemplary preacher might have on the Norwich group. As the well-known Lollard poem "Jack Upland" proposes, priests should preach the gospel, pray devoutly, administer the sacraments, study God's law exclusively, and "be *trewe ensaumpleris* of holi mennes lijf continuli, in doynge and in suffringe" (italics added).[26] Clergymen taught not just in words but by example, according to the Norwich defendants and Lollard writings.

William and Joan's marriage was also a way of teaching through example, and its emblematic function was closely related to the Norwich community's understanding of Christian duty. The Norwich group of course called on its preachers to teach, but this obligation extended to all believers. As Hudson observes, "preaching of the gospel to all" was a duty "imposed on all Christians, according to Lollard thought," and she cites a discussion of this idea in Netter's *Doctrinale* in which he "refers to a book by Purvey which showed that all the laity, including women, should preach, and also alleges that this has been carried out in many places."[27] Traditionally, all Christians (not just Lollard dissidents) were responsible for sharing the gospel with one another, but a seemingly sharp distinction was drawn between public preaching (acceptable only for trained clerics) and teaching. This distinction figures in writings as diverse as the fictional prologue to the *Wife of Bath's Tale* and the autobiographical *Book* of Margery Kempe, and it suggests how difficult it was to actually distinguish preaching from teaching. As Margery retorts when she is accused of preaching—a violation of Saint Paul's pronounce-

[26] Cited in Hudson, *Premature Reformation,* 351–52.

[27] Ibid., 354, citing Thomas Netter, *Doctrinale antiquitatum fidei Catholicae ecclesiae,* ed. Bonavenura Blanciotti (Farnborough, U.K.: Gregg Press, 1967), bk. 2, ch. 70. See also *Premature Reformation,* 185 n. 64: "The duty of the literate is often expressed in Lollard texts . . . 'whoso kan rede bookis in his langage, and so knoweth the better Goddis lawe, he his bounden to spende that kunnynge and that grace to the worschipe of God and to helpe of his euene cristen.' "

ments against women sermonizing—she only uses "communication and good words," which she is obligated to do as a Christian. Preaching, she explains, requires a pulpit, and she has not used one.[28] Women in the Norwich community seem, as Margery Kempe had, to have taken seriously their duty to teach one another, but unlike Margery, one of the ways they taught was through (as opposed to in conflict with) their married lives.

What is especially important in relation to Joan White's ministry is the way that conjugal exemplarity was explicitly and necessarily public: Joan taught by *being* William's wife, and she taught because she *was* William's wife, that is, as an example of conjugal love that figured forth God's love and as an extension of her "traditional," familial role. It would be an exaggeration to claim that this model of pastoral care made it not only possible but natural for Joan to take up her husband's ministry even in a limited way—the logic of medieval family and public life made such a recognition impossible—but the Norwich community's emphasis on exemplarity and conjugal life, despite the real limitations patriarchal culture placed on women, made a difference for the literate practice of Lollard women like Joan. Even if women were not equal with men, Lollard belief in "universal priesthood" coupled with conjugal exemplarity granted women like Joan authority, even if it was limited authority, to teach in the Norwich conventicle and to be respected for it.

All of this may strike the reader interested only in exactly what Joan was teaching as an elaborate and needless aside about Lollard marriage and women's status in the community, but my point is that Joan's teaching was *about* (in its most general sense) her marriage to William. We do not know what the content of her lessons (sermons?) was.[29] Foxe tells us only that she taught and disseminated "the same doctrine" that her husband had taught and that she "confirmed many men in God's truth."[30] Did she own books? Could she read or did she teach from memory? Had her husband taught her? To Foxe it was only her ministry that was important, what she achieved rather than what she knew. Possibly punning on the word "confirmed" and its synonym "bishoped," Foxe described what he felt mattered about

[28] *The Book of Margery Kempe*, ed. Sanford Brown Meech and Hope Emily Allen, EETS, o.s., 212 (London: Oxford University Press, 1940), bk. 1, chap. 52.

[29] Hudson cites a Wycliffite text written before 1413 that seems to be a sermon (although it would have taken "from four to five hours to deliver") left behind by the preacher for the Lollard group to study (*Premature Reformation*, 184).

[30] *Acts and Monuments of John Foxe*, 3:591.

Joan's work (in contrast to the institutional hierarchies of the Roman Church), her success in encouraging individuals to recognize God's truth. What this truth was—the same doctrine as William's—was self-evident and needed no explication as far as Foxe was concerned. Foxe, like William White, and the men who died with him, John Waddon and Hugh Pye, believed they had no choice but to share "God's truth," and they were sure they knew what it was. If Joan actually was involved in the teaching ministry described by Foxe, I suspect she thought about her literate practice in much the same way that Foxe presented it: as required of her as a believer and especially as the wife of William White, who had taught her so well and whose love exemplified and took part in God's love.

This silence about that "truth" and how it was learned and transmitted is nevertheless very frustrating for those of us who are not so sure about what mattered to Lollard teachers. We know from Lollard writings that the primary duty of preachers was to provide believers with God's word, and it appears that the conventicles were thought of as schools for hearing scripture. Biblical recitation was an important part of the conventicles: Joan Colins and her mother Alice, for example, knew a number of religious texts, including the Ten Commandments and five chapters from the book of James, by heart according to Foxe.[31] But how they learned the pieces they memorized is never discussed. Nor is the structure of the conventicles ever described: Were they tutorials? Did preachers deliver the sermons? Did they read tracts such as the *Lanterne of Light* aloud? What form did their discussions take? The court transcripts from Norwich do not say. We are only left with questions: How did Joan White and Hawisia Moon actually learn to read (if they did)? Why didn't Margery Baxter?[32]

What we do know is that regardless of the ways the conventicles were organized (and I imagine that different teachers and communities worked in various ways), their participants did not view the schools as short-term seminars or weekend workshops in which one

[31] Ibid., 4:238.

[32] Hudson describes "Lollard practices" (*Premature Reformation,* 144–57). See also *Premature Reformation,* 178–79, where Hudson cites a letter from 1392 describing "conventicula" in which laypersons, especially craftspeople, were meeting secretly to discuss "heretical" ideas and to study scripture. Ralph Hanna, "Some Norfolk Women and Their Books, ca. 1390–1440," in *The Cultural Patronage of Medieval Women,* ed. June Hall McCash (Athens: University of Georgia Press, 1996), briefly discusses Margery Baxter and Hawisia Moon's literate activities (290–94).

mastered a certain body of information and "graduated." We do not know how often the Norwich group met, but the schools were clearly ongoing concerns; as Hawisia Moon's abjuration states, the teachers "kept, holde *and continued* scholes" (italics added), which she and her husband attended eagerly. Yet if the point of Lollard teaching was the confirmation of God's truth, which seems to suggest that one is either confirmed or not, we are left to wonder why the groups had to keep meeting. It is obvious from the abjurations that certain beliefs were taught consistently in the Norwich area, but if these dozen or so tenets were all that participants learned in the conventicles, they would have needed to meet no more than once or twice. Regular attendance at services was part of traditional religious practice, and one might assume that this accounted for ongoing participation in the conventicles. Whatever activities they were engaged in, it is clear that the ongoing nature of the private meetings was as important to the Lollard community as the teaching itself.

The Norwich group was particularly concerned with "priviness," that is, secrecy. In the late fourteenth and early fifteenth century, some Lollard communities seem to have met openly. Hudson notes that in the 1390s, the Northampton community advertised for Lollard preachers publicly; similarly, those Lollards living near Leicester met without hiding at least during much of the time from 1382 to 1413.[33] This kind of free movement was apparently out of the question for the Norwich community, and by 1425, as Aston observes, "there was no doubt that Lollardy was on par with treason."[34] Official writers imagined that the groups met with such enthusiasm in order to plot against civic and religious orders.[35] Twenty-five years later, attitudes toward sedition had changed, but the Lollards' secret meetings still troubled clerical writers. Reginald Pecock, for example, complained that lay believers, in particular women, met in their homes so they could "avaunten" themselves, that is, put themselves forward, against clergymen; congratulate themselves on their biblical knowledge; and "dispute ayens clerkis."[36] It is difficult to tell which Pecock resented more, the women's secrecy or their knowledge of scripture.

[33] Hudson, *Premature Reformation,* 153.

[34] Margaret Aston, "Lollardy and Sedition, 1381–1431," in *Lollards and Reformers,* 8.

[35] Hudson, *Premature Reformation,* 178.

[36] Pecock, *Repressor,* 1:123.

The Norwich group apparently met in members' homes out of fear of prosecution. Places such as Hawisia Moon's "chesehous chambr" are mentioned in the Norwich records, chosen clearly for their extreme privacy (*T* 76). Attempting to stamp out heretical activity, the authorities responded to the community's efforts to meet privately by declaring that members of the Norwich group had to abjure the secrecy of the Lollard meetings as well as their heretical beliefs. The accused were regularly called on to agree that they would defend no person who continued to hold the errors that had been abjured (either "opinly or prively") and that they were obliged to agree that they would return to "holy Church" who "spereth not hyr bosom to hym that wil turne agayn" (*T* 142). It is hard to imagine that the two sides were not knowingly battling over claims to "priviness." Clerical writers such as Pecock and Palmer described the scriptures as "secreta" and "arcana" but demanded that lay believers attend services regularly and openly; the Lollards insisted that access to the scriptures should be unrestricted and claimed the right to study them in private.

The Moons' house seems to have been one of the places in which the Norwich group met most frequently. "Master" Thomas Moon, as Foxe calls him, supported a large household and offered lodging to a number of well-known heretics, including William and Joan White. In an effort to stop the Moons, the authorities brought the couple before the episcopal court in Norwich—Hawisia on August 4, 1430, and Thomas on August 21 of the same year. Although the transcripts of the abjurations recount standard Lollard heresies such as the rejection of pilgrimages and fasting, Thomas, as Foxe notes, was "especially" attacked because he had "familiarity and communication with divers heretics, and had received, comported, and supported, and maintained diverse of them, as sir William White, sir Hugh Pie, Thomas Pert, and William Callis, priests, with many more." Like Thomas's, the transcript of Hawisia's abjuration shows that she had been "right hoomly and prive with many heretikes" who she had received so they might hold "scoles of heresie yn prive chambres and prive places." The transcript also reveals the extremes to which she went to care for fellow members of the sect. Intimate with the heretics she "harbored," Hawisia stated that she did everything in her power to assist them (*T* 140). When Hawisia's testimony refers to the Moons' hospitality, it differs from her husband's only in the use of the adjective "our" ("in our hous") in place of her husband's "my" ("in myn hous"). The couple clearly worked together to support members of the community, but it is also possible that Hawisia, as McSheffrey suggests, "may in fact have been the motivating force behind the schools held in her house" since she acted independently of her husband, for example, hosting a meal that broke the fast on Easter Saturday illicitly.[37]

Among the women Lollards in Norwich, only Joan White has been identified as performing a public role like that played by William White or Hugh Pye, and McSheffrey is no doubt correct when she observes that, "Like their [orthodox] contemporaries, Lollards saw the subordination of wife to husband, woman to man, as part of God's divine creation."[38] Nevertheless, it is important to note that it was also unusual for men in the community to be identified as teachers, and that Hawisia Moon's hospitality need not be seen as the obvious and "passive" extension of a female role. Believers such as Thomas and Hawisia who participated in the schools but held no obvious spiritual authority were much more numerous than were teachers. Further, hospitality was a Christian duty and demanded of both men and women in the Middle Ages, a common theme in a variety of literary texts, including the poem *Cleanness,* for example.[39] In Lollard writings, both sexes are called on to care for others and to perform acts of mercy "to oure owne kyn, to oure owne parishenys, and to oure owne neighboris," as one sermon puts it. Blending spiritual and secular realms, Lollard involvement in community service anticipated admission to God's city and household. Heaven itself is the site of civic participation; it is the "worshipful cite" of which members of the sect are "not straungers and comelingis" but "burgeysis and cytesyns, and the homely meyne of the kyng of this cite, and his eyris, and euen eris with his son."[40] This is not to suggest that women were considered equal with men. The preacher of a sermon for the second Sunday in Lent explains, for example, that men are accountable for the way "thei han gouernyd her wyues and her children, her

[37] McSheffrey, *Gender and Heresy,* 119.

[38] Ibid., 85.

[39] *The Poems of the Pearl Manuscript,* ed. Malcolm Andrew and Ronald Waldron (Exeter: University of Exeter Press, 1996); see *Cleanness,* ll. 601–1012, in which the story of Abraham's reception of the angels as an act of hospitality is emphasized.

[40] "Sermon of Dead Men," in *Lollard Sermons,* ed. Gloria Cigman, EETS, 294 (Oxford: Oxford University Press, 1989), ll. 1063–65. The sermons edited by Cigman appeared in three separate manuscripts and date from the first quarter of the fifteenth century, making it possible that they were familiar to community members tried at Norwich later in the century.

meyne and her housholde."[41] But although the sermon quite obviously embraces a model of gender relations that is anything but equitable, its impulse toward spiritual equality is also unmistakable. In the sermon, believers care for one another because they are all God's children, and this relationship of equality is shared not just with other members of the sect but with Jesus, their "euen er"—equal heir—to God's kingdom.

"Our hous" in Hawisia's abjuration stands as a barrier against the worldly networks of clerical repression that struck down godly men like William White. Setting up antagonistic relationships between members of her community and those wielding social power, Hawisia refers pointedly to "our houshold," in which she "receyved and herberwed" "divers heretics" whom she then "conceled, conforted, supported, maytened and favored with al my poar" (*T* 140). This supports Steven Justice's sense that the Lollards at Norwich were oriented toward "domestic" understandings.[42] "Domestic" is not, however, a simple synonym for concern with material existence. Rather, the group's domestic impulse, or reconfiguration of familial heritage (as heirs to God's kingdom), was driven by particular intellectual and spiritual commitments. It was of course true that the physical conditions of meeting in a domestic space shaped the group's religious practice, but it was equally true that ideas of domesticity merged spiritual and material concerns. For example, the author of the *Lanterne* mimics the judges' voices, who say to the Lollards, " 'lyue as thi fadir dide & that is ynow for thee or ellis thou schalt to prisoun,' " announcing the political and material distance between members of the sect and worldly authorities—and alluding to the very real dangers of participation in the conventicles. But he also justifies Lollard resistance by claiming that spiritual relations are themselves domestically constructed. Citing the book of James, he asserts that all believers are "born to blisse," begotten so that they may be part of God's "creature," holy church, of which "euery chosen man & womman is clepid a sone or a doughtir."[43]

41 "Second Sunday in Lent," in *Lollard Sermons,* 12: ll. 448–49.

42 Steven Justice argues that Margery "Baxter's faith was, not automatically but elaborately and consciously a *domestic* faith, with the house, family, and the maintenance of both at the center of her religious values, a yardstick to take the measure of doctrine" (Justice, "Inquisition, Speech, and Writing: A Case from Late-Medieval Norwich," *Representations* 48 [1994]: 23).

43 *The Lanterne of Light,* ed. Lilian M. Swinburn, EETS, o.s., 151 (Oxford: Kegan Paul, Trench, Trübner, 1917), 100, 32–33. The *Lanterne* was frequently mentioned in heresy trials; in that of John Claydon, a London skinner, it became grounds for his de-

Hawisia too linked "spatial" domesticity (her cheesehouse chamber) with spiritual birth. Her abjuration states that in those "prive places" she had "herd, conceyved, lerned and reported" the heresies included in the court document. Although this is obviously a formula for describing heretical activity—the verb sequence also appears in her husband's abjuration—it nevertheless emphasizes the dynamism of Hawisia's particular experiences. From hearing to imagining, from imagining to knowing, from knowing to teaching, the abjuration suggests that she not only concealed and comforted members of the sect but made it possible for them to experience true, spiritual growth. The Norwich group associated the community's "prive places" with that growth. The Moons' house was a refuge in Hawisia's abjuration, a safe harbor for those fleeing immediate persecution such as William White, but it was also a haven for members of the household who were learning the basics of faith. In his abjuration Edmund Archer, a former apprentice of Thomas Moon's, for example, distinguishes himself from the "many notorie and famous heretikes" such as "Sir William Whyte, Sir Hughe Pye, Sir William Caleys" and so on, but affirms his familiarity with these well-known Lollards and with Hawisia's home in which he had been a "servant" and "conversant and homly" with all participants in the schools (*T* 165). Archer's growing involvement in the conventicles is implied in the abjuration when it notes that he had "kept and continued" in the schools "longe tyme" and as a consequence "herd, lerned and reported" the beliefs included in the court's document (*T* 165). Hawisia's abjuration, like Archer's, emphasized continuance in the schools but associated that continuance even more closely with "priviness" than Archer's had because the meeting rooms were "prive places of oures," hers and her husband's, and opposed in her abjuration to a number of public places including Rome, headquarters of the pope "fadir Antecrist"; the "tapster['s]" alehouse in which pilgrims wasted their time and money; and "holy Church" itself—which seems to be both "all universall" and local.

The word "homely," which appears in many of the Norwich abjurations including Hawisia's and Edmund's, draws attention to the domestic nature of the conventicles. Members of the community imagined themselves as forming a new kind of family. This included obvious familial relations—marriage partners such as Hawisia and Thomas, and children, like the Moons' daughter, who according to

nunciation as a heretic and encouraged a group of friars to draw up a list of the heretical errors contained in the tract. See Hudson, *Premature Reformation,* 208–14.

Foxe could read, were included—but also extended to interactions among other members of the community.[44] As one Lollard sermon writer puts it, members of the sect were no longer part of the "generation of Cain," that is, descendants of "oure former fadir," but instead had become descendants of Abel.[45] Familial labels were traditionally used to describe relations among believers, but the emphasis was usually on the parent–child relationship of clerical fathers to the laity rather than on the family of believers. Pecock, for example, calls the Lollards ungrateful, lay "children" whose demand for the scriptures showed why they needed clerical "fathers" to discipline them. Pecock maintained that without their "fathers," the Lollards would fall into "childrenys perel." Like children, their love of "sweete meetis" required parental intervention.[46] The Lollards, in contrast, insisted that all believers were equally members of an extended family with membership in "oo passing creature, holi chirche," which in the *Lanterne* is "lickned to a womman with childe."[47] Members of the community understood themselves as a new family, related to one another through their spiritual heritage. Just as the Church instructed earthly families to support one another, Lollard writings admonished believers to love and care for one another.

Hawisia's attention to the needs of Lollard believers led Margery Baxter to refer to her as "privy," identifying Hawisia's person, apparently, with her household. Margery stated in her deposition that "uxor Thome Mone est secretissima et sapientissima mulier in doctrina W. White" (*T* 47). Although it seems clear that "sapientissima" refers to Hawisia's knowledge of White's doctrines, it is less clear what "secretissima," the most "privy," means in this context. One might suspect that Margery's remark was a wry comment on the authorities' ability to detect Lollardy: the proceedings against Margery began October 7, 1428, almost two years before Hawisia's abjuration on August 4, 1430, and perhaps Margery did not think they could de-

[44] McSheffrey speculates that the Moons' daughter may have been rebelling against her parents in that Foxe states she was only "partly" a Lollard (*Gender and Heresy,* 99).

[45] "Second Sunday in Advent," in *Lollard Sermons,* 2: ll. 700–701, 703.

[46] Pecock, *Repressor,* 1:67.

[47] The *Lanterne of Light* actually distinguishes among three churches in chaps. 6–10: the "chosun noumbre of hem that schullen be saued" (23); the physical building; and the actual congregation. See Hudson, *Premature Reformation,* 318–20. The Norwich community seems to mingle these together, and they are in fact less than distinct at points in the *Lanterne* itself.

tect Hawisia's involvement at the time of the 1428 deposition. Or she may have meant that the authorities could do what they liked to Hawisia because her "most secret" knowledge would help her find her way out of any legal difficulties. There certainly appears to have been some sense in the Norwich community that when one abjured, it had no bearing on one's spiritual condition, probably because all oaths were considered illicit. As John Reeve declared in 1430, "censures of holy Churche and sentences of cursyng yoven be bisshops, prelates or other ordinaries be not to be pondred ne to be dred, for as sone as soche bisshops or ordinaries acurse ony man, Crist hymself asoileth hym" (*T* 112). However, it seems likely that Margery's remark, framed as it is in relation to White's teachings, probably referred to the depth of Hawisia's spiritual understanding and her relationship to the "privy places" that she provided for her fellow believers. Although Hawisia is never identified in any of the court transcripts as a teacher, the authorities considered her important enough to be jailed before her trial, unlike the other women tried at Norwich. Incarcerated prior to her husband's arrest, she appears to have been the most knowledgeable and perhaps most independent of the women associated with the Norwich group, but as Hawisia's own abjuration makes clear, she used that knowledge to support the Lollard conventicles, counseling, comforting, and concealing, and not to teach other Lollards, at least not in the same way that Joan White had.

Hawisia's priviness was, in other words, the way that she lived what she learned at the conventicles, and her hospitality was motivated by her "reception" of Lollard teachings. Yet her abjuration suggests that spiritual understanding involved a continuous, spiritual birth, such as that described in the *Lanterne,* which drew on the Epistle of James, rather than intellectual mastery. According to James, God "wilfully . . . gendride vs with the word of treuthe," and as a result "we be sum bigynnyng of the creature of him" (voluntarie genuit nos verbo veritatis ut simus initium aliquod creaturae eius).[48] Like divine incarnation, this engendering is both a "birth" and a kind of self-

[48] Scriptural citations are from two sources. The Latin is from *Biblia Sacra Iuxta Vulgatam Versionem,* ed. Robert Weber et al. (Stuttgart: Deutsche Bibelgesellschaft, 1983). The second is the earlier version of the Lollard Bible (ca. 1385), printed in *The Holy Bible . . . Made from the Latin Vulgate by John Wycliffe and His Followers,* ed. Josiah Forshall and Frederic Madden (Oxford: Oxford University Press, 1850). I have included the Latin in the text and the later Lollard version in the notes; James 1:18, "For wilfulli he bigat vs bi the word of treuthe, that we be a bigynnyng of his creature."

generation: God is not the only creature who acts "willfully" in this process; the believer chooses to "recyue . . . the word insent, or ioyned," so it "mai saue" his or her soul (in mansuetudine suscipite insitum verbum quod potest salvare animas vestras).[49] This interiority equates scriptural understanding with a bodily experience of truth rather than with analytic interpretation, and Hawisia's abjuration makes this point in distinguishing between legality and lived, spiritual experience. She states that the priests make "newe lawes and newe ordinances" so they may go on with their "vicious levyng" (*T* 141). Contrasting her "child-like" knowledge with the "sotel techyng and prechyng, syngyng and redyng" of the "false fadirs," Hawisia makes it clear that Lollard study has little to do with the superficial trickery that the orthodox Church called spiritual knowledge.

Believers such as Hawisia rejected expertise and institutional membership as valid categories by which degrees of spiritual understanding might be maintained. Instead, they considered personal desire and "holy lyvyng" the features that distinguished the righteous children of God from those who belonged to the "devil's church." Hawisia, like other participants in the Norwich community, depended on access to written texts for spiritual understanding, but she also believed that the understanding that resulted was contingent upon desire and not on knowledge or intellectual training. We can see this conviction in her explanation that the sacrament of confirmation is unnecessary because "whan a child hath discrecion and can and wile undirstande the word of God it is sufficiently confermed be the Holy Gost and nedeth noon other confirmacion" (*T* 140). This statement may appear to be another straightforward rejection of institutional authority, but it is also a description of a much more complicated view of reading than one in which knowledge is simply accumulated. Rather, as Hawisia's statement suggests, the ability to read, and the importance of reading, lies in redirection of will. For Hawisia, understanding was sufficient if one, at an early age, desired to understand. The universalist potential granted by such an assumption is obvious and was denounced by clerical scholars. For example, Reginald Pecock, writing a few decades later, asserted that women Lollards were unfit readers of scripture because when they tried to understand God's word, they "puttiden al her affeccioun or motyue in her wil . . . and not in her intelleccioun or resoun."[50] Hawisia, if

[49] James 1:21, "resseyue ye the word that is plauntid, that may saue youre soulis."
[50] Pecock, *Repressor,* 1:67. For discussions of Pecock's emphasis on "reason" as necessary to spiritual understanding, see Janel Mueller, *The Native Tongue and the*

she could have, would no doubt have denounced Pecock for his attempt to use his learning to sell vernacular books. However, although they would have been out of sympathy with one another, she and Pecock seem to have agreed about the nature of Lollard women's reading and study. Reading was understood by members of the sect to require an earnest desire to know and was not dependent on knowledge acquired.

Even though "spiritual transformation through the redirection of will" is an academic-sounding formula that might have struck Hawisia as much like the priests' "sotel techyng," it sums up Hawisia's position neatly. It also suggests why it is so difficult to discover what Hawisia learned in the conventicle. According to Hawisia, anyone who actually wanted to know would have already known. Her job was to make it possible for such people to receive that knowledge safely. The idea that God's truths could be known by the uneducated was not of course new to the fifteenth century. Having been made in God's image, a certain level of spiritual understanding according to "kynde" was considered available to all humans throughout the Middle Ages, and "kynde" was an important concept in literature as disparate in time and genre as *Beowulf,* the cycle plays, and the poems in the *Pearl* manuscript. However, in their focused study of religious texts and tenets, Lollards, including Hawisia, were claiming a great deal more than this. The traditional view was that such truths were universally present but in a very limited way and that the duty of the Church was to analyze, study, and guard knowledge that was too difficult, abstract, or sacred for common consumption. This division clearly supported a hierarchical relationship among Christians based on knowledge. According to the Book of Hebrews, lay believers were "children" who needed spiritual "milk" and were not ready for the "solid food" that they clamored for (Pecock derived his condescending discussion of lay children and their "sweet tooths" from this passage), and there was a clear hierarchy of spiritual maturity that differentiated the least of the clergy from the highest of the laity. Denouncing clerical authority, Hawisia and the other members of the Norwich community insisted instead that each individual was a

---

Word: Developments in English Prose Style, 1380–1580 (Chicago: University of Chicago Press, 1984), 140–47; Ernest F. Jacob, "The Judgment of Reason: Bishop Pecock's Contentions," *Times Literary Supplement,* 29 September 1945, 462; Jacob, "Reynold Pecock, Bishop of Chicester," *Proceedings of the British Academy* 37 (1951): 121–54; and Arthur B. Ferguson, "Reginald Pecock and the Renaissance Sense of History," *Studies in the Renaissance* 13 (1966): 147–65.

"very pope" who had not just a right but a duty to study the scriptures, to understand them, and to teach others.

Although this might look like the argument that is made for all Protestant groups—that they reject clerical mediation in favor of individual spirituality—in Hawisia's case it is the familial sense of "priviness" and not simply rejection of clerical interference that defined her participation in the conventicle. The "genealogy" from the Epistle of James that attracted Lollards authorized lay believers' reading of the scriptures, in which God "gendride" believers with "the word of treuthe," and helped them revise the interpretive dynamic established in one of the medieval Church's central biblical passages, the Gospel of John's description of divine Incarnation:

> Et Verbum caro factum est et habitavit in nobis et vidimus gloriam eius gloriam quasi unigeniti a Patre plenum gratiae et veritatis.
>
> And the word, that is, Goddis sone, is maad fleisch, or man, and hath dwellid in vs, and we han seyn the glorie of him, the glorie as of the oon bigetun of the fadir, the sone ful of grace, and of treuthe.[51]

In the passage from John, the "Word" is, of course, traditionally understood, as we can see in the Wycliffite translation, as Christ in his spiritual, rather than human, essence, and "word" is equated with "truth." God produces his fleshly Son, quite literally, through his Word, thereby achieving, simultaneously, self-generation and reproduction.[52] James, in contrast, encouraged Christians to be "doers of the word" and not "hearers only" and revised the birth sequence described in John by announcing that the human Christian—not a textualized Word—is begotten through the union of God's will and His word. In the later Middle Ages, the Johanine genealogy was used to describe textual production: the Word was conflated with the word of

[51] John 1:14: "And the word was maad man, and dwellyde among vs, and we han seyn the glorie of hym, as the glorie of the oon bigetun sone of the fadir, ful of grace and of treuthe."

[52] Eugene Vance, in *Mervelous Signals: Poetics and Sign Theory in the Middle Ages* (Lincoln: University of Nebraska Press, 1986), suggests that this metonymic relationship between God and Word informs medieval understandings of the relationship between scripture and exegesis and, more generally, between text and interpretation (257). Similarly, Brian Stock argues that several heretical, textual communities considered the source of their faith a literally internalized Word and that in some cases "the birth of Christ becomes an allegory of the birth of interpretation" (*Implications of Literacy,* 106, 219).

God, the divine scriptures, and orthodox writers took this linguistic-textual association and used it to authorize their exegetical writings, as both Gerald Bruns and Rita Copeland have argued.[53] Exegetical texts were positioned in organic relationships to scripture, and their authors claimed an aristocratic pedigree of "canonical" intertextualities through the writings of the saints. What James helped the Lollards do was to reject clerical professionalism and textual production in order to reclaim the scriptures for themselves, and the Epistle did this by encouraging the reading and "doing" of God's word.

A quarter century after the Norwich trials, Bishop Reginald Pecock recognized that members of the sect had appropriated a "divine genealogy" to justify their vernacular studies, and in response he provided his own clerical genealogy to control Lollard interference in clerical affairs. The sense that he, and professionals like him, were "fathers" to lay children is central to Pecock's writings, and this idea takes a particularly telling form at the beginning of one of his treatises, the *Reule of Crysten Religioun*.[54] The *Reule* opens with the narrator, who is identified with Pecock, awaking from a vision in which he had met three fair ladies, the "treuths of vniuersal philsophie." Eager to marry, the ladies tell him that they had "profery[d]" themselves as mates to trained clerics, the "sons of God," but the men ignored them and chose instead the "daughters of men," that is, "worldly trouthis, oolde rehercellis, strange stories, fablis of poetis, newe invenciouns," for their wives. Pecock's story of the clerics' marriage becomes a myth of textual production: the fruit of the marriages between the sons of God and the daughters of men were "bastard" writings, the sort of works that some Lollards might have been interested in studying.[55] In contrast, Pecock proudly announces his own union with the ladies, identifying the *Reule* as his and the truths' own, legitimate child. Although the story is clearly aimed at establishing the authority of Pecock's books, the dream vision does more than legitimize Pecock's written work. Rather, by providing himself

53 Gerald Bruns, *Inventions: Writing, Textuality, and Understanding in Literary History* (New Haven: Yale University Press, 1982); Rita Copeland, *Rhetoric, Hermeneutics, and Translation in the Middle Ages* (Cambridge: Cambridge University Press, 1991).

54 Pecock was ultimately accused of heresy, stripped of his episcopal privileges, and confined. See V. H. H. Green, *Bishop Reginald Pecock: A Study in Ecclesiastical History and Thought* (Cambridge: Cambridge University Press, 1945); and Wendy Scase, "Reginald Pecock," in *Authors of the Middle Ages: English Writers of the Late Middle Ages*, ed. M. C. Seymour (Aldershot, U.K.: Variorum, 1996), 69–146.

55 Reginald Pecock, *The Reule of Crysten Religioun*, ed. William Cabell Greet, EETS, o.s., 171 (Millwood, N.Y.: Kraus Reprint, 1987), 32.

with a whole new family, Pecock's book also conveniently replaced the troublesome lay children who foolishly rebelled against clerical authority. The lady truths took the place of real women, such as Hawisia Moon and Margery Baxter, who with their noisy "iolite" and childish bullheadedness refused to accept the authority of their "fathers' " decisions.

In contrast with Pecockian professionalism, Hawisia, as a "child" of God, was responsible for sharing the scriptures with members of her household, and in her deposition, God's word and Lollard teachings replace the eucharistic bread that the orthodox Church believed sustained faith, which was of course administered by professionals as well. A Lollard sermon explicating John 6:11, a verse from the account of Christ's feeding of the five thousand with five loaves, which the Church used to authorize the sacrament, makes the explicit association between vernacular teaching and spiritual food. The sermon writer offers an allegorical interpretation of the five loaves of bread in which the first is "the lofe of the worde of God." According to the sermon, "alle that eten of this breed effectuelly, of Holy Scripture shullen be fulfillid, for al thing that is necessarie to the gouernaunce of her soulis thei mowen taste and fynde therinne."[56] Hawisia's abjuration associates her attempts to comfort, support, and maintain the group's members with the conventicle's ability to provide spiritual nourishment which the Church, offering only "vigiles" and "fastes," withheld. Priests are supposed to be God's "cheef panteris," that is, stewards in charge of His pantry, and their primary job, which they refuse to perform, according to the sermon writer, is "the setting foorthe and departing" of God's "breed." As the lay believers' hungry cries go unheeded, they are driven to find scriptural nourishment themselves, but when they do "taken it hemself (that is rede it or comoun therof together)," they are beaten and imprisoned. In contrast with members of the sect such as Hawisia, who took loving care of lay believers—who, like the Lollard priests in the sermon, distributed the "lofe of the worde of God . . . tenderly as modiris to children"—the priests behave as "stepmodris" who deny their charges nourishment.[57]

[56] "An Alternative to Sermon 14" (Sermon 14 is for the fourth Sunday in Lent), in *Lollard Sermons,* 15: ll. 118–20. For a discussion of this sermon, see Christina von Nolcken, "Some Alphabetical Compendia and How Preachers Used Them in Fourteenth-Century England," *Viator* 12 (1981): 271–88.

[57] "An Alternative to Sermon 14" in *Lollard Sermons,* 15: ll. 83–86, 77–78.

Criticism of the clergy was widespread in medieval literature, but what differentiated Lollard writing on the subject from more orthodox criticism was its insistence on a connection between the priests' refusal to provide lay readers with vernacular texts and lay/clerical relations. In a sermon for the fifth Sunday in Lent, the author, for example, equates clerical rejection of the vernacular scriptures with the rejection of spiritual procreation, which we saw was so important to the Norwich Lollards, referring to priests who would not provide access to the scriptures as "dispisers of the worde of God" who will be damned "more bitterly . . . then Sodomitis."[58] These priests, according to the sermon writers, are at fault because they refuse to act as mothers who nurture their children. Further, the priests' claims to spiritual authority are, according to the sermon, perverse—masculine, but sterile.

Although we might be tempted, given the emphasis in Lollard writings on maternal care and the vernacular, to argue, as Rita Copeland has, that the "Lollard hermeneutic" was feminine, to do so demands that we disregard the patriarchal structures that shaped participation in the conventicles (McSheffrey's argument) and, in relation to the vernacular, to ignore the ways that some of the Lollard writers described the English-language scriptures.[59] Although Latin was no doubt considered "masculine," as Copeland argues, and similarly, clerical writers such as Pecock clearly took aggressively "masculine" stances in their emphasis on clerical paternity, this did not mean that Lollard writers necessarily embraced the "feminine." The same Lollard sermon from Lent in fact "masculinizes" the vernacular, warning that "it is more perel to distrie goostly seed of the worde of God," which engenders Christ "in mennys soulis," than it is to destroy "bodilie seed by whiche mannys body shulde oonly be engendrid."[60]

Even women Lollards showed little interest in embracing the "feminine," although their trial transcripts exhibit clear disgust with the "masculine" practices of the established church. Hawisia, for example, did not call herself a mother to the Norwich community, but she did contrast her group's practices with those of "fadir Antecrist," that is, "the pope of Roome," and his men. According to Hawisia, clerical authorities, who are "cleped [called] prestes" even though

[58] "Fifth Sunday in Lent," in *Lollard Sermons,* 16: ll. 254–55.

[59] Copeland, "Why Women Can't Read," 253–86.

[60] "Fifth Sunday in Lent," in *Lollard Sermons,* 16: ll. 255–59.

they "ben no prestes" but "lecherous and covetouse" men, lead "vicious" lives of pride, lechery, sloth, and "alle other vices" (*T* 141). Rather than caring for the needs of the laypeople, these priests, stated Hawisia, "pile [rob]" them "of thar good" with "sotel techyng and prechyng, syngyng and redyng." Drawing attention to equality among believers, she contrasts the priests' corrupt lives with those of believers who, if they are "moost holy and moost perfit in lyvvyng in erthe," are "verry pope[s]" (*T* 141) no matter what their social status is. Although Hawisia was contemptuous of the priests' claims to "fatherhood," and was therefore critical of their assertions of masculine authority, she showed little interest in the idea that the vernacular was feminine. Rather, she was concerned to demonstrate that any believer could claim righteousness, that institutional authority was bankrupt, and that crooked priests lacked spiritual superiority over lay believers.

Clerical writers such as Wyclif were careful to avoid comments such as Hawisia's because such remarks were identified with Donatism, the heretical belief that a sinful priest could not perform the sacraments. But the inclusion of these comments in Hawisia's abjuration seems not to have bothered her at all.[61] Instead, her matter-of-fact denunciation of clerical corruption presents an idea of "holiness" that can be associated with the "imitatio christi" tradition. The Lollard sermon on John 6:11, the verse traditionally associated with the eucharist, shows how she might have thought about the relationship between spiritual nourishment and spiritual living. In the sermon, the writer suppresses the Church's reading of the verse and refers elliptically to John 6:51 in which Jesus declares that He is the "bread of life," emphasizing the divine rather than the sacramental. He then associates John 6:11 with Matthew 4:4, "Not oonly in breed lyueth man, but in euery worde that gothe oute of the mouthe of God." The context of the verse from Matthew is the devil's temptation of Jesus after His forty-day fast, and the Lollard writer in this way appropriated Jesus' righteous hunger to justify his demand for the vernacular scriptures. The sermon writer's tropological reading of the verses, his application of scripture to contemporary circumstances, shows Christ hungering for the "lofe of the worde of God" as the writer and his community of Lollard believers hungered.

Hawisia participated in the "imitatio christi" tradition by providing members of her community with a place in which they might

[61] On Lollardy and Donatism, see Hudson, *Premature Reformation,* 316.

consume spiritual food, the "lofe of the worde of God," but because she considered the group's teachings to be nourishment, her interest was, like Foxe's, in the effects of study rather than in its contents. This concern seems to have been typical of believers attracted to Lollardy, including those with clerical training. For example, the Lollard sermon on John 6:11, for all its elaborate scriptural cross-referencing and obvious clerical training, shows a writer with a similar understanding of the grounds for demanding the scriptures. We can see this similarity in his sermon's shift from John's description of the miraculous feeding of the five thousand, the sermon's topic, to a discussion of Matthew 4:4, a passage in which Jesus, after fasting for forty days, speaks to the devil in the wilderness. Jesus' words in Matthew, in which he rejects the devil's attempt to trick him into turning stones into bread, are themselves a citation of Deuteronomy 8:3, "He trauelde thee with scarsenes, and gaf to thee meet manna, the which vnknewe thow, and thi fadres, that he shewe to thee, that *not in oonly breed lyueth man, but in eche word of God,* that goth out of the mouth of the Lord" (italics added). Manna, the miraculous bread that the Lord fed the Israelites as they wandered in the wilderness for forty years, was life-giving and unknown to the Israelites' ancestors. The sermon thus weaves together nourishment (the feeding of the five thousand), righteous resistance (against the devil), and the "word of God." Although the sermon writer is clearly concerned with scriptural access, he, like Hawisia, seems to think of Bible reading in terms of sustenance rather than knowledge.

Hawisia's abjuration, even though it was made because she was known to run schools in her home, demonstrates almost no interest in justifying or explicating what she has learned because what mattered to her was the way that study nourished the community. Hawisia's spiritual understanding contrasted sharply with that of the priests, those "singemesses," who she suggests merely produce the sounds of religiosity. For all her "sapience," her deposition, like those of the others, is made up almost entirely of what seem to be Lollard "commandments," such as "it is not leful to slee a man for ony cause" and "no man is bounde to faste in Lenton, Ymbren Days, Fridays ne vigiles of seyntes" (*T* 142). We might assume that the absence of such discussion is either scribal (the court did not want to record what she had learned) or gendered (Lollard women did not think about such things), but I suspect both assumptions are wrong. Rather, it appears to me that Hawisia's idea of knowledge was that it required little discussion because she *knew,* like Foxe, like Joan White, that she had it. The purpose of the conventicles was to help other believers to know as well.

What could this mean, to run schools without mentioning what was taught? To know things without explaining what those things were? As difficult as this is for modern scholars and readers to conceive, it appears to be exactly the way in which Hawisia thought about the conventicles. Her experience in the schools emphasized the process of learning, of being with other members, of receiving believers into her home and protecting them, and not the material learned or even the comprehensibility of the vernacular scriptures. We might for this reason see Hawisia's participation in the schools as an act of communal dissent. David Aers, for example, observes that Lollard

> women and men organiz[ed] the study of the Scriptures and their forms of devotion within their homes, trade networks and villages, striving to develop communities of worship, resources (material and spiritual), and human solidarity in which orthodox boundaries between laity and clergy, secular and sacred spaces, secular and sacred people, secular (vernacular) and sacred (Latin) were dissolved.[62]

Some of Hawisia's statements in the deposition certainly support Aers's assertion. She admits, for example, that she believes baptism is unnecessary because all believers are "sufficiently baptized in the blood of Christ," and they therefore require no institutional apparatus to consecrate what is already sacred. Similarly, she avows that a valid marriage demands "oonly consent of love betuxe man and woman, without contract of wordis and withoute solennizacion in church and withoute symbred askyng [permission of kindred] is sufficient for the sacrament of matrymoyn," reflecting the same anti-institutional impulse (*T* 140). However, while it seems obvious that Hawisia rejected the Church's institutional authority, I think it is misleading to identify her involvement in the schools as "dissenting." To do so suggests that the practical aspects of lived participation in the conventicles were beside the point: if we consider her involvement in the school as enacting dissent, Hawisia's literate engagement becomes symbolic, meaningful as something else. This, as Asad ex-

[62] David Aers and Lynn Staley, *Powers of the Holy: Religion, Politics, and Gender in Late Medieval English Culture* (University Park: Pennsylvania State University Press, 1996), 58.

plains, is the way that we now think about ritual: as something "interpretable" that stands "for some further *verbally definable*, but tacit, event."[63] Her participation was of course interpretable on a social level—the most obvious evidence was her trial for heresy—but that interpretation came after the fact of her participation and in concert with the forces and exigencies of the trial and its interrogative dynamics. Even if we insist that in her participation she was "sending a message" to the authorities, she was also involved in a learning process upon which she believed her salvation depended.

Learning was important to the authorities as well. The explicit aim of the trials was to stop heresy and to return the accused to the established Church. One of the court's educational instruments was the written "indenture" that was sent home with the accused person following her abjuration. The process of recantation was complete only when the confession was turned into a document made up of two parts. The heretic signed one portion, the authority in charge signed the other, and each party kept a copy. Hawisia's abjuration, for example, concludes with this statement: "In wittenesse of which thinges Y subscribe here with myn owen hand a cross †. And to this partie indented to remayne in your registre Y sette my signet. And that other partie indented Y receyve undir your seel to abide with me unto my lyves ende" (*T* 143). Having taken away the opportunities for study that the conventicles afforded, the authorities offered the heretic her own personal piece of writing whose purpose was no doubt, as Aston observes, "to fortify the fears of recidivism." For members of the Norwich group who were dedicated to regular study in the community's schools, the authority's document must have seemed especially insulting: it asserted authority over the accused for life, treating her largely as an inert entity, and forced her to sign herself over to the bishop. The episcopal authorities put their copy in their register, but one wonders what the heretic was supposed to do with hers: was this public document conceived of as a replacement for the privy ones that the Norwich Lollards studied, and was the indenture to be displayed? kept on one's person? stored in a drawer?[64] No matter where the indentures were kept, Hawisia's abjuration sug-

[63] Talal Asad, *Genealogies of Religion: Discipline and Reasons of Power in Christianity and Islam* (Baltimore: Johns Hopkins University Press, 1993), 57.

[64] The public floggings imposed on many of the accused were clearly more useful in terms of public display—as of course were the burnings of White, Pye, and Waddon—than any document might have been. See Tanner, *Heresy Trials*, 22–25.

gests that members of the community must have imagined the recantation document as a personalized form of the "newe ordinances" that Hawisia asserted "curse and kille cruelly" those opposed to the priests' ungodly habits.

The Norwich community understood their involvement in textual culture, in explicit contrast to the authority's professional writings and practices, as life-bringing. For example, in Margery Baxter's deposition and abjuration from October 1428 to April 1429, Margery, according to one of the witnesses, her neighbor Joan Cliffland, claimed to be immune to the law imposing death by fire on heretics because she "habuit et habet unam cartam salvacionis in utero suo" (had and has a charter of salvation in her womb) (*T* 49). Margery was a relapsed heretic by 1429 (having been formally accused of heresy for a second time by Joan), and she surely knew that immolation was the punishment reserved for repeat offenders. Her teacher William White had been burned at the stake in September 1428, and Margery had attended the execution. Indeed, Joan's testimony concerning Margery's earlier remark may have struck observers as grimly ironic given that Margery stood before the episcopal authorities because of two highly public documents. The first, the 1401 statute "de heretico comburendo," banned participation in conventicles and designated excommunication and immolation as potential punishments. The second, Arundel's Constitutions, forbid the production, possession, and reading of vernacular translations of the Bible except with the local bishop's prior approval. It is not clear why Margery was not finally executed, but the possibility of such a punishment was no doubt on her mind as she sat in her house talking to Joan about her faith, testifying about the "document" that she believed would save her.

We know both more and less about Margery's involvement with written texts than we do concerning Joan White and Hawisia Moon's literate practice. Less because Margery seems not to have been central to the community's functioning—she was neither a teacher nor a hostess of conventicles—and more because her deposition and abjuration describe her actual handling of books. She had secretly helped William White carry his books from Yarmouth to Martham before his death and had then hidden them for him (*T* 41). Hanna suggests that this description of Margery's actions shows that Margery "was clearly engaged in keeping" William White's "teaching alive." It shows even more particularly that the books seemed to her an extension of White's person: just as he needed to be hidden by families such as the Moons, his books needed to be transported secretly and deposited in a safe place.[65] Hanna says she was "preserving" the books, and maybe she was, but given her enthusiastic description of William's saintliness, it seems just as likely that she was preserving William. The books could incriminate him, just as simply carrying them later incriminated her, and as the fact that Margery's husband read aloud from his "lex Christi" in the evenings made him liable to prosecution.[66] In either event, Margery's abjuration, like that of Hawisia, associates written texts with priviness. Margery carried the books "occulte," and she then "abscondisse ibidem" (*T* 41). Her husband read from his book privately in what are specified as "their rooms" (*T* 47).

Even Margery's discussion with Joan Cliffland seems to have been conducted discreetly. One would be hard-pressed to call it teaching: the women were sitting together in Joan's house chatting when Margery made the heretical statements that led Joan to testify against her. Margery did invite Joan to come "secrete in cameram" to hear Margery's husband read aloud, but this seems a far less formal situation than even the most casually organized conventicle. Margery was not offering to teach her to read. In fact, as Hanna suggests, Margery may not have known how to read (although I am surprised Hanna offers Margery's husband's nightly reading as evidence for her illiteracy—surely the nightly reading was a household activity that proves little except that her husband certainly was able to read).[67] But in any case, whether Margery could read or not, it is clear from Joan's deposition and the earlier accusation concerning William White's books that intimate engagement with the written word was a regular part of Margery's life. She did not wait to attend Hawisia's or anyone else's conventicles (and we do not know if she did attend them) in order to learn from the scriptures but heard them and perhaps read them in her own home.

The intimacy of Margery's experience with the written word is echoed in her claim that she has and had a charter of salvation in her womb (*T* 49), which I alluded to above in relation to her possible execution as a relapsed heretic. Copeland has associated Margery's "charter" with the Annunciation, or rather, with "the Virgin who carried the Word incarnate in her womb," and suggests that Margery

[65] Hanna, "Ricardian Prose Translation," 332.

[66] Citing Foxe, Hanna states that Margery's husband was called William Wright; William had implicated many people as Lollards (Hanna, "Richardian Prose Translation," 337–38 n. 31).

[67] Ibid., 332.

herself made the "very connection" between her "textual activity and the central mystery of the faith, the Incarnation of the Word."[68] I have no doubt that Margery made the association between herself and the Word in light of her identification of her own body in the Norwich document with His cross (she spread out her arms and said, "Hec est vera crux Christi" [*T* 44]). I wonder, however, about the emphasis on "textual activity" in Copeland's remarks. I do not mean to suggest that Margery thought that books were unimportant. There is no question about her bravery in carrying William's books or her enthusiasm for her husband's reading. But "textual activity" really seems to mean that she was committed to thinking about what books meant, to studying them, and learning from them, and although it is clear that she heard her husband read in the evenings, the deposition against her offers little more in the way of bookish accusations.

Rather, it seems to me that her "charter" has more in common with James's "divine genealogy," in which the believer is begotten through the "word of truth," than it does with biblical studies. James offered the Norwich Lollards a "readerly" genealogy in which consumption of God's word authorized activities like Margery's husband's nightly reading. But what is surprising about James's genealogy is that the origin of the "word of truth" appears to be both external, a partner in union with God, and internal to the believer. In the circa 1385 version of the Wycliffite Bible, James commands his audience, "receyue ye the word insent, or ioyned, that mai saue youre soules" (in mansuetudine suscipite insitum verbum quod potest salvare animas vestras).[69] In the slightly later version of the Wycliffite Bible the verse reads, "resseyue ye the word that is plauntid, that may saue youre soulis." Both Lollard versions develop metaphors of growth and generation that are present throughout the first chapter of James, but the earlier version is especially interesting in its hesitating, double translation of "insitum" as "insent, or ioyned." "Insitum" can be a botanical term meaning not just implanted but engrafted. Botanically, grafts are unions of two separate plants and are used by gardeners to improve the quality of a root plant. The "scion," a cutting from a superior plant, is joined with the root plant, and it transforms the root plant's composition. The result is that the new, improved plant produces vastly superior fruits and flowers from having been joined with the scion. If the graft takes, the two plants are

[68] Copeland, "Why Women Can't Read," 277.

[69] James 1:21. Cited above.

"ioyned" and not just "plauntid," the parts forming a unified whole that is transformed inside as well as outside.[70]

Belief in the need to receive the word "insent"—on the inside, like Margery's "charter"—may have contributed to the Lollards' attention to memorization of scripture. The practical convenience of memorization during periods of persecution is obvious: it left no evidence of heretical activity. Margery had to hide William White's books, but memorized texts are undetectable, entirely "privy," and require no hiding. Joan Cliffland's testimony against Margery suggests that Margery may have had a great deal of scripture memorized. As Hanna points out, Joan recounted a story Margery had told her about arguing with a begging friar. According to Joan, Margery had told the friar to labor honestly for his money instead of begging, and she had then expanded on the gospel "in lingua Anglicana" to support her point (*T* 48). "Presumably," as Hanna suggests, "she cited passages which show the apostles earning their bread through manual labor."[71]

However, although it seems likely that Margery had memorized verses from her husband's "lex Christi," her "charter of salvation" appears to be a different kind of written document from a remembered scriptural passage. A charter was a legal document, and as Andrew Galloway and Margaret Aston explain in different contexts, the "charters of Christ" became an important genre and image in late medieval literature.[72] In these texts, Christ's crucifixion is presented as a documentary transaction that is "inscribed on the parchment of Christ's body" by pens, which are "scourges" that leave "wounds," letters of the alphabet, on the body/paper. The metaphor was ex-

[70] "May" in both Wycliffite versions of this verse implies a certain anxiety concerning claims to guaranteed salvation that the translators may have associated with "potest."

[71] Hanna, "Ricardian Prose Translation," 334.

[72] Margaret Aston, "Devotional Literacy," in *Lollards and Reformers,* 104–5. She notes that "compositions" that include this image and "the surviving manuscripts of these charters of Christ are fairly numerous" (105). Also see Andrew Galloway's insightful essay, "Intellectual Pregnancy, Metaphysical Feminity, and the Social Doctrine of the Trinity in *Piers Plowman,*" *Yearbook of Langland Studies* 12 (1998): 117–52. Galloway makes an explicit connection between the charters of Christ and Margery Baxter, suggesting that Margery "invoked the 'charter of salvation'—that epitome of the contractual and legalistic world of late-medieval culture—in the way that she used her other bodily lessons: invoking from a certain metaphorical remove her physical existence and generativity as a lay woman to displace the sacred authority of the institutional church, and to locate that authority instead in a place—the secular maternal womb—uncharted by theology and the ideals of a celibate clergy" (121).

tended, and as Aston notes, "It was even possible to conceive of salvation in terms of a chirograph or indenture." Specifically, these charters associate the seal, "that instrument of personal identity," with Jesus' blood. The legal promises of such texts were made explicit, and persons who held such charters could, as one text puts it, "come and claim when thou wilt / the bliss that lost our former friend."[73]

The claims that one could put forward based on memorization were very different from those based on holding such a "charter of salvation." Memorization required both time and experience. One might accumulate a great many texts this way, and Foxe includes a number of Lollards who memorized entire books of the Bible. But even individuals with the most remarkable memories could only do so through practice, and they required either a written book or another person who had already memorized the passage to check their work. A charter, however, was acquired quickly and kept safe until the time it was needed. The verbs used in Joan's deposition to describe Margery's possession of the charter, "habuit et habet," "had and has," draw attention to both the moment of Margery's acquisition and her continued possession of the document. Memory, and oral performance of what had been memorized, might furthermore succumb to time's vagaries. The charter, in contrast, was a material document that could be produced as evidence with guaranteed accuracy and depended on with confidence if it was kept safely.

However, I do not think, as Copeland does, that "the hiding of the text of salvation" in Margery's womb "represents the exercise of private and thus autonomous interpretive power."[74] Copeland calls it a "personalized charter" that allowed Margery to "exercise[] her interpretive prerogative," but the charter seems to me to signify transformation of the kind described by James rather than interpretive control. Margery may have been very interested in interpretive issues, but there is no evidence of this in the deposition. What there is instead is a statement about the salvific power of this charter and its ability to protect her as if she belonged to a species of beings who could not be burned. It is not, in this case, an image that she used to describe her interpretive rights but one that allowed her to differentiate herself from those who could make no such claim. Margery, in other words, seems to have counted herself among the elect, those chosen for salvation, in the language of James, one of those whose re-

[73] Aston, "Devotional Literacy," 104–5.

[74] Copeland, "Why Women Can't Read," 278.

ception of the Word had saved her soul. Wyclif had maintained that the church was made up of the "congregatio predestinatorum." Although technically it was impossible according to Lollard writings to know who was a member of the elect, one writer argues that even though "we may not yit wite for certeyn which persone is of Cristis spouse of all the men that wandren heere," we "may gesse and that is ynow."[75] We might assume, as Hanna does, that this explains how Margery "read": he states that "Lollard reading" was thought to come "only by grace," and as a result Lollards' "textual understanding is predicated upon election."[76]

Margery's "charter" is a sign of her election but not a personally created sign, as Hanna and Copeland propose. Copeland and Hanna might suggest that what I am pointing out is that Margery's reading was literal and that I have misunderstood their arguments. Copeland identifies literal reading as the mode favored by Lollard readers and explains that in the allegorical tradition, a text is read "not just for itself (carnally) but for its significance in love of God (charitably)." Lollard readers, in contrast, argues Copeland, preferred the "literal," a term that at least initially she appears to use to denote what it usually means, the non-metaphorical. She cannot possibly mean this, however, since she goes on in the essay to describe Margery's carrying of the "charter" as a "literal identification" with the Virgin: it is impossible to imagine this identification as anything but metaphorical. And in fact Copeland does not mean non-metaphorical. She subsequently contends that the "literal" instead refers to a "private investment" in which the reader might free herself "from clerical regulation."[77] This is a rather different idea from that in which reading is understood as something that is done "just for itself," and it is much like Hanna's description of Margery's reading. Hanna claims that Margery's reading was literal, and he contrasts that literality with allegorical hermeneutics in which the reader is familiar with a "system with rules for recognizing significance." Margery's reading, according to Hanna, is a "rejection of hermeneutics," and her response to the literal level of the text was "to use the text almost archaeologically," that is, as a "model for current conduct."[78]

[75] Hudson, *Premature Reformation,* 315. She cites *The English Works of Wyclif,* ed. F. D. Matthew (1880; 2d rev. ed., London: Trübner, 1902), 422–27.

[76] Hanna, "Ricardian Prose Translation," 337.

[77] Copeland, "Why Women Can't Read," 256, 278.

[78] Hanna, "Ricardian Prose Translation," 335. That Lollard reading is literal has often been remarked and makes good sense given passages such as "al holy writt is trewe aftir the lettre," but as Hudson notes, despite such remarks, it is difficult to

Although it seems to me that the Lollards at Norwich were taught to read in the allegorical manner (reading a text "not just for itself . . . but for its significance in love of God") to which Copeland alludes, my primary concern at this point is with the association between the literal and private interpretation. Margery Baxter, at least if the deposition offers an accurate account of her words, certainly made some idiosyncratic-sounding statements. My favorite is her warning against swearing: "dame, bewar of the bee, for every bee wil styngge, and therfor loke that ye swer nother be Godd ne be Our Ladi ne be non other seynt, and if ye do the contrarie the be will styngge your tunge and veneme your sowle" (*T* 44). But unless we actually believe that she thought a bee would come to sting someone who swore, her statement cannot be considered "literal" in the non-metaphorical sense. More importantly, her statement clearly requires rules (and not a private investment) for recognizing significance, and therefore it matches neither definition of the literal. The rule (and I might point out that it is a rule and not an interpretation) that led Margery to produce this warning was obviously the Norwich community's position on swearing. Of the Norwich defendants, at least twenty-two of them, more than a third, mentioned that it was never "lawful" to swear. The *Lanterne of Light* argues that taking oaths is an act of idolatry if any name other than God's is used.[79] And taking God's name in vain was of course blasphemy.[80]

Margery's expression therefore may have been idiosyncratic, but her position on swearing was definitely not. Rather, Margery was a member of a community with specific interests and ideas that were shared, and these ideas shaped the way that members of the Norwich group responded to written texts. Her "charter of salvation" is a good example of the ways that an individual in the group might choose to focus on one particular idea. The community, as I have suggested, was committed to ongoing study, to instruction by teachers such as William White, and to informal reading and discussion such as the Baxters' evening reading from the "lex Christi." It seems overwhelmingly likely that her ideas were influenced by all of these interactions. Communal forces did not shape the individual's ideas or interests en-

label Lollard reading literal because Lollard practice "does not entirely bear out the implications" of such comments. Instead, she argues, Lollard writers identified the literal sense with the writer's intentions. See *Premature Reformation,* 271.

79 *Lanterne of Light,* 89.

80 See Hudson, *Premature Reformation,* 371–73.

tirely, but they did lead her to concentrate on particular concerns, much as clerical culture did not produce uniform religious interpretation but influenced medieval scholars' writings. Margery's "charter" reflects the Norwich group's anxieties about prosecution, salvation, and access to the written texts that they believed were able to save their souls. Margery's desire to share that salvation with her neighbor, as she believed she was commanded to do, did not keep her from worrying about prosecution. She even remarked to Joan at a certain point during their conversation that Joan looked like she would betray her to the bishop. That charter of salvation, as she had (presumably) learned in her conventicles and from hearing her husband read at home, was her guarantee that even if Joan did report her, she would be safe from the episcopal fires—as she believed William White was.

The fact that Margery thought of spiritual education as producing a "charter of salvation" suggests that her literate practice differed dramatically from that of Joan White and Hawisia Moon. Joan and Hawisia were both, in different ways of course, committed to spiritual education as a continuous and communal process. Margery, however, seems to have listened to her husband read from the scriptures and to have been devoted to William White but to have been far less concerned with communal education than were the other two women. Although Margery's "charter" was at least in part the product of communal understanding, it was also a personal document that she herself understood without actually having to "read," in any intellectual sense, because it was "written" inside of her. The image of the scriptures written inside the believer appears in orthodox writings, including, for example, Margaret Beaufort's translation of the *Mirroure of Golde,* but it was especially important for heterodox communities that were "deprived" of God's word because it granted them textual authority even when they were without texts. The *Lanterne,* for example, cites Jeremiah's accusations against corrupt priests that "taken from the peple the lawe that God hath writen him silf in myddis of the herte"; as Steven Justice points out, "the law written in the *heart*" in the *Lanterne* "turns out to be identical with the law written in the *book.*"[81] This writing is like Margery's charter—more important for what it is than for what it says. And what it is ultimately is a confirmation of identity. How do you know if you are one

[81] Justice, "Inquisition, Speech, and Writing," 21. For an earlier sect's use of the notion of divine inscription, see Stock, *Implications of Literacy,* 115.

of the elect? God's word is written in your heart. How do you become one of the elect? God writes His word in your heart.

This conclusion may seem a surprising one to draw about a member of a community devoted to vernacular study, even if she may have been unable to read, but it is precisely this sense of writing's significance that informed not only Margery's but Joan's and Hawisia's literate practice: "having" God's word (in your heart, in your home) was more important than understanding it. This chapter has been about a group of readers, or at any rate of believers, who depended on ideas found in written texts, but this "heretical" literate practice has a great deal in common with Margaret Beaufort's "orthodox" self-inscription, which placed her "within" the text itself. It links reading—as the *Chastising of God's Children,* a book associated with a Benedictine abbey, suggests—with "vertuous lyueng" and not necessarily with comprehension.[82] For the Lollard women who were the subject of this chapter, the spiritual effects of communal study far outweighed the intellectual benefits of vernacular reading.

[82] *Chastising of God's Children,* ed. Joyce Bazire and Eric Colledge (Oxford: Basil Blackwell, 1957), 203–4. The passage concerns Saint Hildegard, "an hooli nun," who, despite the fact that she "vndirstode nat" the Latin she read, was able to scare away devils when she read the psalter; the passage turns to consider propitious verses generally.

CHAPTER 4

Reading at Syon Abbey

The Syon Additions to the Bridgettine rule state that when a novice made her profession and entered the abbey, she should bring with her "bokes, beddynge, profession rynge, dyner, offerynge, and such other."[1] This practice must have been intended to save the abbey some money—one might expect that the novice would have had the bedding and "such other" practical items already in possession and that they could be used in the monastery. The mention of unspecified "bokes" in the list of things to bring is harder to explain. Mary Erler suggests that the inclusion of "bokes" "reveals both the . . . expectation of book ownership at entrance and a degree of personal interest in reading."[2] But while it is true that the sisters in the community were to read daily, it is surprising that the order would make such a demand since another Bridgettine injunction prohibited the holding of personal property. The "sin of property" was, according to the sisters' rule, among the "most grievous" crimes one could commit. When a sister was "conuycte of properte," she was required to perform penance, and if she refused to do so she was to be "put into pryson."[3] Property holding was understood as active rebellion against the community, and it figured among the most serious offenses—these included apostasy, insurrection, murder, and "fleschly syn" (both "kyn-

[1] *The Syon Additions for the Sisters from the British Library MS Arundel 146,* vol. 4 of *The Rewyll of Seynt Sauioure,* ed. James Hogg (Salzburg: Institut für Anglistik und Amerikanistik, 1980), 83.

[2] Mary Erler, "The Books and Lives of Three Tudor Women," in *Privileging Gender in Early Modern England,* ed. Jean R. Brink (Kirksville, Mo.: Sixteenth Century Journal Publishers, 1993), 5–17.

[3] *Syon Additions for the Sisters,* 15.

[4] See, for example, Roger Ellis, *Viderunt eam filie Syon: The Spirituality of the*

dly or vnkyndly").[4] Given the seriousness of this restriction, we might assume then that the sisters used the practical items they brought with them, which were no doubt so similar as to be almost impersonal anyhow, but donated their books to their communal library. This appears to be what the Bridgettine brothers did. Toward the end of the fifteenth century, many of the brothers at the monastery, which was a double order and housed monks and nuns in separate quarters, were university-trained scholars, and these men were used to having books with which to work. The brothers' library catalog survives, and it shows that many of the books in the library were donated by the brothers themselves.[5]

Although no catalog is extant, we know from Syon legislation that the sisters had their own library as well.[6] But even if they donated their books to the abbey library, some also undoubtedly owned books as personal possessions. Erler describes several personally owned books from the sixteenth century, including those of the Syon sister

English House of a Medieval Contemplative Order from Its Beginnings to the Present Day (Salzburg: Institut für Anglistik und Amerikanistik, 1984), 85–86. Ellis describes Syon's Additions to the Bridgettine Rule, noting that "open rebellion" is associated with "receiving letters or gifts" (85) and "especially" with "the sin of property" (86). For the Additions themselves, see *Syon Additions for the Sisters,* 12, 15. Roger Ellis, "The Visionary and the Canon Lawyers: Papal and Other Revisions to the *Regula Salvatoris* of St. Bridget of Sweden," in *Prophets Abroad: The Reception of Continental Holy Women in Late-Medieval England,* ed. Rosalynn Voaden (Cambridge: D. S. Brewer, 1996), remarks on the "gravity" of the ban on private property (84).

[5] Roger Lovatt notes that some of the brothers' collections were extensive (we know this because the catalog for the men's library was organized by donor). See Lovatt, "The Library of John Blacman and Contemporary Carthusian Spirituality," *Journal of Ecclesiastical History* 43 (1992): 225; and Mary Bateson, *Catalogue of the Library of Syon Monastery Islesworth* (Cambridge: Cambridge University Press, 1898). Vincent Gillespie mentions that "over 1200 out of 1465" books in the men's library "are donations from the brethren themselves or from well-wishers" (Gillespie, "Dial M for Mystic: Mystical Texts in the Library of Syon Abbey and the Spirituality of the Syon Brethren," in *The Medieval Mystical Tradition,* ed. Marion Glasscoe [Cambridge: D. S. Brewer, 1999], 267).

[6] The most recent discussion of the nuns' library at Syon is in David N. Bell, *What Nuns Read: Books and Libraries in Medieval English Nunneries* (Kalamazoo, Mich.: Cistercian Publications, 1995), 171–210; Bell incorporates much of the bibliographic material from Christopher F. R. de Hamel, *Syon Abbey. The Library of the Bridgettine Nuns and Their Peregrinations after the Reformation* (London: Roxburghe Club, 1991). I cite both Bell's and de Hamel's catalog numbers. No catalog is extant for the nuns' library. On the practical concerns of book maintenance, see Mary C. Erler, "Syon Abbey's Care for Books: Its Sacristan's Account Rolls 1506/7–1535/6," *Scriptorium* 39 (1985): 293–307.

Eleanor Fettyplace, whose name was written in four books, for example.[7] Eleanor might have left her name in the books even after she donated them to the library, of course. Or, probably less likely, Eleanor wrote her name in the books when she borrowed them from the library, to practice writing or just because she felt like it. At any rate, a name written in a book is not definitive proof of individual ownership that continued after enclosure. A copy of the *Scale of Perfection,* given to the Syon sister Joan Sewell by a Carthusian, offers firmer evidence that at least some of the sisters owned books personally. The copy is de Worde's 1494 printing, the same edition that Margaret Beaufort and Elizabeth of York gave to Mary Roos, and Joan Sewell's contains the spectacular ex libris shown in figure 1.[8]

The monogram in which James Grenehalgh, the donor, linked his initials with those of his book's recipient leaves little doubt that this was a personal gift to Joan and not a book to be shared with other members of the Syon community.

Although much has been written about Syon as a center of learning, little has been said about the discrepancy between the rule's prohibitions on property and the sisters' ownership of books. Ann Hutchison comes close to acknowledging the contradiction between the rule's restrictions and the sisters' book-owning. She notes that "poverty is stressed" in the rule, which she cites, " 'therfor be it / lefull to none to haue eny thyng propir: no / manere thing. be it neuere so lityll. nor for to haue / oon halpeny in possession or towche it wt hondys' "; she goes on to remark that "even the number of service books [was] stringently regulated."[9] However, although Hutchison acknowledges the severity of the rule in relation to book ownership, rather than working out its implications she puts aside the restriction, suggesting only that "it is all the more impressive" that the sisters were to have " 'Thoo bookes . . . as many as they wyll in whyche

[7] Erler mentions that four books—three service books and a copy of Whytford's *Pype of Perfection*—contain Eleanor's signature; Eleanor joined the Syon community sometime in the early 1520s ("Books and Lives of Three Tudor Women," 5–17).

[8] Reproduced in Michael G. Sargent, *James Grenehalgh as Textual Critic* (Salzburg: Institut für Anglistik und Amerikanistik, 1984), 1:173.

[9] Ann Hutchison, "Devotional Reading in the Monastery and in the Late Medieval Household," in *De Cella in Seculum: Religious and Secular Life and Devotion in Late Medieval England,* ed. Michael G. Sargent (Cambridge: D. S. Brewer, 1989), 217. See also *The Rewyll of Seynt Sauioure and Other Middle English Brigittine Legislative Texts,* vol. 2 of *The Rewyll of Seynt Sauioure,* ed. James Hogg (Salzburg: Institut für Englische Sprache und Literatur, 1978), 8–9.

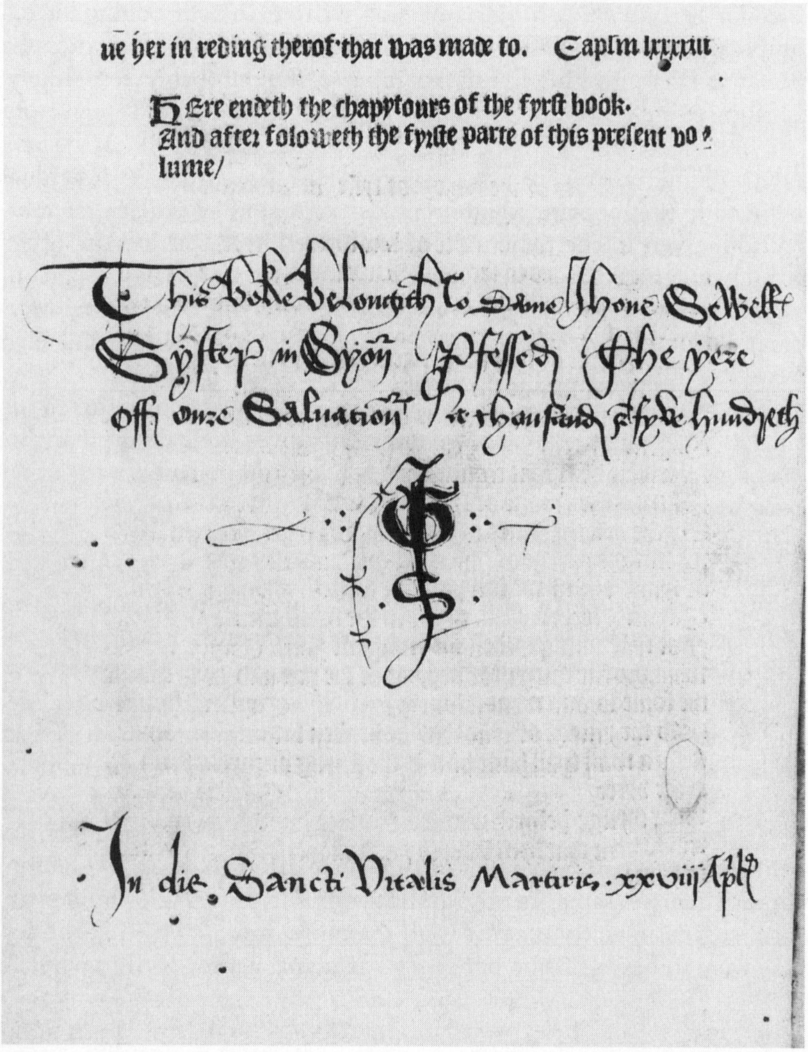
ue her in reding therof that was made to. Caplm lxxxxiii

Here endeth the chapytours of the fyrst book. And after foloweth the fyrste parte of this present vo lume/

This boke belongyth to dame Jhone Sewell Syster in Syon professed the yere off owre Saluation a thousand fyve hundreth

In die Sancti Vitalis Martiris xxviij Aprilis

Fig. 1. Walter Hilton, *Scala perfectionis,* fol. 4v (lower two-thirds of page). Philadelphia, Rosenbach Incun. 494h. Reproduced by permission of the Rosenbach Museum and Library.

ys to lerne or to studye.' " Hutchison's cheerful assessment is echoed by most scholars who mention the sisters' studies. J. T. Rhodes, for example, assumes that the Syon brothers' involvement in the production and composition of devotional books at the close of the Middle Ages was motivated by their "obligation to provide the sisters—who were expected to be literate—with a suitable range of reading matter in English." He clearly believes that the sisters considered the books at Syon personal property and suggests that "there are extant a considerable number of books bearing the names of individual nuns at Syon," which demonstrates their individual, scholarly enthusiasm.[10] Christopher de Hamel's remarks are definitive: "Strictly, the nuns were allowed no personal possessions whatsoever, but surely the rules were flexible enough to permit the keeping of a prayer-book on indefinite loan for private use in the cell or cloister."[11]

In contrast, I am hesitant to put aside the discrepancy between the rule's prohibitions on ownership and the sisters' book-owning. This is not because I am convinced the sisters followed the rule to the letter; houses always modified their relationship to the order's rules when it suited their purposes (for example, the Carthusians at the London Charterhouse counseled lay believers in direct disobedience of the order's regulations, as I observed in chapter 2 of this book). It is, rather, because I think this inconsistency can tell us a great deal about the sisters' literate practice and about how they negotiated between individual investment in books and the demands of communal, "familial" life. Broadly, this chapter is about the ways in which the nuns' reading changed from the monastery's foundation in 1415 up to the early sixteenth century. Bridgettine emphasis on individuality as part of a collective identity, which is most strongly reflected in the liturgy and in Bridget's *Life,* was part of a religious, disciplinary program of lived performance. Private, devotional reading constituted one aspect of this program, and was intended to occupy the nun when she was not involved in liturgical performance. What seems to have changed over the course of the fifteenth century is the centrality of the material book—the actual, printed copy and its writing—to the lives of the sisters both before and after they entered the monastery. Increasingly, the nuns' private reading at Syon Abbey involved an intense experience of identification with books as both material and spiritual objects. What personal ownership of books offered the nuns at Syon was the sense, even as they were "mirrors" of Bridget and of one another, as daughters of Syon, of readerly individuality.

Monastic programs were based on the understanding that "virtues" should be "formed by developing the ability to behave in

[10] J. T. Rhodes, "Syon Abbey and Its Religious Publications in the Sixteenth Century," *Journal of Ecclesiastical History* 44 (1993): 15.

[11] De Hamel, *Syon Abbey,* 74.

accordance with saintly exemplars."[12] It was easier to recognize what aspects of the lived life were imitable in the lives of saints long dead than it was to find such aspects in those of saints such as Saint Bridget, who had lived in personal as well as written memory.[13] Bridget had died in 1373. When Syon was founded in 1415, people who had been acquainted with the saint were still alive—and many others who had never met her had detailed knowledge of her life because she was a well-known public figure.[14] This meant that Bridget's followers had an abundance of facts about the saint and the way in which she had lived her life. Although this observation may seem to be a neutral one, it was of central importance to the establishment of Bridgettine monasteries. Weinstein and Bell have observed that written accounts of saints' lives must be "treated with skepticism" as factual documents because they tend, generically, to emphasize (and construct) those aspects of the life that conform to ideals of holiness.[15] Writing with the modern scholar in mind, Weinstein and Bell's point is, in other words, that looking at the written lives may allow us to know about saintly paradigms but will offer little biographical "truth."

Conversely, Bridget's followers knew a great deal about their saint's life but were in far less agreement about the particular brand of holiness to be derived from its components. The two best-known of Bridget's English devotees, Margery Kempe and King Henry V, illustrate the extremes to which her exemplarity was stretched. Margery, on the one hand, imitated Bridget's mystical spirituality as a woman who had been part of the secular world. Margery's *Book* is said to have been written beginning on Saint Bridget's day, July 23, 1436, and it is filled with echoes of Bridget's life, including the Swedish saint's experiences of maternity, pilgrimage, textual transcription, prophecy, and, most importantly, visionary episodes. In her *Book,* Margery al-

[12] Talal Asad, *Genealogies of Religion: Discipline and Reasons of Power in Christianity and Islam* (Baltimore: Johns Hopkins University Press, 1993), 63.

[13] On this distinction, see Aviad M. Kleinberg, *Prophets in Their Own Country: Living Saints and the Making of Sainthood in the Later Middle Ages* (Chicago: University of Chicago Press, 1992). Chapter 2, "Negotiating Sainthood," is especially helpful in its description of the relationship between social and sacred forces.

[14] Margery Kempe's quest to learn about Bridget is significant in this regard. Margery, unwilling to take for granted the diffuse information she already had about the saint, hunts down Bridget's former maid while in Rome to learn more about Bridget's life. See *The Book of Margery Kempe,* ed. Sanford Brown Meech and Hope Emily Allen, EETS, o.s., 212 (London: Oxford University Press, 1940), bk. 1, chap. 39.

[15] Donald Weinstein and Rudolph M. Bell, *Saints and Society: The Two Worlds of Western Christendom, 1000–1700* (Chicago: University of Chicago Press, 1982), 8.

ternately held up for admiration and competitively set aside Bridget's mystical experiences as she constructed her own visionary authority. The Lord Jesus Christ, for example, tells Margery that He speaks to her "rygth as I spak to Seynt Bryde [Bridget]" but also that He showed Himself to the Englishwoman in a special, eucharistic guise—the form of a fluttering dove and a trembling chalice—in which "wyse" his "dowtyr, Bryde" had never seen Him.[16] On the other hand, Bridget was celebrated as a political leader and prophet. Henry V, for example, founded Syon to honor her as a "lover of peace and tranquillity" who intervened in difficult situations and prophesied a truce between England and France following the Hundred Years' War.[17] The name Syon itself alludes to the hill in Jerusalem on which the city of David was built. Like the biblical city's prominent location, Syon's position between Westminster and Windsor, the river on one side, the main road on the other, allowed the monastery to stand as a visual reminder of Henry's devotion.[18] As different as Henry's and Margery's emulations of Bridget were, both were drawn to imitate her in rela-

[16] *Book of Margery Kempe*, bk. 1, chap. 20.

[17] In his *Regement of Princes*, a text written expressly for Henry V, Thomas Hoccleve rewrites Bridget's predictions concerning Edward III to comment on Henry's relationship to France. See Hoccleve, *Regement of Princes*, ed. Frederick J. Furnivall, EETS, e.s., 72 (Millwood, N.Y.: Kraus Reprint, 1978), 194. On Hoccleve's *Regement* and Henry's political concerns, see Derek Pearsall, "Hoccleve's *Regement of Princes:* The Poetics of Royal Self-Representation," *Speculum* 69 (1994): 386–410. For Syon's founding documents, see *William Dugdale's Monasticon Anglicanum: A History of the Abbies and Other Monasteries, Hospitals, Frieries*, ed. John Caley, Henry Ellis, and Bulkeley Bandinel (London: James Bohn, 1846), 6:540–44; and G. J. Aungier, *The History and Antiquities of Syon Monastery* (London: J. B. Nichols and Son, 1840).

[18] The most recent discussion of Syon's founding occurs in Neil Beckett, "St. Bridget, Henry V and Syon Abbey," in *Studies in St. Birgitta and the Brigittine Order*, ed. James Hogg, 2 vols. (Salzburg: Institut für Anglistik und Amerikanistik, 1993), 2:125–50. See also Margaret Deanesly, *The Incendium Amoris of Richard Rolle* (Manchester: Longman, Green, 1915), 91–130; Grenehalgh had annotated the short and long versions of Rolle's text. Deanesly's discussion is summarized in David Knowles, *The Religious Orders in England* (Cambridge: Cambridge University Press, 1955), 175–84. See also Aungier, *History and Antiquities of Syon;* John Henry Blunt, introduction to *The Myroure of Oure Ladye*, EETS, e.s., 19 (London: Trübner, 1873), xi–xix (hereafter, most page references to *Myroure* are found in parentheses in the text); and the *Bridgettine Breviary of Syon Abbey*, ed. A. J. Collins (Worcester: Boydell Press for the Henry Bradshaw Society, 1969), i–v. Legend has it that Henry IV had planned the foundation of a convent to perform due satisfaction for the murder of Archbishop Scrope and that Henry V's founding of Syon and Sheen was part of this act of penance. Jeremy Catto disputes this claim, in passing, in "Religious Change under Henry V," in *Henry V: The Practice of Kingship*, ed. G. L. Harriss (Oxford: Oxford University Press, 1985), 111. In 1431, the Syon community moved from Twick-

tion to their participation in public life. Margery leaned on the saint's involvement in public teaching and prophecy to authorize her own (perhaps less successful and more controversial) efforts to instruct other believers (an effort that culminated in the composition of her *Book*—just as Bridget's ministry led her to write down her *Revelations*); Henry named himself "a true son of the God of peace, who gave peace and taught peace and chose Saint Bridget as a lover of peace and tranquillity,"[19] cementing his political image as the king who, like Bridget, worked to resolve political differences.[20]

In contrast with both Henry and Margery, enclosed Bridgettines, by the very nature of their religious life, were cut off from direct involvement in the world outside the abbey. The walls of the convent circumscribed their imitation of the saint literally and imaginatively. As contemplatives, their ability to imitate Bridget, who is generally referred to as having combined visionary experience and "active spirituality," which included prophetic, political statement and missionary activity, was clearly constrained.[21] The rule in fact suggests that, with the exception of the abbess, it was only the priests at Bridgettine monasteries who should imitate Bridget's active life and her exercise of social authority; although the brothers were to engage in public preaching on feast days and on Sundays to provide vernacular translations of the gospel from the day's Mass for their audiences, the nuns were cloistered and encouraged to perform their liturgy for God alone.[22] It is no doubt true, as Roger Ellis observes, that "the example of Saint Bridget" provided "a clear inspiration" for every aspect of the sisters' lives. It is also true that the sharp contradictions between a public saint and her contemplative order demanded that exemplary imitation involve interpretive adjustments.[23]

Perhaps "imitation" is the wrong word for the Bridgettine pro-

---

enham to Isleworth, the new site just across the river from the Charterhouse of Sheen.

19 *Dugdale's Monasticon Anglicanum,* 6:540–44.

20 Henry established an explicit connection between his rule and Saint Bridget's efforts to make peace between England and France during the Hundred Year's War—and consequently between his actions and England's political designs on France in 1415. On politics and Bridget in England see F. R. Johnston, "English Defenders of St. Bridget," in *Studies in St. Birgitta,* 1:263–75.

21 Bridget Morris, *St. Birgitta of Sweden* (Woodbridge, Suffolk: Boydell, 1999), concludes that Bridget "anticipates the shift that took place in the later medieval period . . . away from extreme affective states, toward a more active spirituality" (175).

22 Morris, *St. Birgitta,* 165, 166.

23 Ellis, *Viderunt,* 12; see more generally 11–19.

gram, at least if we think of it as involving individual attempts to reenact specific events from a model life.[24] Rather, Bridgettine legislation imagined the enclosed sisters' reading, devotional as well as liturgical, as the specific act by which they would "copy" their founder. The emphasis on reading was in part drawn from the saint's own life. Raised in a noble household in Sweden, Bridget had grown up reading and writing in Swedish. Later, she learned to read Latin by studying along with her young sons, an episode that suggests the extent of her enthusiasm for learning. Her vita praises her scholarly interest and represents her as a teacher who, for example, encouraged her husband Ulf to read, especially books of hours and legal texts.[25] But it was her fame as a visionary writer and prophetess, and not simply as a reader or teacher, that garnered the attention of the clerical establishment and the general public. In fact, given the primacy of accounts that describe the manner in which Bridget recorded her mystical experience, we might suppose that the sisters would have become writers (and the direct recipients of God's words) themselves. And yet, at least at Syon, this seems not to have happened. The only evidence of writing by enclosed women that was not corrective (involving the emending and bettering of liturgical texts) or inscriptive (encompassing signatures in books and casual annotation) at the Bridgettine house is the possible scribal activity of a Swedish nun, who had come over from Vadstena to help establish the English house.[26]

Rather, Bridgettine imitation involved reception of God's words through the performance of the liturgy. In the English rubrics found in one of the extant copies of one of the Syon breviaries, probably from the early fifteenth century, the writer describes the relationship between God and Bridget as he explains that the book is written for

[24] On exemplarity and imitation, see Giles Constable, *Three Studies in Medieval Religious and Social Thought* (1995; reprint, Cambridge: Cambridge University Press, 1998), 143–248. Constable explains that "Some late medieval mystical writers went beyond image and likeness to identity and vision, merging the imitator with the exemplar" (246). See also Jeffrey Hamburger, *The Visual and the Visionary: Art and Female Spirituality in Late Medieval Germany* (New York: Zone Books, 1998), 233–78; and Caroline Walker Bynum, *Jesus as Mother: Studies in the Spirituality of the High Middle Ages* (Berkeley: University of California Press, 1982), 95–102.

[25] Biographical anecdotes are widely used in discussions of Bridgettine history: see, for example, Morris, *St. Birgitta,* 57.

[26] De Hamel describes the possible scribal activity of Anna Kaarlsdottir, a Swedish Bridgettine who came to England to help found the monastery (*Syon Abbey,* 56–57).

the "sustres of the ordir of seynt sauiour" and "ordeynd of the precept of the hooly modir seynt birgitt and more verily and groundly of ihesu crist."[27] The breviary's rubrics make it clear that Bridget's words are really the savior's. Rather than an act of authorial creation, Bridget's writing is portrayed as the verbal expression of perfect obedience to God. The breviary, for example, includes these lines, translated as follows in a Middle English work, which allude to Bridget's composition of the *Revelations:* "O. Brygytte kinges spouse. techer of lawe. folowyng the ensamples of strengthe. thow bondest thy lyppe with a red lace whyle thow louedest the sonne of god bothe in spekyng and in scylence" (136). In this passage, drawn from *Song of Songs* 4:3, "sicut vitta coccinea labia tua et eloquium tuum dulce," Bridget's mouth is controlled entirely by God, her performance perfectly obedient to His will; her writing is an act of verbal chastity, the movement of her lips divinely regulated. Consequently, the sisters' imitation of Bridget was understood as an act of becoming, like the saint, a perfect channel for Jesus' words: by performing the liturgy perfectly, reading Bridget's words aloud, the sisters should conform themselves to Bridget's image and ultimately to God's.

This kind of imitation was not necessarily gendered; it is found, for example, in Paul's command to the Corinthians, "Be ye imitators of me, as I also am of Christ."[28] Visionary writers, both men and women, were authorized by their direct experiences of God's presence and not by their own words. The prophet or mystic was a vehicle for the divine, and technically it made no difference if that vessel was male or female.[29] However, while this model of mystic experience may not have been inflected by stereotypes of female piety, its implementation at Syon divided the burgeoning community along gender lines.

[27] *Bridgettine Breviary,* 13.

[28] 1 Corinthians 11:1. The passage is cited frequently in discussions of exemplarity. See Hamburger, *Visual and Visionary,* 234; and John A. Alford, "The Scriptural Self," in *The Bible in the Middle Ages: Its Influence on Literature and Art,* ed. B. S. Levy (Binghamton, N.Y.: Medieval and Renaissance Texts and Studies, 1992), 1–21 (Hamburger cites Alford). Giles Constable makes this point generally in *Three Studies,* 246.

[29] Gender was nevertheless a central concern in the struggles involved in Bridget's canonization. See Dyan Elliott, "Dominae or Dominatae? Female Mysticism and the Trauma of Textuality," in *Women, Marriage, and Family in Medieval Christendom,* ed. Constance M. Rousseau and Joel T. Rosenthal (Kalamazoo, Mich.: Medieval Institute Publications, 1998), 51, 55–57, 62–63; and Eric Colledge, "Epistola solitarii ad reges: Alphonse of Pecha as Organizer of Brigittine and Urbanist Propaganda," *Mediaeval Studies* 18 (1956): 19–49.

The controversy resulting in the dismissal of Matilda Newton, Syon's first abbess, is a case in point. Although preparations had been started by 1406, it was not until May 1415 when a group of nuns and priests arrived from Vadstena, the motherhouse, that English nuns and priests were recruited actively. They seem to have drawn heavily from Benedictine houses; Matilda was a Benedictine nun at Barking before she accepted the position at Syon. Although we have no clear idea what had brought Matilda to the attention of Henry V, his advisers, and the Swedish Bridgettines, it probably had to do with her work at Barking. Benedictine monasteries often had schools attached to them, and this may have attracted the Bridgettines to Matilda and Matilda to the new foundation; for an order explicitly concerned with reading, it would be important to have a person in charge who could read and write, probably in Latin, French, and English, and who was also concerned with the education of her charges.[30] Barking itself was a convent with a long history of women's involvement with devotional writings, and which according to Phyllis Hodgson, "prefigured Syon itself in the encouragement of learning."[31] At Barking, books were distributed to the sisters at least once a year beginning in 1404 at the latest, and the abbess, Sibyl Felton, is known to have herself owned several, including the *Chastising of God's Children.*[32] The book, as its modern editors point out, is especially concerned with the demands of liturgical performance and "the problem of illiteracy," and it seems likely that Matilda shared these considerations with Sibyl, her superior.[33]

[30] Marcia L. Colish, *Medieval Foundations of the Western Intellectual Tradition, 400–1400* (New Haven: Yale University Press, 1997), 55. On Bridgettine legislation and reading, see Ellis, *Viderunt*, 76.

[31] The quotation appears in Phyllis Hodgson, "The Orcherd of Syon and the English Mystical Tradition," *Proceedings of the British Academy* 50 (1964): 235. It is cited by Hutchison ("Devotional Reading," 218) along with the information about Barking.

[32] *The Chastising of God's Children*, ed. Joyce Bazire and Eric Colledge (Oxford: Basil Blackwell, 1957), 37. Anne Clark Bartlett lists other books associated with Sibyl Felton, including the *Mirror of the Life of Jesus Christ* and *Cleansing of Man's Soul*, both in English; a Latin ordinal; and a French book of the lives of the saints and fathers (Bartlett, *Male Authors, Female Readers: Representation and Subjectivity in Middle English Devotional Literature* [Ithaca, N.Y.: Cornell University Press, 1995], 151–53). It appears that Sibyl read all three languages.

[33] *Chastising of God's Children*, 66. Expectations that nuns would be literate at Barking appear to have been quite high. For example, Katherine Sutton, abbess immediately before Sibyl Felton's tenure, had revised the dramatic offices to be performed at Easter at Barking. See Nancy Cotton, "Katherine of Sutton: The First English Woman Playwright," *Educational Theatre Journal* 30 (1978): 475–81.

We can only guess why Matilda was chosen for the position, but there is no doubt about the sequence of events that led, ultimately, to her dismissal: Matilda refused to submit to the authority of the monastery's general confessor. Although the order's revised rule stated that the abbess was the head of the monastery "in temporalibus" and the confessor general "in spiritualibus," Syon's own 1415 charter declared that the abbess was the ruler of the entire double monastery and had authority over spiritual and temporal affairs—"ac regimen universale monasterii praedicti, tam in spiritualibus quam in temporalibus super se assumant."[34] Matilda wholeheartedly endorsed the charter's formulation, and, according to Swedish sources, she declared not only that "by the rule of S. Saviour" the abbess was "head of the monastery in every particular, to be obeyed by the general confessor and the brothers," but also that the modifications added by the Swedish prior Peter Olafson were invalid.[35] Of particular concern to Matilda was legislation that included domestic labor, such as baking, among the sisters' duties. The sisters at Syon, including those who had come to England from Sweden, supported Matilda in her rejection of the Additions, which had not yet been confirmed by Pope Martin V and the council of Constance. A series of discussions were held about the dispute, and at a January 1416 meeting arranged by Henry and a council of distinguished clerics, including William Alnwick, the confessor general, Matilda "was deprived of her dignity by the king, and succeeded in that honour and enclosed state by the nun of Markyate."[36] By May 1417, the records show Matilda was again at Barking, now as a recluse.

Generally, scholars have treated this episode as an example of Matilda's personal failure, yet her removal also illustrates the difficulty of Bridgettine imitation. The phrase "a dignitate sua per Regem exonerata est" indicates that Henry's actions were punitive. Swedish accounts of the dispute describe rancorous, public meetings in which "brothers made assertions against the sisters, and the sisters against . . . the brothers." Matilda seems to have been unwilling to compromise her principles. Her leadership skills, for which she may have been offered the assignment in the first place, were apparently

[34] *Dugdale's Monasticon Anglicanum,* 6:542.

[35] Deanesly, *Incendium Amoris of Richard Rolle of Hampole,* 111.

[36] Ibid., 111–16. Joan's connection with Markyate, as I discuss later in this chapter, probably recommended her to Syon's clerical officials. On Alnwick, see Knowles, *Religious Orders in England,* 180.

strong enough to persuade the sisters of her point of view, but from the information that remains there seems little question that, as Deanesly concludes, "she was not possessed of sufficient tact to guide the heterogeneous community."[37]

Perhaps more importantly, however, Matilda's removal suggests that she and the clerical authorities differed in their view of the legitimacy of "exegetical" material associated with Bridget's writings. Having been recruited to head a Bridgettine monastery, Matilda had become intimately acquainted with Bridgettine writings and believed that legislation composed by the order's patron constituted the only "rule" that the community should follow. Because the rule had been directly revealed to Bridget, "shewid" to her by "oure lord ihesu crist" "with his blissid mouthe" as one account of Bridget's life describes it, Matilda was unwilling to accept legislation written by Peter Olafson as Bridget's own; Matilda's refusal was based on what she saw as her obligation to defend her newly adopted order from noncanonical intrusions in the Bridgettine collection of writings.[38] When she assumed the position at Syon, it seems to have been unclear, at least to Matilda, how the Bridgettine mission was to be carried out. Perhaps she believed she was to institute a program of study similar to the one she may have been involved in at Barking. As Marcia Colish observes, the Benedictines aimed to provide "an institutionalized framework" in which "nuns as well as monks . . . could pursue learning and the arts and in which they could exercise leadership roles."[39] The Syon Additions to the sisters' rule make it clear that the dream of uniform women's literacy at Syon was unrealized. The Additions make provisions for "Sustres that be not lettred," "They that kan not rede," "to say dayly in stede of matens, fourty Pater nostres with as many Aues and oo crede."[40] Matilda's fundamentalist zeal made it impossible for her to compromise her educational goals or to accept the authority of the confessor general as anything but bankrupt.

This is not to say that reading was an element of the Bridgettine program that failed to "take" when it was transplanted from Sweden to England. Even if Matilda failed to establish a rigorous program of study or to introduce a fundamentalist approach to Bridgettine legis-

[37] Deanesly, *Incendium Amoris of Richard Rolle of Hampole,* 112–15.

[38] Aungier, *History and Antiquities of Syon,* 19. Matilda's stubborn refusal of Olafson's writings may have struck Henry as similar to the Lollards' demands for *sola scriptura.*

[39] Colish, *Medieval Foundations,* 55.

[40] *Syon Additions for the Sisters,* 152.

lation, the monastery was nevertheless associated with women's reading and devotional study from its inception. Particularly interesting in this regard is the donation of a Middle English copy of Walter Hilton's *Scale of Perfection* made, probably, very close to 1415. Christopher de Hamel notes that during the foundation's early years, patrons began to donate books to the abbey, and the purpose of the bequests seems to have been to ask for the Bridgettines' prayers. A thirteenth-century Bible given by the duchess of Clarence to the brothers, for example, includes such a request.[41] Although many of the donations were of a general nature, books such as Bibles and psalters that lay supporters imagined the monastery would need, the gift of the *Scale* seems to have had a more specific purpose. Donated by Margery Pensax, an anchoress at St. Botolph's at Bishopsgate in London between 1399 and 1413, the book's bequest may have been motivated explicitly by the donor's sense that the sisters at Syon might need such a guide: the *Scale,* a book written to introduce a "ghostly sister" to the contemplative life, pays a great deal of attention to the relationship between devotional study and spiritual understanding. Early in book 1, for example, Hilton draws his reader's attention to the necessity for balance between study and affection in the pursuit of spiritual goals and concludes this part of the *Scale* by noting that the purpose of his book is to help his reader "to travail more busily and more meekly" by considering the "simple words" that God had given him the "grace to say." Margery's ownership of the *Scale* suggests that she shared Hilton's reader's concerns, and the fact that she left the vernacular book to Syon, even though her own associations with the monastery are unknown, indicates the extent to which its promotion of women's learning was recognized as part of the monastery's mission.[42]

But there is a great difference between the fairly loose idea that devotional reading was beneficial—that nuns should have some familiarity with books—and the strict notion of liturgical performance as imitation. As if to compensate for the "laxness" of the additions to Bridget's (Jesus') own words, a model of reading in which rigorous at-

[41] De Hamel, *Syon Abbey,* 57–61.

[42] Veronica Lawrence, "The Role of the Monasteries of Syon and Sheen in the Production, Ownership and Circulation of Mystical Literature in the Late Middle Ages," in *The Mystical Tradition and the Carthusians,* ed. James Hogg (Salzburg: Institut für Anglistik und Amerikanistik, 1996), notes that A. I. Doyle suggests Thomas Fishbourne might originally have given this copy of the *Scale of Perfection* to Margery Pensax; if this is the case, "her decision to donate the volume to Syon Abbey is readily understandable" (111).

tention to external conformity with the saint was demanded, and which encompassed visual and verbal representations, was introduced at Syon. Ultimately, this model, combined with the increasing availability of books to lay readers, resulted in the concentration on physical books and claims to personal ownership that characterized reading at the monastery in the early sixteenth century.

The coupling of reading and visual information began even before the candidate's initiation. Before her enclosure, the candidate was required to study a banner with the image of Christ's suffering on one side and the Virgin on the other. The purpose of this exercise, as the rule explains, was that in "beholdyng the signe of the newe spouse sufferyng on the crosse," the initiate would learn patience and poverty; similarly, in "beholdyng the virgyn moder," the candidate might perceive the meaning of chastity and meekness.[43] At the time of initiation, the individual herself became the image of divinity as she imitated Bridget (who imitated the Virgin and Jesus). The Bridgettine initiation rites demanded that the novice sign a document of obedience and submission, an act of inscription in which she signed over her familial identification from the world to the monastery, and it coupled this documentary gesture with a ceremony in which the novice was undressed and reclothed in Bridgettine garb—the clothes that she would wear for the rest of her life. Ellis points out that each piece of clothing was associated with one of Bridget's virtues—the mantle with faith, its large button with Christ's Passion, the sister's shoes with repentance, and so on. Written texts such as the *Revelations* and rule, as Ellis observes, allegorize these articles of clothing; the precedent for this is no doubt the New Testament injunction to put on the "new man."[44] Bridgettine dress was not, however, merely "symbolic" of the knowledge the novices had acquired. Rather, the clothes, like the sisters' reading and liturgical performance, were understood to constitute each nun's obedience and devotion. Every minute of her life she *was* Bridget and so were all of the nuns around her.

Jeffrey Hamburger has recently argued that for late medieval nuns, "The process of vision is detached from the process of reading" and images are "assimilated to experience."[45] Hamburger, an art histo-

[43] *Rewyll of Seynt Sauiore and Other Middle English Brigittine Legislative Texts*, 22.

[44] Ellis, *Viderunt*, 15.

[45] Hamburger, *Visual and Visionary*, 148.

rian, is particularly concerned with the ways in which drawings such as those he studied from the convent at St. Walburg in Germany gave nuns "an *immediate* point of entry to a world that lay beyond ordinary experience" (italics added).[46] At Syon, emphasis was placed on the nuns' status as living images of Bridget and of each other, as we saw in the previous paragraph, but reading too was construed as an act of visual perception and reflection. For example, the *Myroure of Oure Ladye,* an English Bridgettine text printed in 1530 but believed to have been written in the first quarter of the fifteenth century, associates reading explicitly with seeing.[47] The purpose of the treatise is to explicate Bridgettine liturgical practice for the sisters, and in doing so the author explains that his book is a special kind of "mirror" in which his readers will see the Virgin, to whom Bridget and all Bridgettines were devoted. Just as each sister put on Bridget's clothes and became a reflection of the saint, each sister who read the *Myroure* (and, more importantly, who performed the liturgy faithfully and correctly) became an image of the Virgin. The idea is Augustinian both in the broad sense that to know God we must become like Him, espousing imitation, and in the specific notion that reading (of scripture) "presents a kind of mirror to the eyes of the mind, that our inner face may be seen in it."[48] However, although the concept was widely known and the Bridgettine rule was in part Augustinian, the *Myroure*'s author does not depend on his readers' familiarity with Augustine.[49] Instead, he carefully explains what sort of mirror his book

[46] Hamburger, *Nuns as Artists: The Visual Culture of a Medieval Convent* (Berkeley: University of California Press, 1997), 215.

[47] Ann Hutchison, "What the Nuns Read: Literary Evidence from the English Bridgettine House, Syon Abbey," *Medieval Studies* 57 (1995), suggests that the *Myroure* "was composed either late in the first quarter, or before the end of the second quarter, of the fifteenth century" (209). Hutchison's new edition of this work is not yet available; all references to the text refer to Blunt's edition (full citation in n. 18) and hereafter are noted parenthetically in the text. For an overview of the treatise's contents, see Ellis, *Viderunt,* 115–23.

[48] On Augustine and the relationship between knowledge of God and becoming like God, see Marcia L. Colish, *The Mirror of Language: A Study in the Medieval Theory of Knowledge* (New Haven: Yale University Press, 1968), 80. The quotation is from Mary Carruthers, *The Book of Memory: A Study of Memory in Medieval Culture* (Cambridge: Cambridge University Press, 1990), 168; it is her translation of Gregory the Great's quotation of Augustine.

[49] An English edition of Augustine's rule was translated for the sisters by Richard Whytford; on Whytford, see *A Werke for Housholders, A Dayly Exercyse and Experyence of Dethe,* ed. James Hogg (Salzburg: Institut für Anglistik und Amerikanistik, 1979). See also James Hogg, "Richard Whytford," in *Studies in St. Birgitta,* 2:254–66; and Bell, *What Nuns Read,* 74. On "mirrors," see Ritamary Bradley, "The

is: it is not an object in which "oure lady shulde se herselfe" but rather one in which his reader should see the Virgin (4). Blurring the distinction between his book and Bridget's words in a manner that would have exasperated Matilda Newton, the author melded the reflective quality of the performed liturgy together with his own treatise: he advises that the *Myroure* offers a perfect image of Mary for the reader to see when she looks in his book.

The *Myroure* opens with a quotation from the *Song of Songs* that correlates external appearance and liturgical reading. The book begins "Viderunt eam filie Syon, et beatissimam predicaverent," which it translates as "The doughtres of Syon haue sene hyr (that is to say oure lady) and they haue shewed hyr mooste blessyd."[50] In this translation the author establishes a relationship between the sisters' outer appearance and the Virgin's holiness. The "showing" that the sisters perform is their visual testimony to the holiness that they have witnessed with their "spiritual eyes." Glossing "predicaverent," a verb generally used to refer to verbal affirmation in the sense of "proclaim," as "shewed," the passage replaces a verbal term with a visual one: the testimony of their liturgical performance becomes something that, most importantly, can be seen. In supplying the referent "oure lady" for the pronoun "hyr," the author insists that reading results in external practices that testify visually to the Virgin's sanctity: by seeing the Virgin, the sisters will be seen as witnesses to her blessedness.

David Lawton has observed that Margery Kempe's account of her experiences in her *Book* involves "a metonymy between vision and locution."[51] At Syon, reading depended on seeing and being seen, but

---

Speculum Image in Medieval Mystical Writers," in *The Medieval Mystical Tradition in England,* ed. Marion Glasscoe (Cambridge: D. S. Brewer, 1984), 9–27. Bradley explains that "In Christianity the inner self is simply a stepping stone to an awareness of God. Man is the image of God, and his inner self is a kind of mirror in which God not only sees Himself, but reveals Himself to the 'mirror' in which He is reflected" (9) and notes that the "Scriptures are the mirrors which help the literate" and "the teachings of those who can read assist the unlearned" (15). She goes on to cite the *Cloud of Unknowing* on this subject: "Goddes word, outher wretyn or spokyn, is licnid to a mirrour" (15).

[50] *Myroure,* 1; Ellis suggests that "Syon" is inserted into the biblical text to increase the nuns' identification with their abbey (*Viderunt,* 119 n. 63). This seems unlikely to me because the insertion also appears in both late-fourteenth-century editions of the Lollard Bible.

[51] David Lawton, "Voice, Authority, and Blasphemy in the *Book of Margery Kempe,*" in *Margery Kempe: A Book of Essays,* ed. Sandra J. McEntire (New York: Garland, 1992), 104.

it also involved hearing and being heard. In Bridget's *Revelations*, the "book of life," for example, announces itself as a text that "speaks" visually. Bridget explains that she had seen a book on a pulpit "shynyng as gold moste bryght, that had the shap of a boke." Emphasizing the book's form in order to broaden her reader's usual definition of a written text, she goes on to explain that in this book "the scriptur ther-of was not write with ynke." In fact, this book does not need to be read. Rather, "ych worde in the boke was qwhik and spak itself as yf a man shuld say, doo thys or that, and anone it wer do with spekyng of the word." "No man redde" those speaking words. Rather, "what euer that scriptur contened, all was see in the pulpyte and in the iij colours.[52] Bridget's "book of life" seems to fit the traditional definition of pictures as the books of the unlettered, fixing the way those pictures are read by insisting on the absolute perlocutionary force of the book's "speaking" words, but it is also a description of an actual book (or at least the shape of an actual book) and the experience of reading.

Although this model of "hearing" God by "seeing" His words may seem to encourage only private reading, the nuns' public, liturgical reading stands as the model for all reading at Syon, both communal and private, because it provides a "script" against which an individual can measure her devotion in terms of the accuracy and consistency of revealed truth that she re-expresses through her performance. According to the *Myroure*'s author, during prayer "man spekyth to god," and in reading "god spekyth to man" (66). Because God is speaking when one reads, the author feels that the reader should attend to His words with "meke reuerence," which "causeth grace and lyghte of vnderstandynge to enter in to the soulle" (66). Bridgettine liturgical texts, like the angel of Bridget's experience who whispers God's words into her ear in some Bridgettine illustrations, "speak" the truth directly to the reader if she listens carefully, and she in turn "speaks" that truth herself.

The guarantor of the truth of the words spoken and read was phys-

[52] These quotations are all from *The Revelations of St. Birgitta. Edited from the Fifteenth Century Ms. in the Garrett Collection,* ed. William Patterson Cumming, EETS, o.s., 178 (London: Oxford University Press, 1929), 68. It seems likely that the nuns had a copy of the *Revelations* in Middle English, and the *Myroure* draws heavily on Bridget's book. There is, however, no record that any single nun or the nuns' library had a copy until Cecily of York left hers to her granddaughter Anne de la Pole, who was Syon's prioress at the close of the fifteenth century. See Hutchison, "What the Nuns Read," 210–11.

ical discipline as a condition for reception. If Bridgettine devotional reading had not demanded bodily obedience, statements in which God speaks and the reader hears could easily have been misconstrued as heretical, particularly in the troubled climate following Arundel's broadcast of his *Constitutions* in 1409. In addition to obtaining a license from the bishop for his book, "so that bothe oure consyence in the drawynge and youres in the hauynge may be the more sewre and clere" (71), the author of the *Myroure* insists on the institutional (and impersonal) nature of Bridgettine spirituality. Of particular importance is the identity of verbal accuracy and spiritual understanding, and he qualifies Isidore's statement that "prayer longeth to the harte, not to the lippes" to stress the apt performance of the liturgy (40). The nuns are warned to pronounce their words carefully when they read their service, because if they mumble or misspeak, they are like "clyppers or falsers of the kynges money" who deserve to be punished with death if they "clyppe away . . . eny wordes or letters or syllables, & so false yt from the trew sentence, or from the trewe maner of saynge therof" (53–54). Money "clipping"—chipping off bits of gold or silver and keeping them for one's self—and forgery devalue the payment to God that must be made through bodily obedience, that is, by training the tongue to speak carefully and keeping nothing back for oneself.

Like money clipping, inattentive reading is a problem because it pits the individual against the community. In this regard the appearance of Titivillus, the infamous devil who, as the Wakefield *Last Judgment* puts it, collects "briefs" recounting deadly sins, in the *Myroure* is especially interesting. In the Bridgettine text, Titivillus appears to a Cistercian abbot with a "great poke" around his neck in which Titivillus had collected all of the "letters, and syllables, and wordes, and faylynges" performed by the members of the order.[53] Titivillus is often invoked in situations, as in the *Last Judgment,* when individual souls must face up to a final accounting, but in the *Myroure* the emphasis is on communal singing as a sacrifice to God and not on final judgment. Immediately before Titivillus's appearance in the *Myroure,* the nuns' performance is compared with Aaron's sacrifice of a calf in the Old Testament. In this context a comparison is drawn between the calf, which has been "cut in gob-

[53] See "*The Last Judgment* (From Wakefield)," in *Medieval Drama,* ed. David Bevington (Boston: Houghton Mifflin, 1975), 645, l. 225; *Myroure,* 54. Titivillus is also featured in *Mankind* (Bevington, *Medieval Drama,* 903–38).

ettes," and the division of the sisters' song into "wordes and syllables." Butchery requires accuracy, as does song, and according to the *Myroure* the sisters must perform the liturgy distinctly "in eche member and in eche parte thereof" (53). To modern readers it is perhaps an unappealing comparison, but the author's point is to imagine Bridgettine performance as one sound, just as the calf is one sacrifice. It is as if the collective daughters of Syon are one person who produces a single sound. In the *Myroure* the disciplined unity of liturgical performance assures the orthodox, and spiritually powerful, nature of their worship. Further, performance is described as utterly impersonal except insofar as the individual must discipline herself: the nuns are described in another passage as wax impressions, all identically "reformed to the lykenesse of God," or "pennies" that are "impressed" with "the image of the kynge" (98). The "daughters of Syon," as similar as if they were mass-produced in God's factory, perform their service, according to the *Myroure,* as one voice praising their "mother," the Virgin.

It might seem obvious that liturgical reading would have as its aim accurate, disciplined production. What is less obvious, however, is that this same function was imagined as the goal of private, devotional reading at Syon. On the one hand, reading was described as a regularized program for training one's rational understanding. The *Myroure* begins its discussion of nonliturgical reading with a heading that states in part "how ye shall be gouerned in redyng of this Boke and of all other bokes" (65). It divides books into three groups, the first of which includes those that "enforme the vnderstondynge," such as devotional guides and pastoral manuals that "tel how spiritual persones oughte to be gouerned in all theyr lyuynge that they may knowe what they shall leue & what they shall do" (68). This knowledge includes the "clensyng of theyr conscyence," the "gettyng of vertewes" to withstand "temptacyons & suffer trybulacyons," and "how they shall pray & occupy them in gostly exercyse" (68). Such information appears to have been considered pellucid, and these books allow the reader to ascertain whether her "lyfe is rewled in verteu" through comparison: she is advised to "beholde in [her]selfe . . . whether [she] lyue & do as [she] rede[s] or no," to measure her desire to fulfill the terms laid out in such books, and to consider whether her actions accord with their instructions (68). Just as liturgical performance could be evaluated in terms of accuracy, these books, according to the author, should be used as scales by which the reader can measure her spiritual condition. Although the verb describing action in this passage is always "feel" rather than "think," the *My-*

roure's author presents such reading and self-examination as an absolute process. If the reader is not "reckless" in her study, being careful not to proceed as if the authors had "roughte not thereof"—that is, if she does not ignore parts of the reading as if they had not been written—she can determine with confidence what she "lacks" and find ways to work toward her own amendment (68). Understanding in this description is not limited by the reader's sensory perceptions as it is, for example, in Augustine; in the *Myroure* (and more generally, in English pastoral guides included under the first category of books), the author's words are assumed to address the reader directly, allowing her to see her own life and providing her with a practical remedy for her failings.[54]

On the other hand, the second group of books, those that "sturre vp oure affecyons of loue and of hope" in God, are conceived of as instruments to be used in response to one's own emotional state. So, for instance, when one reads "maters of drede," the reader is to "conceyue a drede" in herself. Similarly, when she reads an encouraging work, she should "fele comforte of the same hope" (69). This kind of reading is like medication that produces certain effects under specific emotional conditions: when one is feeling the "bytternes of temptacyon or of trybulacyon," for example, it is best not "to study in bokes of heuynes & of drede," which might encourage one to feel even more dispirited, but instead at such times to study those that "mighte sturre vp [the reader's] affeccyons to comforte and to hope" (69). The *Orcherd of Syon,* a translation of Catherine of Siena's *Dialogo,* written for the nuns at Syon, probably near the time that the community was enclosed, exhibits a similar sense of reading as self-medicating. In its *Prolog* the author explains that his book will lead the reader to the "fruyt where you lust to feed you" but also that "bittire wedis" are to be found in its "garden"; these weeds, although "bittir & soure" to the "taaste," are "profitable to knowe" and should be "tasteth"—but not "sauoureth."[55]

It may appear that the two groups of books work at cross-purposes,

[54] On Augustine's sense of the limitations of words, see Brian Stock, "The Self and Literary Experience," *New Literary History* 25 (1994): 841. On the relationship between "understanding" and affective response, see the headnote to the excerpt from the *Mirror of Our Lady,* in *The Idea of the Vernacular: An Anthology of Middle English Literary Theory, 1280–1520,* ed. Jocelyn Wogan-Browne, Nicholas Watson, Andrew Taylor, and Ruth Evans (University Park: Pennsylvania State University Press, 1999), 258–59.

[55] *Orcherd of Syon,* ed. Phyllis Hodgson and Gabriel Liegey, EETS, 258 (London: Oxford University Press, 1966), 16.

and that the third group, those that combine the evaluative qualities of the first group and the responsiveness of the second, is an empty category. The *Myroure,* however, sees them as interdependent. Books that inform the understanding set "external" goals that spur the reader on to greater spiritual understanding. They do this by letting her understand what she lacks. The written book is in this regard instructive, and it demands that the reader reflect both on what she has done and what she will do. Although such books may seem to be aimed only at regulating the reader's understanding from the outside, they are important not because they limit her knowledge but instead because they help her prepare for the second kind of books; through their disciplinary demands, the first group of books strengthen her for the rigors of works that experiment with affective response and that may ultimately unite the reader and the divine. This progression perhaps seems backward—we might expect that the books that respond to our feelings would be read before others—but it is study that allows the reader to know and desire God. In the passage just before the treatise on reading in the *Myroure,* Proverbs 4:23, "Omni custodia serua cor tuum, quia ex ipso vita procedit. that ys Kepe they harte with all dylygence, for thereof commeth thy lyfe" is glossed to explain how "contynuall studyes" help to keep the "treasure of grace," our only "rychesse" (64). According to the *Myroure,* the reader depends on God for this safeguarding because the "harte may neuer be kepte but only in god" and "there is nothyng may fylle the soulle but god alone" (65). Reading is the way in which "all scaterynges of the mynde may be oned in hym," and the reader herself becomes part of God who is "more then the soule" and in whom "the harte & soulle is rested on eche syde" (65).

The assumption that drives the *Myroure*'s observations is that devotional reading involves a relationship between the reader, God, and the book itself. So, for example, when the author explains that "worldely bokes" should not be read, he excludes them not because they contain false information but because to read them is the same as speaking "ydel wordes" (66). This remark is puzzling only if one forgets that according to Bridgettine legislation, reading is a manner of both listening and speaking to God. To read secular writings would be the same as relaying worldly information to God, pointless and spiritually empty. Rather, private reading is like conversation with God through the language of a book; choosing the wrong book is like trying to talk to someone who does not speak the same language. The book is the conversation, and in its contents the reader finds herself in God. Because reading is relational, it is important to keep one's conversational partner in mind and to forget what people outside of the "conversation" might think of one's reading. For this reason, the *Myroure* explains that studying to impress other people with one's cleverness and failing to apply what is read to one's life is typical of the reader who "laboreth agenste hymselfe"—and who will be "beten with many woundes" like the servant in Luke 12 who knew his Lord's will and yet "dothe yt not" (67). In "laboring" for herself, the reader is ultimately "speaking to" and "listening to" God, effortlessly resting in Him, her desire, her reading, and her soul all "oned in hym." Reading those books that respond to and train the reader's affective response does not just prepare her for spiritual growth but instead allows her to rest in God. Just as Saint Anthony was able to fend off the demons in the desert because, as the devils told him, "when we wolde lyfte they vp by to moche hope, thou berest downe they selfe in drede and sorow of thy synnes & when we wolde brynge the in ouer moche drede and heuynes, then thou rerest vp thyselfe to hope, & comforte of mercy" (69), Bridgettine reading is a way to commune with God fully because it gives the reader the emotional strength she needs in every situation.

The relationship between God and believer was often figured in literature written for nuns as erotic, usually referred to as "Brautmystik," or romantic, "la mystique courtoise."[56] Texts such as the *Ancrene Wisse,* written for enclosed nuns, draw on these traditions, which are largely based on allegorized readings of the *Song of Songs,* and Bridget's own description of herself as Christ's "sponsa" in the *Revelations* clearly takes part in this discourse. Yet although Bridget's writings employ the rhetoric of spiritual marriage, as does the Bridgettine office, works concerned with the nuns' affective responses at Syon seem less interested in erotic relationships than in relationships between parents and children.[57] The Middle English *Life,* for example, opens with an anecdote concerning Bridget's grandmother, a story told from the perspective of a nun who, as a young woman, had seen the grandmother from a window in a monastery. As if worried about reconciling the enclosed Bridgettines with the fact that Bridget had a secular life before she started her new, spiritual

[56] See, for example, Barbara Newman, *From Virile Woman to WomanChrist* (Philadelphia: University of Pennsylvania Press, 1995), 137–67.

[57] It should be noted, however, that the term "sponsa" is used regularly, especially in the *Revelations.* See, for example, *A Ryght Profytable Treatyse Compendiously Drawen Out of Many and Dyvers Wrytynges of Holy Men by Thomas Betson* (Cambridge: Cambridge University Press, 1905).

family, the *Life* begins with a traditional description of the saint's noble "stok and lynage," but immediately shifts to address the concerns of the Bridgettine "daughters," the imagined audience for this particular vita. In the anecdote, the nun has seen Bridget's grandmother and her servants walking past the monastery. Looking at the grandmother's lovely clothes and physical beauty, the nun "despysed hir [the grandmother] for the great pryde that she adiuged to be in hir."[58] While the general purpose of the story is to honor Bridget—the subsequent lines concern the saint's birth and the "great grace" granted to the grandmother, her good fortune in having such a "daughter to come of her progeny"—the *Life* also offers a shorthand account of the way to understanding. The truth is finally revealed to the nun in a vision of beauty that reinterprets the beauty the nun had misjudged: the following evening the "sayd Nonne" had a vision of a "certayne person of a meruaylous beaute," clearly the Virgin, who reprimanded her for having "bakbyten" her "handemayde." It is only when the nun has her vision of the Virgin, that is, when she "sees" her, as the reader is supposed to do as she consumes the *Life,* that the nun can understand Bridget's history and, subsequently, amend her own life.

The *Life*'s association of the Virgin with Bridget's grandmother by way of their (aristocratic) beauty points out one of the problems with this model of imitative reading: it demands that the reader not only "forget" certain elements of her exemplars' lives (those of the Virgin and Bridget) entirely—if, as a "daughter of Syon," she desired to follow their example in the confines of the monastery—but also that she reconstrue certain life events, in this case childbirth and social status, spiritually. The practice of sifting through the corn and the chaff was always part of any exemplary or exegetical reading, of course, and it was something with which medieval writers were equipped to deal (one need only think of the Wife of Bath's reading of the traditional exegetical treatment of Jesus' invitation to the wedding at Cana to see how true this was). Bridgettine literature worked out this difficulty by drawing attention to Bridget's children, her son Byrgerus and especially her daughter Katherine, as her spiritual as well as biological descendants. By transferring their mother's bones to Vadstena from Rome and working to secure her canonization, Katherine and Byrgerus are positioned as the original Bridgettine followers.

Katherine in particular is portrayed as Bridget's attendant and disciple. According to the *Life,* Katherine was married but she and

[58] *Myroure,* xlvii.

her husband lived in chastity. He died early, and after his death "she was alwayes with hir moder seint Birget & lyued in the estate of wydowhood." Katherine remained a "daughter" throughout her entire life, committed to celebrating her mother's holiness, and never bore any children of her own. The *Life* argues that, on this account, Bridgettine readers should emulate Katherine's life: "This blessyd virgyne Katheryne bycause she was feruent in deuocion & excellent in grauite of maners of fayre of body & lyued a blessyd lyfe to gyue other example of good lyuyng." Although Bridget is to be worshipped by readers at Syon, it is Katherine, Bridget's biological and, more importantly, spiritual daughter whose situation most closely resembles that of the Bridgettine reader. Katherine ultimately became Vadstena's first abbess; as the sisters at Syon thought about her, they must have imagined her wearing the same clothes that they themselves, as Bridget's "daughters," were wearing.[59]

Asad, drawing heavily on Leclercq, has remarked that Bernard developed a monastic program in which the secular experiences of the recruits at Clairvaux were used as "the material for exercising virtue."[60] The Bridgettine program seems to have worked in a similar manner, drawing explicitly on the nuns' earlier experiences of family life to help them identify with their maternal exemplars. In the rule, Christ explains that the order is intended to follow a matrilineal principle by which His "beloved Mother" would be honored especially by women, "daughters" of the Virgin, among whom Bridget counted herself.[61] Like Bridget, the Bridgettine abbess is both a daughter of the Virgin, just as all the Bridgettines are daughters of their Mother, and a "mother" to the monastery. As a consequence, Bridget's social and familial authority is transferred to the abbess, whose job it is to transform her exemplar's familial standing. This spiritualization of maternity would have been extremely important at Syon because by the early fifteenth century, Bridget inspired devotion that celebrated her motherhood. The poet Audelay, for example, began his *Salutatio Sancte Birgitte,* written in 1426, by emphasizing her femaleness and

[59] Morris mentions that Katherine was the "de facto abbess"; Katherine died in 1381, three years before Vadstena was formally consecrated, but "the beginnings of the community were forming well before official recognition was granted" (*St. Birgitta,* 168).

[60] Asad, *Genealogies of Religion,* 142.

[61] The Middle English translation reads, "This religion therefore I wyll sett and ordeyne fyrst and principally by women to the worshippe of my most dere beloued moder, whose ordir and statutys I shall declare most fully with my owne mowthe" (*Rewyll of Seynt Sauiore and Other Middle English Brigittine Legislative Texts,* 8).

maternity: "Hayle! maydyn and wyfe. hayle! wedow Brygytt."[62] Margery Kempe, herself a mother and wife, was particularly devoted to Bridget precisely because she identified with the saint's experience of divine revelation as part of her active life in the world.[63] In contrast, Bridgettines aimed to transform their familial affection for their parents and siblings into love of God, the Virgin, and Bridget.

Reading was one part of this system not because it programmed the reader but because it gave her the opportunity to remake herself spiritually. By drawing on her memories of family life, Bridgettine writings allowed the nun to "redescribe," as Asad calls it, her affective relationships.[64] This can be seen in the Bridgettine breviary, which juxtaposes the Virgin's paradoxical family roles with concrete, often natural, metaphors. She is, for example, described as blessedly procreative: "Beata es virgo maria. que dominum portasti creatorem mundi genuisti eum qui te fecit et in eternum permanes virgo," which the *Myroure* translates, "Blyssed art thow marye. that haste borne the lorde, maker of the worlde. thou haste broughte fourthe hym that mad the. and endelesly thow abydest vyrgyn."[65] Although Mary's position as Heaven's Queen is central to the Bridgettine liturgy, Bridgettine texts also emphasize her motherhood, praising her fecundity and maternity in homely, natural terms. She is the Virgin who gave Jesus "suck," who her children can ask to "show" herself "to be a mother," who intervenes on behalf of her offspring, and who comforts and heals.[66] A reader/performer of this liturgy who understood its meaning (or who had read the *Myroure*'s English translation) would have little trouble imagining this Virgin as an affectionate, loving mother, and her performance would have formed part of a constructive process in which she actively "collaborated" with the Bridgettine program.[67]

[62] Cited in *Revelations of St. Birgitta*, xxxi.

[63] Karma Lochrie, *Margery Kempe and Translations of the Flesh* (Philadelphia: University of Pennsylvania Press, 1991), discusses Margery Kempe's attraction to Saint Bridget and visit to Syon in 1434 (76–79). See also Julia Bolton Holloway, "Bride, Margery, Julian, and Alice: Bridget of Sweden's Textual Community in Medieval England," in *Margery Kempe: A Book of Essays*, 203–22; and Gail McMurray Gibson, *Theater of Devotion: East Anglian Drama and Society in the Late Middle Ages* (Chicago: University of Chicago Press, 1989), 47–65, 97, 98.

[64] Asad, *Genealogies of Religion*, 144. Ellis makes a similar claim about the collaborative nature of Bridgettine devotion (*Viderunt*, 83).

[65] *Bridgettine Breviary*, 30; *Myroure*, 155–56.

[66] See, for example, *Bridgettine Breviary*, 80–81; *Myroure*, 235–37.

[67] On "medieval images of the maternal," see Bynum, *Jesus as Mother*, 133–34.

At the same time, the Bridgettine liturgy also presented the celebrants with a "new vocabulary," as Asad refers to this aspect of the Bernardine program, with which they could "redescribe, and therefore in effect construct, their memories in relation to the demands of a new way of life."[68] In the Bridgettine breviary, Mary is a woman—a mother, a daughter, and a queen—but she is also an imagistic "gloss" on the *Song of Songs,* and to "see" her is to hear the biblical text's metaphors. She is described as the sun, the moon, a rose among thorns, the sweet song of birds, a star, a shining pearl, an olive, and a vine—to name only a few of the objects with which she is compared.[69] The metaphors are obviously traditional, but their appearance alongside the familial language redirects the affective response of the now-enclosed reader. Mary is a mother, but she is also beautiful, concrete, and inexpressible: she is something that can only be described by isolating and then multiplying images that stand apart from human relationships.[70] By juxtaposing these natural metaphors and familial descriptions, the liturgy plays on the reader's experience of love for her family, associating Mary with personal affection and transforming that emotion. In drawing on concrete, natural images from the *Song of Songs,* it encourages love for the Virgin that goes beyond her relationship to humans and reaches toward the ineffability of her being. Although it also includes utilitarian images that relate Mary to the celebrant as helper to helpless—as gate to the one who would enter, light to the blind, way to the crooked, Martha (who provides clothes) to the naked, and so forth—in employing concrete, natural imagery the breviary simultaneously helps the reader to think beyond the interpersonal, to worship Mary for herself alone.[71]

[68] Asad, *Genealogies of Religion,* 144.

[69] The echoes from the *Song of Songs* are striking. For these images, see especially *Myroure,* 180, 198, 241, 282–85 (a catalog of trees), 306. Bynum notes that "*Brautmystik* (the use of nuptial and erotic imagery to describe the soul's union with God), the use of maternal names for God, and devotion to the Virgin did not occur together in medieval texts; the presence of some kinds of feminine imagery seems to have inhibited the presence of other kinds" (*Jesus as Mother,* 141).

[70] In an aside about affectivity and maternal imagery, Bynum remarks that "a mystic like Ruysbroeck . . . whose writings are filled with metaphors from the natural world" but who "studiously avoid[ed] physiological (including erotic or nuptial) imagery" might be an example of someone writing "an implicit critique" of the tradition (*Jesus as Mother,* 135).

[71] For these images, see especially *Myroure,* 307. E. Catherine Dunn's observations about certain aspects of the *Myroure*'s prose style are interesting in this regard. Dunn notes that the author at times "gathers paradoxical ideas into a delicately suspended unity of thought," and her example (from the *Myroure,* 86) concerns "the hyghnesse and depnesse of mounteynes he beholdeth" ("The *Myroure of Oure Ladye:*

Like the liturgy, the Middle English *Life* of Bridget also encourages its reader to draw on her previous understandings of family life in order to reimagine her spiritual life and, more to the point for this discussion, to read with her "ghostly eye." The *Life,* for example, relates the story of Bridget's third daughter, Ingeborg, a nun at the monastery of Rysaburga, who died suddenly. Ingeborg entered the monastery while she was still "in hir youth," and only a "shorte tyme" after she had made her confession she died. The *Life* takes a self-evidently sad episode and highlights its sadness: when Bridget had discovered that her daughter was dead, she "fell vpon great wepynge and sobbynge," her exclamations so loud that "all that were nygh" heard her and remarked, "loo, howe she weepeth for the deth of hir doughter." Although the episode seems to affirm the value of natural, human emotion, the audience to Bridget's grief has, however, misunderstood her tears (just as the nun who saw Bridget's grandmother earlier in the *Life* misunderstood her finery). Bridget's sobbing is produced by remorse. She explains that she weeps because she believes she has given her daughter "examples of pryde" and "neclygently corrected hir when she hath offendyd" and not because Ingeborg was dead.

The *Life* presents Bridget's "reading" of her tears as a model for devotional study. Bridget's audience had relied on what it understood as the "mocions of the flesshe" to interpret the saint's tears. The saint, however, looks with her "gostely eyne" in order to come to greater spiritual understanding. Following her emotional upheaval, the *Life* describes Bridget's vision of Christ in which He tells her that "euery moder that wepyth bycause hir doughter hath offendyd god and enformyth hir after hir best conscyence she is a very moder of charite and moder of terys and hir daughter is the doughter of god for the moder." The *Life* thus suggests that the nuns read as Bridget understands her maternity, that is, by "seeing" an event and imagining themselves in relation to it, using each occasion to move closer to God and further from human ties. Employing this pattern of spiritual "reading" rather than emotional reaction repeatedly, the *Life* shows Bridget as equipped to understand the spiritual significance of situations that appear to be merely human. We see this again, for example, when Bridget learns that her small son Benedict was ill. She cries

---

Syon Abbey's Role in the Continuity of English Prose," in *Diakonia: Studies in Honor of Robert T. Meyer,* ed. Thomas Halton and Joseph P. Williman [Washington, D.C.: Catholic University of America Press, 1986], 125–26).

only because she thinks he is being punished for her failings and not because she was concerned he would die or that he was in pain. Jesus again reassures her that this is not the case.

Another anecdote, in which Bridget's aunt finds the saint wandering naked at night, extends the *Life*'s work with familial motivations and reading to include childhood. In the story, the aunt is about to beat her twelve-year-old niece after finding Bridget "out of hir bedde knelynge all nakyd." Mistakenly believing that Bridget's behavior is evidence of "the lyghtnesse of the virgin," the aunt has a servant fetch a "rod" to correct her niece. She lifts the rod to strike Bridget, but as she places the rod on Bridget's back, it "breke all in small pecys" in a strange, failed movement that leaves Bridget's innocence intact and the aunt's violence impotent. Underscoring the *Life*'s educational aims, the aunt ultimately renounces her accusations against Bridget when she learns that she has misread her niece's actions; Bridget explains that she had not learned some "false" teaching but had rather risen to pray to Jesus, who the saint had seen "of late." The pattern in the *Life* is striking: other people misinterpret Bridget's familial responses (the reader is sometimes positioned as one of these people, sometimes as the misunderstood saint), and Bridget then reveals the spiritual content of her response, which is inevitably related to a visionary experience. In this way, the *Life*, like the liturgy, makes use of the reader's familial understanding in order to enlarge and reshape her spiritual understanding, demanding that she respond emotionally to the described domestic situation and demonstrating, after she has had the opportunity to anticipate the "correct" answer, what the proper response would be.

One might expect that the sensitivity to familial imagery and attention to domestic relationships expressed in Bridgettine texts reflected a strong commitment to monastic solidarity, a renunciation of the natural family in favor of the spiritual family and its needs. This is true at least in part given that the nuns at Syon were invited to think of themselves as "daughters of Syon" and encouraged to renounce their earthly families, a Bernardine directive, to achieve a deeper spiritual life.[72] The Additions to the sisters' rule, which were composed sometime after 1425 and available to the nuns in English, include an anecdote describing the virtues of keeping one's window

[72] For example, Bynum, *Jesus as Mother,* 145–46. On the softening of family strictures at Syon and concerning the nun's relationship to her family more generally, see Ellis, *Viderunt,* 91–92, 101.

shut when friends and family stand outside and might see the inhabitant.[73] The value of "invisibility" in relation to the secular family contrasts with the intense, visual identification of each sister with the other as they engaged in daily devotions, most importantly the performance of the liturgy. Although Bridgettine writings return to images of the family repeatedly, that material, as we saw in the paragraphs above, was read in order to redirect emotional attachments from the secular to the spiritual. To renounce the secular family for the monastic family involved more than a simple transfer of emotional investment, however. Rather, Bridgettine communities, although composed of "daughters," were to be little concerned with relations among siblings: the aim of Bridgettine communal reading was to establish a collective, visual identity, but that identity was in *singular* presence before God. The purpose was not to support, edify, love, or influence one's sister but to worship and contemplate, and communal practices were designed, paradoxically, to unify the nuns' devout aims individually through imitation of a common model. Each reader was to see herself as a particular, but interchangeable, part in the Bridgettine service, with the common goal of honoring the most singular of women, the Virgin, through identification with Bridget. The emphasis in Bridget's *Life* on the spiritual unnaturalness of natural emotion, on the emotional significance of remorseful tears but the inappropriateness of crying about a child's death, for example, is not only about secular family life but also concerns the monastic family. Bynum notes that the monk's "concentration on the salvation of the individual rather than on his obligation for his fellows" is what "underlies the widely disparate conceptions of the cloistered life found in twelfth-century monastic treatises."[74] Syon's founding, as well as that of the Carthusian house at Sheen, can be seen, as Jonathan Hughes observes, as "a revival of old contemplative ideals" in which ascetic concerns were emphasized over the good deeds of the active life.[75] The ideal of the Bridgettine family was to direct all affection toward God, the Virgin, Bridget, and the monastery itself: the sisters were to serve as mirrors for one another, exhibiting, most

[73] *Syon Additions for the Sisters*, 75.

[74] Bynum, *Jesus as Mother*, 72.

[75] Jonathan Hughes, *Pastors and Visionaries: Religion and Secular Life in Late Medieval Yorkshire* (Woodbridge, Suffolk: Boydell, 1988), 74–75. See also his discussion of Rolle's treatment of the active and contemplative lives: Rolle "claimed that he found it necessary to flee the wilderness because he found it impossible to live harmoniously with other men who were an obstacle to his inner joy" (115).

importantly, familial identity and, less centrally, familial love. The affective state of separation from one's earthly family was also supposed to apply to relationships with other "daughters" of Syon.

At least that was the theory. In practice, the implementation of a model of reading that depended on visual conformity with and affective distance from fellow inhabitants was complicated by the monastery's recruitment patterns. From its founding, Syon had strong affiliations with an influential network of lay believers from the north of England, as Hughes demonstrates.[76] These included Henry Lord FitzHugh, the king's chamberlain, who had visited Vadstena ten years before Syon's founding, his brother-in-law Henry Lord Scrope of Masham, and Thomas Fishbourne, Henry V's chaplain, who had been "a devout Yorkshire squire" before his ordination and enclosure in a cell at St. Germain's; Fishbourne became Syon's general confessor in 1420.[77] Scrope and FitzHugh were among Henry V's most trusted advisers, and their influence over the king, as well as the fact that Henry's sister Phillipa was married to Eric of Sweden, linked northern religious enthusiasts and aristocratic patrons associated with the court. The direct impact of this social dynamic on the composition of Syon was that many of the inhabitants had family ties to these influential lay communities. The most striking example from Syon's early years is the admission of two women named Fishbourne, Joan and Isabella, in 1420; it seems very likely that they were the general confessor Thomas Fishbourne's sisters. Despite the order's discouragement of familial affection, recruitment within families appears to have been common: in 1428 there were at least three separate families represented at Syon, including the Fishbourne sisters, who survived their brother; four women named Sukelyng—the prioress Juliana, Margaret, Katherine, and Joan; and three named Swethe (or de Sweth)—Cristina, Marina, and Margaret.[78] More generally, social ties

[76] Syon was planned as a northern institution; supporters originally worked to found the abbey on the land on which stood the hospital of Saint Nicholas in York. See Hughes, *Pastors and Visionaries,* 75; and J. H. Wylie, *The Reign of Henry the Fifth* (Cambridge: Cambridge University Press, 1914), 1:221.

[77] The quotation is from Hughes, *Pastors and Visionaries,* 75, and alludes to a remark made by Thomas Gascoigne. The information about Syon's northern affiliations is also from *Pastors and Visionaries,* 75, 112–13. Henry V was encouraged to act by FitzHugh and by Phillipa, Henry's sister, who was married to Eric of Sweden.

[78] F. R. Johnston, "Joan North, First Abbess of Syon, 1420–33, 'Qui Celestia Simul et Terrena Moderaris,' " *Birgittiana* 1 (1996), includes a table listing "family links" at Syon (64–65). See also Aungier, *History and Antiquities of Syon,* 51–52. Johnston

between aristocratic patrons and religious at Syon were very strong, especially from the first third of the century on.[79] Thomas Fishbourne had served as confessor to aristocratic women who belonged to the lay confraternity associated with St. Albans's, including Lady Eleanor Hull, who translated the penitential psalms and some prayers from French into English, and the earl of Warwick's wife Elizabeth Beauchamp, who was a patron of Walton's translation of Boethius's *Consolation of Philosophy.*[80] Alnwick, who had been appointed confessor general by Henry V, had also been at St. Albans's, and Joan North, the abbess who replaced Matilda Newton, was originally at Markyate, the Benedictine nunnery affiliated with St. Albans's.[81]

The "inbred" social composition of the monastery meant that recruits, drawn from the same social backgrounds and in some cases the same families, were often personally acquainted with one another. The point of Bridgettine enclosure was to reconstitute one's familial relationship as a (singular) daughter of Syon, and each nun was to perform the liturgy, as the *Myroure* explains, "only for god" and not so that any "creature shulde here" or "see" her, that is, as if she were alone by herself, concentrating on her own "defaulte and lacke," which she shall "se in [her]selfe" by reading repeatedly, "lok[ing] theron" at the book, and "on [her] selfe" (60, 68). Devotional reading became one way for the nuns at Syon to achieve the spiritual

suggests that the "first recruits" may have been "from rather lower social circles than historians have usually assumed" and that they "do not seem to have established any family tradition for joining the community" ("Joan North," 52–53). He contrasts them with the nuns after enclosure in 1420, who appear to have been from more elite families. It should be noted that Joan North is referred to as the first abbess, not Matilda Newton, according to Bridgettine tradition; similarly, Fishbourne, not Alnwick, is called the first confessor general.

[79] By the end of the fifteenth century, aristocratic women, including Anne de la Pole, Edward IV's daughter, her grandmother Cecily of York, and Margaret Beaufort, were affiliated with Syon.

[80] Concerning Eleanor Hull, see Hughes, *Pastors and Visionaries,* 112; Alexandra Barratt, "Dame Eleanor Hull: A Fifteenth-Century Translator," in *The Medieval Translator: The Theory and Practice of Translation in the Middle Ages* (Cambridge: D. S. Brewer, 1989), 87–101; and in relation to Elizabeth Beauchamp, see Carol Meale, " 'Alle the bokes that I haue of latyn, englisch, and frensch': Laywomen and Their Books in Late Medieval England," in *Women and Literature in Britain, 1150–1500,* ed. Carol M. Meale (1993; reprint, Cambridge: Cambridge University Press, 1996), 137.

[81] Gillespie observes that the Benedictine influence on Syon was especially pronounced and that St. Albans's was particularly important in this regard. See "Dial M for Mystic," 252, 252 n. 31.

goal of communal isolation that personal acquaintance must have made difficult, and books were written for the nuns that addressed such issues.[82]

The *Orcherd of Syon,* for example, approaches the distractions of living among other people explicitly. It opens with the translator's description, not found in the original, of the book as an orchard in which solace and quiet can be found by walking alone among its trees. The *Orcherd*'s reader is encouraged to wander through the fruit trees, walking with her "mynde & resoun" among any of the "xxxv aleyes" she likes.[83] Inviting the reader to imagine the pleasures of solitude, the *Orcherd* suggests that the book itself is a place in which the individual might sit in magnificent silence, free from the distractions of communal life.[84] The *Orcherd* in fact pointedly juxtaposes its private universe with the busyness of monastic life, opening with an address to the "Religyous modir & deuoute sustren" of Syon who "labor" at the monastery together.[85] The reader's place is at Syon, but

[82] On this point, see Eileen Power, *Medieval English Nunneries* (Cambridge: Cambridge University Press, 1922): "The inmates of a house spent almost the whole of their time together. They prayed together in the choir, worked together in the cloister, ate together in the frater, and slept together in the dorter" (315).

[83] *Orcherd of Syon,* 1.

[84] The relationship between concrete, natural images and reflection was often evoked in devotional literature. In a less comforting vain, another work associated with Syon, *Disce Mori,* suggests, for example, "the leeves of forestes, the fedres of briddes, the dropes of the rayne, and the grauel of the see, if a man may nombre, than may he nombre the synnes that springe of the tunge" (fol. 177r, cited in Edwin D. Craun, *Lies, Slander, and Obscenity in Middle English Literature: Pastoral Rhetoric and the Deviant Speaker* [Cambridge: Cambridge University Press, 1997], 4). A manuscript in which *Disce Mori* appears, along with selections from Walter Hilton, Richard Rolle, and other works, was owned by a sixteenth-century Syon nun, Dorothy Slyghte (see Bell A.39). Lee Patterson has suggested that the treatise was written at Syon (Patterson, *Negotiating the Past* [Madison: University of Wisconsin Press, 1987], 118). Ann Hutchison, referring to E. A. Jones's dissertation, an edition of *Disce Mori,* notes that "there is no evidence that the dedicatee, Alice, was a nun" and states that "there is no evidence that the work was *written* for the nuns of Syon, or that it was written at Syon" ("What the Nuns Read," 219 n. 65). The best account of *Disce Mori* is still *Chastising of God's Children,* 1, 6, 25–27.

[85] *Orcherd of Syon,* 1. Denise Despres, "Ecstatic Reading and Missionary Mysticism: *The Orcherd of Syon,*" in *Prophets Abroad: The Reception of Continental Holy Women in Late-Medieval England,* 141–60, considers the ways in which the *Orcherd* "advocates ghostly comfort and, in doing so, subtly discourages pious fantasizing or recreation of ecstatic experience" (160). She suggests this is a "narrow" way of treating Catherine of Siena's mystical experience. On this subject, see also Elizabeth Psakis Armstrong, "Informing the Mind and Stirring up the Heart: Katherine of Siena at Syon," in *Studies in St. Birgitta,* 2:170–98.

it is also in this garden of reading that the translator has planted for the sisters during his own "tyme of pleienge" for their "confortable recreacion."[86]

The aloneness of a silent universe of visualized signs is evoked repeatedly in writings associated with Syon; language itself seems to have been understood as explicitly visual. This may remind some readers of Richard Rolle's emphasis on sensory experience, especially of the affective, contemplative tradition in which an "overwrought intensification of contemplation," as Lovatt calls it, results in visual experience, "where the imagined becomes concrete and where the physical and the spiritual elide."[87] Rolle's influence was increasingly important at Syon during the fifteenth century—the *Myroure,* for example, recommends that the nuns read his *Psalter*—but it is the verbal and visual (rather than the loosely imagined and real) that collided at Syon: communication itself was literally visual at Syon. During periods of silence, for example, inhabitants used a form of sign language in which gestural language replaced spoken communication. The signs are described in a fifteenth-century book written in Thomas Betson's hand.[88] Betson, a brother at Syon and author of *A Ryght Profytable Treatyse,* an instructive text written in rhyming couplets, appears to have been concerned with teaching of a more pedestrian sort than Rolle or even the author of the *Myroure* had been. Betson provides members of the community with a chart of hand signs. Approximately one hundred items are included in the table, and most of them are physical objects—salt, spoons, massbooks, ink, for example—things that would be necessary in the daily lives of Syon's inhabitants. The gestures are simple and mimetic: to signify "broom," for example, one should "Swepe with thy open hand to and for on thy left cowll sleue," and to ask for a book one should "Wagge and meve thy right hande in maner as thou shulde turne the leues of a boke."[89] But although the signs are themselves straightfor-

[86] *Orcherd of Syon,* 16–17.

[87] Lovatt, "Library of John Blacman," 212.

[88] Generally scholars assume that Betson compiled the signs (but did not invent them himself). See A. I. Doyle, "Thomas Betson of Syon Abbey," *The Library,* 5th ser., 11 (1956): 115–18; and *The Syon Additions for the Brethren and The Boke of Sygnes,* vol. 3 of *The Rewyll of Seynt Sauioure,* ed. James Hogg (Salzburg: Institut für Anglistik und Amerikanistik, 1980), viii–ix.

[89] *Syon Additions for the Brethren and The Boke of Sygnes,* 135. Eileen Power suggests that "the sort of dumb pandemonium which went on at the Syon dinner table must have been more mirth provoking than speech. The sister who desired fish would 'wagge her hande displaied sidelynges in manere of a fissh taill,' she who wanted milk would 'draw her left little fynger in maner of mylkyng'; for mustard one

ward, the exercise of using them is more complicated than the easy maintenance of silence. Rather, the point seems to have been to communicate only what could be conveyed visually, and ultimately to encourage inhabitants to imagine that the elements from the table constituted an entire universe in themselves. The purpose in other words appears to be, like that described by the author of the *Cloud of Unknowing,* to promote the experience of "inward stering after the prive sperit of God," but with one great difference: in Bridgettine practice the goal was not to "purify" one's "mind from every image," as it was in the *Cloud,* but to concentrate on those simple signs, much as the *Cloud* recommends meditation on one-syllable words, as a means of "working" toward God.[90] As Ellis points out, the aim of Bridgettine texts was "To make desire rather than need the term of one's reading." Therefore, as he goes on to state, Bridgettine books such as the *Myroure* maintain that "the primary duty of the religious is to 'kepe the harte' in prayer," and they express this through attention to "secondary and outward forms of 'relygious beryng.' "[91] The use of sign language was another vehicle by which the external world could be regulated, freeing up one's attention for "a grete and vyolente applyeng of the harte to do a thynge wyth a grete & a feruent wyll," as the author of the *Myroure* suggests.[92]

The peaceful reading that the *Orcherd*'s author imagines for the sisters and the use of visual, mimetic sign language during times of silence are both examples of the Bridgettine, liturgical impulse that linked the inhabitant with her community and which also separated her from her "family." I have been arguing that the social composi-

---

would 'hold her nose in the uppere part of her righte fiste and thombe and his forefynger ouere the left thombe' "(*Medieval English Nunneries,* 287). Nevertheless, one suspects that daily use of the signs detracted from the comedy Power imagines.

[90] *The Cloud of Unknowing and the Book of Privy Counselling,* ed. Phyllis Hodgson (Oxford: Oxford University Press, 1944), 3, lxi. The *Cloud,* for example, recommends that one pray "not in many wordes" but rather "in a lityl worde of o silable," such as "synne" or "God" (76–78). Robert A. Barakat, *The Cistercian Sign Language: A Study in Non-Verbal Communication* (Kalamazoo, Mich.: Cistercian Publications, 1975), observes that "The silent language of the Cistercians is an excellent example of a system of technical gestures utilized to communicate simple messages. Such a visual system . . . is intended in no way to be as effective as speech, even though some of the features of spoken language are incorporated into it. The rather small inventory of signs is evidence of this. This flows from a desire on the part of the Order to restrict communication. The smaller the list the great the restriction on communication" (27).

[91] Ellis, *Viderunt,* 29, 122.

[92] *Myroure,* 63. On the connection between silence and sensory regulation, see Ellis, *Viderunt,* 99.

tion of Syon, its admission of sisters and friends from the same region and same social background, influenced the monastery's literate practice. By encouraging those writers affiliated with the order to provide the sisters with reading material and devotional exercises that would help them manage the disjunction between their secular, familial experiences and the demands of life in the monastery, the sisters' social affiliations shaped Syon's literate agenda indirectly: as imagined readers, the sisters influenced the kinds of texts that authors drew up for them.

The nuns also shaped literate culture at Syon in more direct ways. In particular, having come from the same social milieu that produced wives of great landholders, Syon's recruits, especially those who had not already been affiliated with other convents, came to the monastery with preconceived ideas about literate culture. Because women entered the Bridgettine monastery only after their eighteenth birthdays, nuns at Syon, by and large, shared the literate interests and understandings of the aristocratic and highborn laywomen who were their mothers, sisters, and cousins. Although admission to Syon involved the study of Bridgettine writings, the women who entered the monastery had already had eighteen years in which they had learned what the relationship between highborn women and written texts was, and this experience too influenced literate practice at the convent.

The use of books of hours at Syon provides the most striking example of the ways in which the nuns' previous experiences with the written word exerted pressure on literate culture within the monastery. In his description, Christopher de Hamel notes that "Books of Hours, almost by definition, were not for monastic use . . . one would not expect Benedictines or Carthusians, for example, to have been regular readers of Books of Hours." Collins explains that Bridget's routine was to recite the Hours of the Virgin daily, a habit that she shared with her husband, according to the *Life* used during the canonization process. On the basis of Collins's evidence, de Hamel concludes that it must have "seemed suitable for the sisters at Syon, in private, to own Books of Hours."[93] In supporting his claim, he explains that except for MS Bodley 62, which appears to have been a "routine (but nice) London Book of Hours of about 1390 which came into the possession of someone at Syon a hundred years later," the books of hours at Syon seem to have been "commissioned or ac-

[93] De Hamel, *Syon Abbey,* 76; *Bridgettine Breviary,* xxiv–xxv.

quired as specially prepared gifts." The seven that de Hamel catalogs "seem to have been intended for nuns" and "are all odd in some way"; many do not include the Hours of the Virgin, and some open with the Hours of the Holy Spirit or Holy Trinity. All, however, show definite signs of Bridgettine use, such as the appearance of Bridget's name immediately after Saint Anne's in the litany; the classification of Bridget's nativity, canonization, and translation as "maius duplex"; lists of obits that include Henry V as founder and Thomas Fishbourne as confessor general; and so forth. Observing that it might be easier to assume that the books of hours accidentally ended up at Syon but that that does not seem to have been the case, de Hamel concludes that the use of books of hours at the monastery "represent[s] a spirituality which is halfway between the secular and the monastic, and between the chapel and the library" and that their use is "unique to Syon."[94]

The earliest of the Syon books of hours are thought by Ker to be from the 1430s, and it seems likely that their appearance corresponded with the arrival of increasing numbers of nuns who had no previous monastic experience. Matilda Newton and Joan North, for instance, had been Benedictines before Syon was founded, and their reading habits were shaped by the literate cultures of Barking and Markyate. In contrast, once the Bridgettine house became more firmly established, it began to recruit young laywomen as members, and these women were likely to have been used to having books of hours for their devotions, much as Margaret Beaufort and the female members of her family had. It is unclear who at Syon decided that the books would be used; perhaps the chantress, the sister responsible for procuring service books, began to acquire them in response to the new nuns' suggestions. De Hamel mentions that a "clutch of rather grand liturgical books" had been ordered in the 1440s and observes that this "suggests a rather zealous Chantress"; it is possible that her love of books extended to books of hours.[95] In any case, someone was clearly responsible for the books' arrival at Syon: they share a number of distinct features. In addition to the obvious Bridgettine markers found in the calendars and litanies and the frequent use of feminine endings in prayers, all of the Syon books of hours, for example, include the Hours of the Holy Spirit, a common feature in lay primers, and most include the Office of the Dead, also frequently found in sec-

[94] De Hamel, *Syon Abbey*, 77.

[95] Ibid., 70.

ular *horae.* A lay reader would have felt very much at home with these devotional selections. But the Syon books of hours were also very different from traditional primers. Many as mentioned earlier, for example, exclude the Hours of the Virgin, the most traditional element of primers. And others include features that a lay reader would have been less accustomed to finding in books of hours. The canticles, liturgical songs, such as the *Benedictus, Magnificat,* and *Nunc dimittis,* drawn from biblical texts and regularly found in breviaries, for example, appear in many of the Syon primers, as does the Athanasian Creed, also known from its opening as the *Quicumque vult,* a text largely concerned with the Trinity and written, as the *Myroure* says, "agenst the heretykes."[96] Both the canticles and Athanasian Creed were important elements of Bridgettine liturgical performance, and their appearance in the books of hours supports de Hamel's surmise; it appears that the person who commissioned the primers thought that Bridgettine readers needed to have access to these texts even when they were not saying their office.

Over time, the content of the books of hours at Syon appears to have become increasingly similar to that of books laywomen were reading. Syon Abbey MS 2, which Ker dates as "xv med," for example, includes many of the same prayers found in Margaret Beaufort's prayer books: the *Fifteen Oes* (in Latin), "Deus propicius est[o] michi peccatrici et custos mei," prayers to the angels Michael, Gabriel, and Raphael, to one's guardian angel, to the Trinity, and to the Cross.[97] In fact, by the early sixteenth century, books such as Cambridge, Magdalene College MS 13 can be found at Syon, a manuscript whose liturgical calendar is followed by tables for determining such things as the tide, the new moon, and "auspicious days for blood-letting," as well as Latin and English prayers such as the Fifteen Oes, the Golden Litany, and the Stabat Mater.[98] Although the usual way of thinking about lay culture and Bridgettine literary practice is, as Virginia Bainbridge puts it, that the Bridgettines "popularised" their ideas "among the elite laity," the relationship is, as we can see from the books of

[96] *Myroure,* 140. The Athanasian Creed was sung daily in English usage but at Syon said only on Sundays. Perhaps it was included in the primers to compensate for its omission on the other six days of the week.

[97] Cataloged by Bell as A.46 and by de Hamel as no. 78; listed in N. R. Ker, *Medieval Manuscripts in British Libraries* (London: Oxford University Press, 1969), 4:336–42.

[98] Bell, *What Nuns Read,* 180. Cataloged by Bell as A.10 and by de Hamel as no. 39.

hours, more complicated than it appears from this statement.[99] The nuns themselves were originally lay readers who shared literate habits and interests with their lay contemporaries, and the relationship between lay literate culture and Bridgettine practice was dynamic. Literate experiences outside of the convent shaped literate practice within Syon, and the nuns' engagement with written texts contributed to changes in lay devotion as well. The year spent studying Bridgettine writing outside of the monastery before initiation may have been the single most important factor contributing to the remarkable similarities between the devotional interests of aristocratic laywomen and Bridgettines. Especially after printed books became available in England, that year could be spent reading with one's family and close friends, allowing lay devotions and Bridgettine writing to drift together over the course of the fifteenth century.[100]

Bridgettine nuns and lay readers of books of hours shared not only a similar interest in particular devotional writings but a common understanding of book ownership. Bernard J. Muir observes that books of hours, in contrast with breviaries and psalters, laid "greater emphasis on the individual and personal prayer" and "involved their readers at a very intimate level."[101] Individual readers of primers attended closely to their books, sometimes choosing their contents and, even when those contents were chosen for them, literally and imaginatively writing themselves into the books. Lay readers often wrote important events of their lives into the books' calendars, as I mentioned in chapter 2 of this book, linking individual experience with the written word. A lay reader might, for example, note the dates on which her children were born or a relative died. By the early sixteenth century, Bridgettine nuns were making similar annotations in their books. Agnes Smith, for example, apparently entered the

[99] Virginia Bainbridge, "Women and the Transmission of Religious Culture: Benefactresses of Three Bridgettine Convents c. 1400–1600," *Birgittiana* 3 (1997): 55.

[100] "Vowesses," laywomen, almost always widows, who took religious vows but were not members of religious communities appear to have been affiliated with Syon as well and may also have had an influence on reading at Syon. See Susan Marie Burns Steuer, "Widows and Religious Vocation: Options and Decisions in the Medieval Province of York" (Ph.D. diss., University of Minnesota, 2001). Burns points out that Margaret Beaufort's grandmother, Margaret duchess of Clarence, had such an affiliation with Syon in the late 1420s.

[101] Bernard J. Muir, "The Early Insular Prayer Book Tradition and the Development of the Book of Hours," in *The Art of the Book: Its Place in Medieval Worship*, ed. Margaret M. Manion and Bernard J. Muir (Exeter: University of Exeter Press, 1998), 12.

obits of her parents in Bell A.44 (De Hamel no. 56), a psalter with, among other items, the Hours of the Holy Spirit and the Office of the Dead, and which Bell explains was originally intended for a brother of Syon.[102] Agnes was at Syon in 1518, the year by which it seems to have become regular practice for the nuns to write in *their* books: examples include the insertion of "C. Browne" in a processional (Constancia Browne was the abbess in 1518); "Rose Pachet, professyd in Syon" in a copy of Hilton's *Ladder of Perfection,* parts 1 and 2 (Rose was at Syon in 1518; by 1557 she was prioress of the restored community); "Thys boke is ssuster Anne Colvylle" and other notes of her possession in a manuscript that included Hilton's *A Treatise of Eight Chapters* and *A Treatise of Discretion of Spirits* (Anne was at Syon in 1518); and "Tressham," with first name erased in a manuscript of John Cressener, *The Psalter of Mercy,* written in Latin with English rubrics, followed by Latin prayers with English rubrics, and an English version of Jordan of Saxony's *Meditations on the Life and Passion of Jesus Christ* (Clemence Tressham too was at Syon in 1518).[103]

By the turn of the century, readers at Syon had come to consider their books, and not just the words in the books, as intermediaries between themselves and God. The most striking example of this is a copy of the *Scale of Perfection* owned by Joan Sewell. On a blank page at the end of Joan's copy of the *Scale,* the Carthusian James Grenehalgh had drawn the diagram shown in figure 2.[104]

The large picture, as Michael Sargent has observed, resembles "the plan of a walled city or, perhaps, convent."[105] Because, as Sargent proposes, Grenehalgh seems to have given Joan the book at the time of her profession, it is difficult not to see the drawing as a "you are here" diagram of Joan's new home: "Johanna Sewell" is at the center of the diagram and is surrounded by the four saints most closely associated with Syon—Saint Bridget, the Virgin Mary, Saint Augustine, and Saint Saviour. The annotation places Joan in the company of the Saviour (Syon itself was often referred to as Saint Saviour), Saint Augustine, who was venerated at Syon because the adoption of his rule

[102] Bell, *What Nuns Read,* 199. De Hamel makes the suggestion on the basis of what he concludes are the obits of Agnes's parents, William and Isabel Smith (*Syon Abbey,* 94).

[103] For descriptions of these manuscripts, see Bell and de Hamel: Constance's book is Bell A.45 (de Hamel no. 68), Rose's is Bell A.38 (de Hamel no. 55), Anne's is Bell A.25 (de Hamel no. 37), Clemence's is Bell A.16 (de Hamel no. 49).

[104] Sargent, *Textual Critic,* 1:201–3.

[105] Ibid., 1:87.

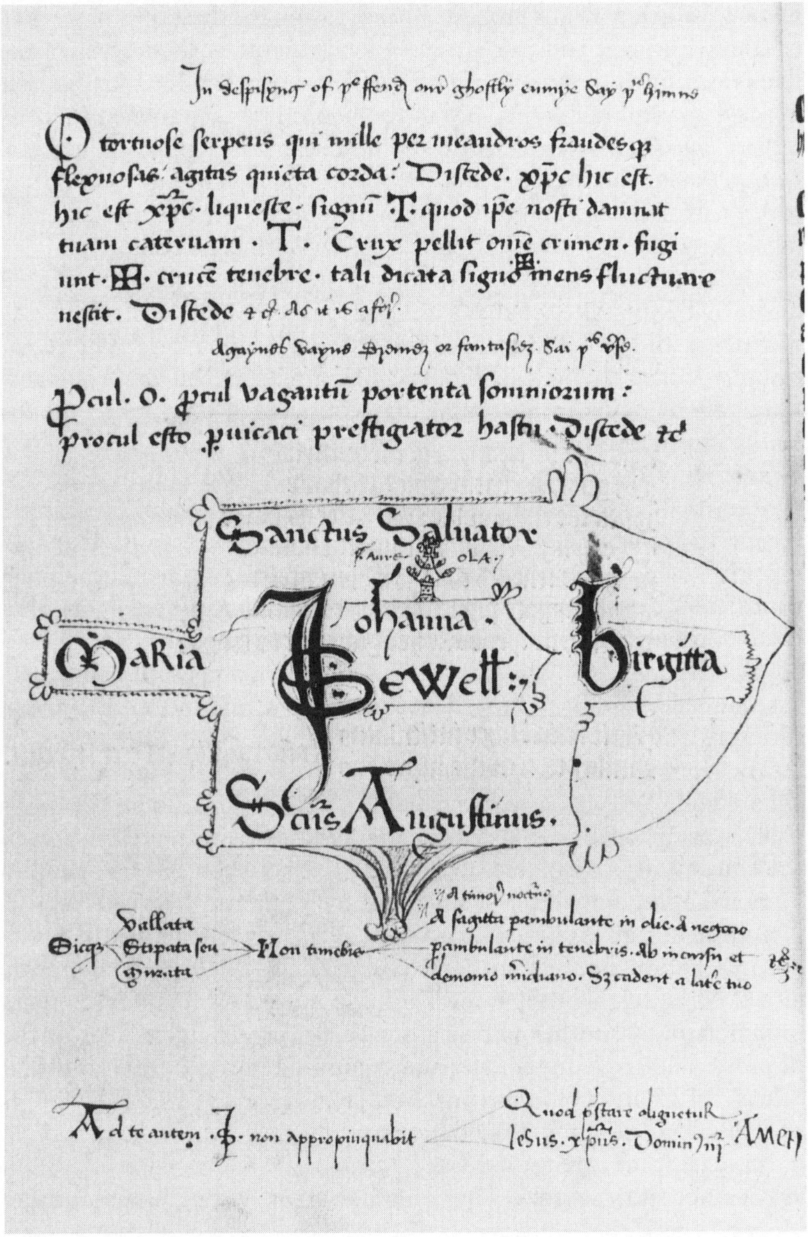

Fig. 2. Hilton, *Scala perfectionis,* fol. 135v. Philadelphia, Rosenbach Incun. 494h. Reproduced by permission of the Rosenbach Museum and Library.

helped the Bridgettines procure authorization for their own order, and of course, Bridget and the Virgin.[106] Joan's name is the largest in the diagram, and it is positioned to suggest both her location (in the monastery) and her ownership of the book. Bridget's name is second largest, and Joan's name "points" toward hers. The physical association between the diagram and the abbey itself is strengthened even further by a charming detail, the picture of a "golden" (Grenehalgh labels it "Aureola") fountain in the center of the enclosure.

Although they were no doubt meant to help Joan adjust to her enclosure at Syon, Grenehalgh's annotations encouraged the reader to identify with her books rather than with other members of her community. It is of course true that the diagram described above is elaborately about being at Syon and that Grenehalgh's notations, in the *Scale* and in the other works he annotated for Joan, show a sharp awareness of the conditions of enclosure. The writing below the diagram of Syon, for example, includes phrases from Psalm 90 that are meant to reassure and encourage Joan in her profession. The subscription reads, "Sicque, Vallata, Stipata seu, Murata, Non timebis: A timore nocturno, A sagitta perambulante in die, A negocio perambulante in tenebris, Ab incursu et demonio meridiano. Sed cadent a latere tuo &cetera" (So that fortified within, encompassed about, and surrounded by walls, you will not be made afraid by the nighttime terror, by the arrow passing by day, by trouble moving in shadows, by attack from the midday demon; rather, they will fall down at your side, etc.)[107] Yet although Grenehalgh's annotations figure the walls of Syon as protective, the marginalia also seems to represent life in the community as isolated. Joan needs phrases such as "Ad te autem JS non appropinquabit / Quod prestare dignetur / Iesus Christus Dominus noster AMEN," which Grenehalgh wrote beneath the previous inscription, because she is, in Grenehalgh's description, intensely alone. Although, as Bazire and Colledge note, "Ad te autem non appropinquabit," another phrase from Psalm 90, is a reminder of the promise made to Saint Bridget and recounted in her *Revelations* that "the devil should not be permitted to approach her," and therefore is an explicit association with the community, the phrase is part of an entire page that offers the reader "weapons" she can use by herself against her spiritual foes. These include signs, verses, and phrases of

[106] On the Bridgettine rule and its permutations, see Ellis, *Viderunt*, 40–41; and Ellis, "Visionary and the Canon Lawyers," 71–90.

[107] Sargent transcribes the Latin; see *Textual Critic*, 1:201.

the sort found in personal prayer collections. For example, a passage taken from Prudentius, a hymn known as *Cultor dei memento* that was thought "efficacious in exorcism," appears at the top of the page. The passage is peppered with tau crosses, which the editors of the *Chastising of God's Children* note were also believed to be valuable in driving away demons and which, as we saw in Margaret Beaufort's prayer books, were also used to prevent the plague.[108] Joan was not safe even while she slept; Grenehalgh includes a few lines in Latin to drive away "vagantum portenta somniorum" for the times when she suffered from troubled dreams.

In light of Joan's actual situation at Syon, it is almost astonishing how intensely solitary Grenehalgh suggested she would be in her fight. Syon writings from the early fifteenth century, in contrast, considered the busyness of community as the condition under which one read. Even when the author of the *Myroure* describes private, devotional reading, for example, he makes concessions to communal life, encouraging the individual to help others to read and to ask for help herself when she does not understand what she has read. Similarly, the *Orcherd of Syon* presents itself as a brief respite from the strain of living among other people. When Grenehalgh annotates Joan's book seventy-five or so years later, he suggests that her only companion is her book, and her "picture" in Grenehalgh's diagram drew attention to her isolation. In place of the matching Bridgettine garb of her fellow inhabitants, Grenehalgh marked Joan's copy of the *Scale* as a glass in which she could see her own reflection. As she looked at his diagram, she saw herself literally enclosed in Syon and, more to the point, reflected inside her own book. The annotations assume the same role as the Bridgettine clothing, allowing the individual to "see" the details of enclosure that define her, yet they differ from the sartorial practice in their exclusion of other inhabitants: Joan's companions were her book and the saints.

Drawing his reader's attention to the physical pages of her book,

[108] *Chastising of God's Children,* 298. The *Chastising* associates Prudentius's hymn with the tau cross and with the "hooli name iesu." See *Chastising of God's Children,* 297. The drawing representing Syon as a fortress may also have a Bridgettine source: Roger Ellis, " 'Flores ad Fabricandam . . . Coronam': An Investigation into the Uses of the Revelations of St. Bridget of Sweden in Fifteenth-Century England," *Medium Aevum* 51 (1982), describes material incorporated into the *Revelations* in which spiritual advice is "presented by way of an elaborate allegory of a walled stronghold which the enemies of the king are striving to breach" (175). The passage Ellis alludes to is from *Revelations,* 7:5.

Grenehalgh encouraged Joan to imagine herself inside its pages. He did this by linking Hilton's text together with his own annotations. For example, next to the passage in the *Scale* that begins, "How a man shall see the grounde of synne wythin hymselfe," Grenehalgh had drawn a large trefoil. It is well known that medieval readers and writers often used visual signposts to emphasize significant passages in manuscripts, and this practice was sometimes picked up by producers of printed books. The author of the *Myroure,* for example, differentiates between colors of ink for the Latin and English elements in his book and uses two sizes of capital letters to distinguish Latin from English: the printed edition makes similar distinctions. But Grenehalgh's annotations do more than direct his reader's attention: they "textualize" Joan. For example, next to the trefoil in the passage from Hilton alluded to above, he wrote, punning on Joan's last name, Sewell, as Sargent observes, "Se wele fro this to the end of the first boke & begyn at such a sygne."[109] If Joan read the treatise according to "signs," such as the trefoil that appears to the left of his notation, Grenehalgh suggested she would learn the best way to "see" her own sin "well." In this way the *nota bene* are explicitly directed at Joan and intersect with the text, offering visual cues to the text's verbal character and placing her within the meaning (and pages) of the book. It is Sewell who is supposed to "see well," and what she was supposed to see, according to the *Scale,* was inside herself. Reading the *Scale* along with Grenehalgh's annotations, Joan Sewell might learn to move closer to God.

Yet although Grenehalgh's intention seems to be to advance Joan's spiritual training, his marginalia ask Joan repeatedly to look at the book itself. Although he eagerly annotated passages that describe spiritual insight, such as the special note in which he, glossing a passage from Hilton describing the "openynge of the ghostly eye" and "ryche nought," had written "Quid sit interior oculus diffinitiue," he could not help himself from drawing Joan's attention to the physical page.[110] Explaining that the mysteries of the Trinity "passithe ferre both you & me," he instructs her to "loke vppe." We might think this was a joke about seeing with Joan's inner eye—did one ever look up with a ghostly eye?—but far more likely, he was advising her to look up at the top of the page, where he had written a note about the Trinity: Father, Son, and Holy Ghost are all God, and yet "None of thees

[109] Sargent, *Textual Critic,* 1:172.
[110] Ibid., 1:188.

is othir, but alle these ooned [vnyd *gloss*] togedyr is oo god in oon substance."[111] Even in making the point that this unity is spatial, active, and invisible, Grenehalgh fixes his reader's attention on the material text.[112]

I have been arguing that private reading at Syon in the late fifteenth and early sixteenth centuries was characterized by an intense, personal relationship between the reader and her book. It is of course possible that Joan's reading, and more generally, her intimate relationship with Grenehalgh, which resulted in the book's annotations, was atypical. Evidence suggests that Carthusian authorities considered the relationship to be unacceptable. Grenehalgh was removed from Sheen (which was directly across the river from Syon) in 1507 or 1508 and placed in a guesthouse at the Charterhouse in Coventry. This move suggests, as Michael Sargent speculates, that Grenehalgh's superiors wished to break off what was seen as an increasingly unacceptable attachment to Joan.[113] We know far less about Joan's part in this affair, although a reference to Joan as "Syonita Reclusa" in one of Grenehalgh's later manuscripts suggests that she too may have been disciplined in that "recluse" was not a term used at Syon.[114] Ultimately, Grenehalgh's pun on Joan's name seems to have turned back on itself: no longer was Joan to "see well" what the text had to say, but the text itself became a substitute for "Sewell"—Grenehalgh linked the couple together through their book, and the annotations themselves became the visual cues that ordered their reading. Perhaps it was a strange version of Paolo and Francesca's story, one in which the book carried the emotional weight of the relationship both as a physical object and for its description of mystical union.

Yet even if it the relationship was irregular—and since Bridgettine legislation included explicit rules forbidding the sisters to send or receive "lettres of lewde affeccion, or of sclaunder of any persone, or

[111] Ibid., 1:196.

[112] Grenehalgh explains that where one member of the Trinity is, "alle beenn: & what oonn dothe: alle doenn" (ibid.).

[113] Ibid., 1:79–83.

[114] Sargent observes that Grenehalgh himself must have felt that his attachment to Joan was hindering his spiritual life: in a manuscript of Richard Rolle's *Contra Amatores Mundi,* Grenehalgh marked particular passages with his or Joan's initials, noting, for example, after a passage describing "the love of fleshly friends" as an obstacle to spiritual insight, "Sewellam Renue [Forsake Sewell]" (Sargent, *Textual Critic,* 1:101, 125).

therto make bylles or rymes, inwarde or outewarde," it seems it was—the practice of male religious advising nuns concerning devotional reading, and specifically, of suggesting that personal, devotional books were central to religious experience, appears to have become not just acceptable but standard practice in the late fifteenth century.[115] Anne Clark Bartlett has argued that a "discourse of familiarity" characterized relationships between spiritual advisers such as Grenehalgh and "religious sisters" like Joan Sewell. According to Bartlett, male clerics composed devotional works for female religious that offered women "the role of spiritual friend" and represented "a form of mixed-sex intimacy that could contradict or compensate for the official restrictions on gender relations."[116] Grenehalgh's annotations place Joan Sewell in such a role, and it seems that the authorities at Syon in the late fifteenth century may in fact have encouraged such supervision.

By 1518, two impulses made book ownership by the nuns at Syon common: the first, as I discussed earlier, was the elite status of many of the initiates who were used to owning books already; the second was support of women's devotional study by the Carthusians and the Bridgettine brothers. Sometimes these relationships were between brothers and sisters at Syon. Thomas Betson, for example, the men's librarian during the time that Joan Sewell was there, probably beginning in 1481, wrote a pamphlet titled *A Ryght Profytable Treatyse Compendiously Drawen Out of Many and Dyvers Wrytynges of Holy Men,* for women who were studying to enter the monastery. As well as providing certain kinds of information that would help initiates adjust to enclosed life, such as reflections on the importance of transcending secular, social distinctions, Betson's book offers the kind of information available in traditional pastoral manuals such as "English versions of the Pater noster, Ave and Creed, together with instructions on the standard catechetical 'sevens': vices and virtues, sacraments, degrees of humility, obedience and patience, and a selection of prayers."[117] Betson's treatise shows great familiarity with the

[115] *Syon Additions for the Sisters,* 15–16.

[116] Bartlett, *Male Authors, Female Readers,* 96, 100–101. Bartlett notes that "Late medieval England saw a dramatic increase in the production of literature that uses these conventions of mixed-sex familiarity" and offers examples of readers and writers from the mid and late fifteenth century (111).

[117] This information is included in the section titled "A lytell Instruccion for them that shall entre in to religyon"; the summary of the treatise is in Rhodes, "Syon Abbey and Its Religious Publications," 18.

concerns of novices; a number of clerics from Syon composed works to aid the nuns, including Richard Whytford, who wrote his *Daily Exercise and Experience of Death* (a book that, considering its title, is much more concerned with lived life than one might expect) for Elizabeth Gibbs, the abbess at Syon during the time that Joan Sewell was a member of the community.[118] While the brothers at Syon were influential, especially in regard to pragmatic, religious instruction, often, as Vincent Gillespie observes, the relationships appear to have been between Carthusians at Sheen and the Bridgettine nuns.[119] For instance, at about the same time that Grenehalgh was directing Joan Sewell's reading, the abbess at Syon, Elizabeth Gibbs, had asked another Carthusian at Sheen, William Darker, for an English translation of Thomas à Kempis's *Musica ecclesiastica,* better known as the first three chapters of the *Imitation of Christ.*[120] Because there was no English translation of the book and it was, as Roger Lovatt has demonstrated, closely affiliated with the English Carthusians, the abbess's interest implies that she was receiving some kind of instruction about her and her charges' reading from the brothers at Sheen.[121] The copy that remains includes explicit identification of Elizabeth as the person "cuius cura hic liber conscriptus est," and the scribe, William Darker, is also named.[122]

De Hamel notes that beginning in the "early sixteenth century there were clearly no major inhibitions about nuns receiving personal presents of books. . . . There are names of nearly two dozen nuns inscribed in different books from Syon, and all are later than about 1500."[123] These inscriptions are almost overwhelmingly signs of ownership: the insertion of one's name, the inclusion of important family events in the calendar, even in some cases monograms and family escutcheons. In the century after Syon's founding, books became both media through which the reader could experience God's presence (an anglicized version of continental mystical experience, perhaps) and

[118] Bell, *What Nuns Read,* 74; *A Werke for Housholders, A Dayly Exercyse and Experyence of Dethe;* on the preparations for death in particular, see Hogg, "Richard Whytford," 256–59. Concerning works composed at Syon more generally, see Rhodes, "Syon Abbey and Its Religious Publications," esp. 16–24.

[119] See Gillespie, "Dial M for Mystic," 243.

[120] See Hutchison, "What the Nuns Read," 217; this book is Bell A.19/de Hamel no. 11 and includes an inscription describing the abbess's request of Darker.

[121] Roger Lovatt, "The *Imitation of Christ* in Late Medieval England," *Transactions of the Royal Historical Society* 18 (1968): 97–121.

[122] See Bell, *What Nuns Read,* 186; Bell A.19.

[123] De Hamel, *Syon Abbey,* 97.

physical icons that gave readers direct, material connections to the divine and to other believers. Syon's ascetic traditions, the demands for accurate performance, for visual identity, for suppression of family emotion, made the companionship of books supremely desirable.

In this chapter I have considered how nuns at Syon read, and my argument, to a great degree, has been concerned with the way that disciplined isolation was central to religious practice at the monastery. Reading was conceived of as explicitly visual (involving the written text and identically clothed readers) and invisible (during liturgical performance, the nuns' only audience was supposed to be God). However, this isolated invisibility was only part of the story. Rather, Syon's heavy investment in externalization should be seen at least in part as an outcome of its mode of acquiring property and not simply as a spiritual or disciplinary phenomenon. The money to allow the sisters to purchase books and to read with their "ghostly eyes" had to come from somewhere; where it came from were the order's landed holdings and from lay supporters' donations. A document from 1490 makes these sources very clear. In that year, a survey of all of Syon's possessions was taken and the income from these holdings recorded. Aungier has printed an abstract of the document, which shows that the monastery held land in Sussex, Gloucester, Lancaster, Cambridge, Essex, Wilts, Devon, Cornwall, Somerset, and Kent. The total value of the revenues, according to Aungier, was just over £1,616.[124] This survey was made just a decade before Grenehalgh drew his diagram of Joan Sewell isolated within the monastery, and the contrast between the survey, drawn up under Elizabeth Gibbs's administration, and Grenehalgh's image is astonishing: a small and empty-seeming convent, in Grenehalgh's description, versus the survey's landholdings so vast that it is hard to imagine the two had anything to do with one another. And yet, of course, they did. For Syon to succeed financially it had, paradoxically, to maintain its reputation for austerity. Donations depended on donors' willingness to leave their lands to the monastery, and that meant they needed to believe Syon was worthy of their property: regardless of what the rule said about performing only for God, the sisters needed to be present in the minds of lay believers.

The abbess at the turn of the century, Elizabeth Gibbs, worked very hard to maintain Syon's associations with austere piety and in-

[124] Aungier, *History and Antiquities of Syon*, 76–78.

tense, devotional spirituality for the secular public. Syon was known widely and often visited by lay believers on account of the indulgences associated with the monastery. Although some of these indulgences involved religious instruction, such as the one that granted three hundred days' indulgence for hearing a sermon preached in English by one of the brothers, the most famous of the pardons associated with Syon involved the black, red, and white prayer beads that, like the image of Saint Bridget, were intimately associated with the monastery.[125] There were five beads, two white, two black, and one red, and the following verse was to be said on the beads: "Ihu for thy holy name / And for thy bytter passion / Save us from syn and schame / And from endles damnacion / And bryng us to the blysse / whych never shal mysse / Swete Ihu amen."[126] Unlike attendance at a sermon, the pardon associated with the prayer beads could be obtained anywhere one prayed, and the beads for this reason seemed to have been especially popular. Elizabeth, in fact, apparently handed them out freely: Aungier notes that in 1486, Edward Plumpton had written to Sir Robert Plumpton that "the first gift that my lady of Syon [Elizabeth Gybbes] gave to me was a par of Jeneper beads pardonet, the which I have sent to you by the bringer."[127] If this was the "first" present that Edward received from Elizabeth, were there others?[128]

The prayer beads and the simple prayer associated with them were intended for believers outside of the abbey, and Elizabeth was clearly interested in making Bridgettine spirituality available to the world beyond Syon. This did not mean that she was merely an administrator or marketer of the externals of Bridgettine spirituality. In fact, as I mentioned above, Elizabeth was one of the early readers of the first three chapters of the *Imitation of Christ,* having gotten a copy of the English translation from William Darker. However, she apparently

[125] Rhodes notes that Thomas More visited to hear one of the vernacular sermons ("Syon Abbey and Its Religious Publications," 12). The tradition seems to have been established early: Margery Kempe visited Syon/Sheen to purchase a Lammas Day pardon (see her *Book,* bk. 2, chap. 10).

[126] Rhodes, "Syon Abbey and Its Religious Publications," 13.

[127] Aungier, *History and Antiquities of Syon,* 426; he reprints several documents concerning the indulgences to be obtained at Syon (421–26). See also *The Plumpton Letters and Papers,* ed. Joan Kirby (Cambridge: Cambridge University Press, 1996), vol. 8, no. 44.

[128] Elizabeth Gibbs is worthy of much further study. She was apparently a remarkable administrator who worked ceaselessly for the monastery. She managed to get royal support in some of her causes, bringing one of the monastery's legal claims before Margaret Beaufort in 1492 (Aungier, *History and Antiquities of Syon,* 74).

understood her position as abbess to involve public relations for the monastery as well as spiritual guidance. She received support in this endeavor from the Bridgettine clerics, who, at the turn of the century, began readying their works for print production and distribution among lay readers.[129] Betson in particular understood the value of the nuns' image to the outside world and exhorted his Bridgettine readers in *A Ryght Profytable Treatyse* that they should "Lete none see you from the seruyce of God or unoccupyed. In redynge of prophetes, epystles, gospelles, sayntes lyues, and other dedes of vertue doynge, *hauynge euer bokes in your handes studyenge or wrytynge*" (italics added). According to Betson, the reason they should do so was so those "people seynge you may saye, 'Beholde here the seruant of God and the lanternes of the worlde.' "[130] Finally, as Martha Driver has observed, certain woodcuts of Saint Bridget were used by the early printers to capitalize on and simultaneously promote the prestige of the monastery; according to Driver, the woodcuts, which appeared in eighteen printed books between 1519 and 1534, each functioned as "an imprimatur, a seal of approval, and bookplate, assuring the reader of the authenticity of the textual contents."[131] Although this began the year after Elizabeth died and the next abbess, Constancia Browne, took over, it fits in well with Elizabeth's efforts to promote the Bridgettines as pious readers.

Despite the justifiably appropriate ends of Bridgettine appeals to a broader public, the means conflicted with the ascetic, contemplative goals of the order, and I wonder if the sisters themselves came to question the monastery's emphasis on the material world. A puzzling story about a book called the *Ymage of Love* suggests that as the Syon prayer beads made their way throughout England, the sisters themselves were turning even more intently toward the kind of inner spirituality associated with Rolle's and Hilton's writings.

In 1525, sixty copies of John Gough's translation of John Ryckes's *Ymage of Love* were sold by Wynkyn de Worde to Syon Abbey.[132] This in itself is unsurprising: de Worde had by this time taken over the market in devotional printing, and Syon was one of his best cus-

[129] Rhodes, "Syon Abbey and Its Religious Publications," 18.

[130] *Ryght Profytable Treatyse,* sig. c. v.

[131] Martha Driver, "Nuns as Patrons, Artists, Readers: Bridgettine Woodcuts in Printed Books Produced for the English Market," in *Art into Life,* ed. Carol Garrett Fisher and Kathleen L. Scott (East Lansing: Michigan State University Press, 1995), 249, 250.

[132] *Ymage of Love, STC* 21471.

tomers. The record does not explain who ordered the copies. Perhaps the confessor general was interested in Ryckes's book, perhaps the abbess or prioress had heard about it. It may possibly have been written explicitly for the nuns by Ryckes, as E. Ruth Harvey suggests, in that its author "appears to be addressing a community of nuns," much as the author of the *Orcherd* had, and Ryckes is known to have been acquainted with at least two important benefactors of Syon's library.[133] Whoever ordered it, there was no reason to suspect that its distribution at Syon would have caused any trouble at all. The sixty copies would have meant that each member of the community would have had her own to read.

But there was trouble. In the same year, according to the consistorial records of the vicar general of the bishop of London, de Worde and Gough were ordered to retrieve all printed copies of the *Ymage* because it was "alleged to contain heresy."[134] Gough and de Worde were fortunate enough to escape any serious punishment, but the public scandal that the recall must have created could have had nothing but a negative impact on the reputations of the author and the printer. The consistorial record offers no grounds for labeling the *Ymage* a heretical text, and we are left to wonder what could have troubled the bishop of London enough to have a book that was distributed among and perhaps written for one of the most "orthodox" and wealthiest communities in England recalled?

The answer seems to involve the bishop's sense of Syon's exemplary function for London. The official record is silent on the matter, but in his *Dialogue concerning Heresy,* Thomas More offers a fictive conversation between a bright but misguided young man, the Messenger, and the Author, an orthodox layman who roughly resembles More himself, which presents both sides of the case. The *Dialogue* gave More the opportunity to respond to current events: in the months before its writing, he had been attending heresy trials such as that of Thomas Bilney, the leader of an elite group of Cambridge scholars. It is in this context that More suggests that the dismissal of external, religious ritual formed the basis for the accusations of heresy leveled against de Worde and Gough's printing of the *Ymage.*

[133] E. Ruth Harvey, "*The Ymage of Love,*" in *A Dialogue concerning Heresies,* ed. Thomas M. C. Lawler, Germain Marchadour, and Richard C. Marius (New Haven: Yale University Press, 1981), 729; the benefactors were Thomas Edyman and Richard Reynolds.

[134] A. W. Reed, "The Regulation of the Book Trade before the Proclamation of 1538," *Transactions of the Bibliographical Society* 15 (1918): 163.

Early in the *Dialogue,* the Messenger cites the *Ymage* to dismiss the Church's reliance on "carued & paynted ymages," explaining that the *Ymage*'s author has demonstrated that images are for lay believers and that therefore "relygyous men and folke of more parfyte lyfe" should "let all such dede ymages passe." Instead, says the Messenger, the religious should work to find the "lyuely quycke ymage of loue and charyte." In dismissing "outward observance, bodyly seruyce, gay and costely ornamentes, fayre ymages, goodly songe, flesshly fastynge & all ye rable of such vnsauoury ceremonyes," the *Ymage,* according to More, seemed to deny the authority of external ceremony and played into the hands of men who misunderstood the significance of institutional authority. Although the Author tells the Messenger that the *Ymage* "sayth not fully so farre as ye reherce," he sees comments such as the Messenger's as the unintended outcome of the *Ymage*'s teaching. If, says the Author, external ritual is not observed, it is possible that spiritual people may be led astray by an evil "spyryte" who may "destroy all suche deuocyon as euer hath hytherto shewed it selfe."[135]

Ryckes's *Ymage* suggests that the believer can experience God's presence directly through His word. The orthodox position was that this unmediated understanding was impossible: as Christ explains in Bridget's *Revelations,* "he that perfytely desyrith to be Marie muste fyrst be Martha, laboryng bodely to my wyrship."[136] Although this may have been the strict view of things, Bridgettine readers were in fact trained by works such as the *Myroure* to think of reading as a way to experience God. They were of course cautioned to read and perform the liturgy "accurately," emphasizing bodily obedience, but at the same time they were encouraged to distance themselves from other people and to concentrate on books. Apparently familiar with this tradition, the *Ymage* shows how external images rather than God's words leave the reader empty. The book opens with the narrator's account of his attempts to purchase an "image of love" to give the nuns for New Year's. Weary from his failure to find a true image among those he has seen, including love of family, friends, and the world, the narrator nearly purchases an "inferior" image of fine material—that is, a sacred object that might "stere a man to deuocyon and to the loue of god." However, as he is about to do so, a "holy doctour" appears before him and tells him that his money will be ill spent if he

135 *Dialogue concerning Heresies,* 40, 43, 44.

136 *Revelations of St. Birgitta,* 35.

wastes it on a material image. Rather than seeking for a physical object, the narrator should, according to the doctor, look for his "image" in the scriptures. At first the narrator ignores his advice, but after exploring various places of worship and failing to find the image of love there, the narrator does, in fact, find it by reading the scriptures. As he reads, he recognizes that the image is the "ghostly" reflection of God in the soul, and he writes his treatise to teach the nuns to follow his example.

One way of understanding the bishop's ban and recall of the *Ymage* is to compare it with "heterodox" attacks such as those of the Lollards on pilgrimages, devotional images, and liturgical singing. By displacing the importance of external ritual, the *Ymage* came dangerously close to advocating the "inspired" reading some groups proposed, and perhaps this was why the books were recalled, as More's *Dialogue* suggests. Maybe the bishop thought that sixty individual copies of the book would have created an epidemic of heresy at Syon and decided he would rather not see the sisters fall into sin. This is possible and supported by More's book, but I suspect that the bishop ultimately was worried not about what the sisters at Syon would have thought about the *Ymage* but rather about what influential lay believers might conclude à propos Ryckes's "gift." One of the reasons that Bilney, the heretic whose trial More had been attending, and his friends were causing such trouble for the bishop was their social position: the Cambridge scholars were influential in large part because they knew the same people the bishop knew. He had to worry about the impression that the sisters' reading might have on his "constituency." What if they found out that the nuns, and not just one but the whole community, were reading Ryckes's book? Would it validate Bilney's point of view? And would Syon's influential followers embrace Bilney's ideas? The bishop was not inclined to learn how the nuns' would interpret Ryckes's book or to discover how their reading might be seen by London's spiritual elite.

Medieval Syon's "orthodoxy" was taken for granted, as it perhaps should have been, not because the ideas and practices central to the institution were inherently orthodox, whatever that would have meant, but rather because the people, especially the laywomen who entered the monastery and became nuns as well as those who supported it from the outside, believed themselves to be "orthodox." By the end of the fifteenth century, ownership of vernacular books had become a common aspect of many women's lives. Many of these works encouraged forms of devotion that granted the reader a good deal of interpretive authority and intelligence, and although, as Bilney's trial suggests, clerical authorities were still concerned with heresy, the impulses that encouraged "heretical" reading were in many ways similar to those that encouraged the seemingly ultra-orthodox reading at Syon.[137]

[137] On this similarity, see Nicholas Watson, "The Politics of Middle English Writing," in *The Idea of the Vernacular,* esp. 338–43 (but see also 345, where he maintains that despite this similarity, fifteenth-century readers of the vernacular were "in retreat from the radicalism of the late fourteenth century").

Conclusion
Medieval Women Authors?

If, as I have suggested throughout this book, many Englishwomen, especially by the end of the fifteenth century, had acquired the skills necessary to read and write, or had discovered how to have things read or written for them, why (to use the Wife of Bath's language) did so few of them "paint lions" at the end of the Middle Ages? Why were "clerks" still writing books while women, even fully literate, wealthy, and industrious women such as Margaret Beaufort and her peers at Syon Abbey, read, wrote letters, and (occasionally) translated devotional tracts? Growing numbers of women were certainly busy acquiring literate skills, as letters sent by and to women make clear. Katherine Chadderton, for example, wrote to her brother, George Plumpton, in 1450 concerning a book she had asked that he give his niece.[1] In 1477 Thomas Betson remarked to his future mother-in-law, Elizabeth Stonor, that he was "wrothe" with his fiancée Katherine Riche "by cause she sendith me no writtynge" and suggested Katherine "myght gett a secretary" if she would rather not write herself.[2] By 1462 the abbess of Denny recognized the written word's ability to eliminate physical distance, observing in a letter sent to John Paston I that she and her sisters "be closyd wyth-jnne the ston wallys" and might "non odyrvyse speke wyth [him] but only be wrytynge."[3] Similarly, although it is more difficult to prove that women were reading

[1] *The Plumpton Letters and Papers,* ed. Joan Kirby (Cambridge: Cambridge University Press, 1996), vol. 8, no. 2.

[2] *Kingsford's Stonor Letters and Papers, 1290–1483,* ed. Christine Carpenter (Cambridge: Cambridge University Press, 1996), no. 185.

[3] *Paston Letters and Papers of the Fifteenth Century,* ed. Norman Davis (Oxford: Clarendon, 1971), no. 656.

than it is to show they were writing, the number of women book owners enumerated by Susan Cavanaugh in her important work on private ownership indicates, given the diversity of social situation and the remarkable range of book prices and kinds represented in her catalog, that many women were avid readers.[4] There is no doubt that there were many more readers than writers, but even with that qualification, the question still remains: Why were there so few women, even among those few who were able to write or who had access to scribes who could, who wrote what we would now think of as "works"—literary texts—or, if not literature, at any rate personal accounts such as Julian of Norwich's *Revelations,* diaries, or autobiographies like Margery Kempe's *Book?* Two kinds of answer have been proposed to this question. The first, summed up neatly by Alexandra Barratt, has to do with medieval women's psychological and emotional relationship to the written word. According to Barratt, the "tacit assumption that 'authority,' and therefore authorship," was "incompatible with feminity" had the effect of limiting the production of literature by women. She makes the point that the inability to read and write was not necessarily a hindrance to women who were determined to have something written or read (her example is Margery Kempe's *Book,* which was dictated to scribes by its author, who was, apparently, unable to read). Rather, Barratt suggests, "the real obstacles were as much psychological as practical" and consisted in women's sense of themselves as "subordinate to all forms of male authority," which meant, because the written word held authority, that women "were inevitably resistant to the idea of authoring texts."[5] Essentially, Barratt surmises that medieval women's sense of the social and psychological stakes of authorship made it unlikely that they would become writers. Another version of this category of response, one that emphasizes patriarchal control, is that proposed by Margaret Hannay. In a discussion of women translators in Tudor England, Hannay asserts that women turned to translation, rather than original authorship, because men "encouraged" them to do so: because "such activity 'did not threaten the male establishment as the expression of personal viewpoints might,' " women could read and translate but not write.[6] In this account, the pressures of patriarchal

[4] Susan H. Cavanaugh, "A Study of Books Privately Owned in England: 1300–1450" (Ph.D. diss., University of Pennsylvania, 1980).

[5] Alexandra Barratt, ed., *Women's Writing in Middle English* (London: Longman, 1992), 5, 7.

[6] See Margaret Patterson Hannay, introduction to *Silent but for the Word: Tudor Women as Patrons, Translators, and Writers of Religious Works,* ed. Margaret Patter-

culture, both the limits it placed on women's educational opportunities and the psychological barriers it erected, restricted women's ability to become authors of original texts.

In contrast with the first variety of answers, the second group, rather than ascribing the lack of women's writing to medieval psychology, emphasizes contemporary critics' misunderstanding of the past and our failure to recognize or uncover literature by women. It is suggested that scholars have misgauged women's participation in literate culture because we know so little about medieval authorship. Laurie Finke, for example, observes that "literary critics are now poised to consider Virginia Woolf's suggestion, made over half a century ago, that 'Anon, who wrote so many poems without signing them, was often a woman.' " Our problem, according to this way of thinking, is that we may not have recognized how much women have actually written.[7] Related to this position is the sense that critics have misunderstood women's writing because they have failed to take it seriously as literature. For example, in writing about Margery Kempe and Julian of Norwich, Lynn Staley argues that women's writing has been studied "in terms of the stereotypes of gender" and not in relation to its artistic merits.[8] Although some critics, in other

---

son Hannay (Kent, Ohio: Kent State University Press, 1985), 8–9. The quotation comes from another essay in the collection, Mary Ellen Lamb, "The Cooke Sisters: Attitudes toward Learned Women in the Renaissance," 107–25. Also in that collection see Rita Verbrugge, "Margaret More Roper's Personal Expression in the *Devout Treatise upon the Pater Noster,*" 30–42.

[7] Laurie Finke, *Women's Writing in English: Medieval England* (London: Longman, 1999), 85. Finke, however, also suggests that even if anonymously authored texts were written by women, the number of women writers we can study is still "fragmentary" (213).

[8] Lynn Staley, *Margery Kempe's Dissenting Fictions* (University Park, Pa.: Pennsylvania State University Press, 1994), 3. Margery Kempe's strong, authorial control of her *Book* figures in Staley's discussion as an antidote to the conflation of women's experience and women's writings; she seeks to resist what critics such as Gayle Margherita and Karma Lochrie have characterized as a "mimetic" impulse in which text and authorial experience are one. See Margherita, *The Romance of Origins: Language and Sexual Difference in Middle English Literature* (Philadelphia: University of Pennsylvania Press, 1994), 20; and Lochrie, *Margery Kempe and Translations of the Flesh* (Philadelphia: University of Pennsylvania Press, 1991), 226. In *Powers of the Holy: Religion, Politics, and Gender in Late Medieval English Culture* (University Park: Pennsylvania State University Press, 1996), Staley and her co-author David Aers make similar claims about Julian of Norwich: turning to models of authorship that have been applied to literature written by men, Staley suggests, "Like Chaucer, Julian needed to evolve a rhetorical strategy that allowed her the freedom to say what she needed to say; like him, she found it necessary to create an authorial self, or, in her case, selves" (109).

words, argue in terms of "quantity" and others in relation to "quality," both groups believe it is essential to treat medieval women's writing in terms of its literary importance.

Whatever the virtues of these answers to the question—and they have many since in various ways they have allowed scholars to consider medieval women's relationship to literate culture seriously—these approaches have had the effect of defining the field of study almost exclusively in terms of the production of (literary) texts.[9] In wondering about women's authorship, modern readers tend to assume (perhaps as Chaucer did) that the natural result of becoming literate or of learning to use written modes is the composition and distribution of written texts and, ultimately, that the highest form of such production is literary authorship.[10] I hope it has become clear in the course of this book that, at least for medieval women, this seems not to have been the case. Rather, women in fifteenth-century England were intensely concerned with books as part of lived experience, and they responded to writing dynamically, not in terms of

[9] Despite work on reading as a dynamic process, authorship continues to be valued in studies of women in the Middle Ages because it seems to "prove" that women were important during that time. Joan Ferrante, *To the Glory of Her Sex: Women's Roles in the Composition of Medieval Texts* (Bloomington: Indiana University Press, 1997), looks at written texts as evidence of women's social power and suggests that her book's aim is to make women's courage from the past available to modern readers. She argues that "To concentrate too much on the negative is to play into the hands of the patriarchal view that women were able to do little, therefore they did nothing valuable, therefore we do not need to include them in our studies" (5). On reading as a dynamic process, see Jonathan Boyarin, ed., *The Ethnography of Reading* (Berkeley: University of California Press, 1992), especially the essay by Johannes Fabian, "Keep Listening: Ethnography and Reading," 80–97, which includes a useful and extensive bibliography of theoretical writing on the subject.

[10] Studies of Julian of Norwich and Margery Kempe unintentionally emphasize artistic production without noticing how acts of authorial validation necessarily ignore what it meant for the vast majority of women to take part in literary culture. This is because to claim that a writer is worthy of literary study, scholars have been required to build a case for her significance by identifying the genius, originality, and especially autonomy of the writer. Paradoxically, canonical authors (Chaucer is the best medieval example) must be both quintessentially "of their time" and outside of it: intensely identified with what it meant to be alive in the Middle Ages, but also far above their contemporaries, original in every regard. For example, Denise Baker Nowakowski writes that the text of Julian's *Revelations,* "Though it did not circulate widely during her lifetime," demonstrates "much the same comprehensiveness and complexity as the literary texts of her more widely admired male contemporaries" and therefore "deserves to be acknowledged as the prose masterpiece of Ricardian literature" (Nowakowski, *Julian of Norwich's "Showings": From Vision to Book* [Princeton: Princeton University Press, 1994], 164).

"consumption" and "production" of discrete texts but as forces that shaped their (familial) lives. Responding personally, imaginatively, and directly, women experienced involvement with written texts in late medieval England as transformative, a means for learning to change, and not primarily a process of learning to produce. When women's literate practice involved attention to audience, as was the case in Margaret Paston's letters, that audience was immediate, specific, and intimately known. Certainly her letters involved strategic representations, but even those representations were part of a process of creating an identity—in the Pastons' case, a gentle one. And even when a seemingly impersonal piece of writing was produced, such as Margaret Beaufort's translation of the last book of the *Imitation of Christ,* the act of translation itself was personally productive, a means for reading oneself through the written word. The text that resulted was available for other readers, but only in the same way that it was "for" the translator herself—something that spoke personally and directly to the Reader. We tend to think of "personal" as individualistic, peculiar to someone in particular, but as was the case at Syon and, rather differently, among the Lollards, it could also be communal. This was, in part, the result of women's close involvement and dependence on familial structures, but it also accords with a broader sense of the relationship between readers and texts in the very late Middle Ages. David Lawton suggests that in the fifteenth century the poet's role was "to know on behalf of, together with, and as well as any man living. It is to be any man living—a supreme commonplace."[11] Like the poet, the fifteenth-century woman thought of herself both individually and emblematically, imagining that her textual concerns were, without question, without reflection, those of other people. I have shown this connection, perhaps most obviously, in the way that books of hours (texts that followed a uniform script) often included the individual's name in their prayers and in the manner in which women at Syon wrote their names into their books. But even the act of textual distribution, such as Margaret Beaufort's commissioning of *Blanchardyn and Eglantine,* might be conceived of as personally relevant, a gift of sorts to help readers precisely as it had helped her. The Lollard memorization of scriptures worked the same way, their message personal and also, to those who were willing to understand, universal. Even Margaret Paston's letters were written out of a sense of common understanding with her recipients (al-

[11] David Lawton, "Dullness and the Fifteenth Century," *ELH* 54 (1987): 771.

though the addressees did not of course always read them as she had intended them to be read). For that matter, the work of the two best-known women "authors" from this period, Margery Kempe and Julian of Norwich, also fits into this category: Julian's *Revelations* and Margery's *Book* both assume readers who would share in their revelatory experiences, readers who would understand the relevance for their own lives of the events and reflections contained in the books, just as the authors' themselves had.

Still these particulars do not explain why women so rarely wrote books. In *Reading Families* I have tried to think of literate practice neutrally—rather than defining the period in terms of failure (women's failure, for whatever reason, to produce literary texts) or triumph (women's ability to overcome the obstacles that kept them from becoming authors)—and have been concerned with the ways that women in the later Middle Ages responded to, and ultimately reshaped, the imaginative and practical circumstances of family life through their literate practice. My basic argument was that the familial context, construed very broadly, was the means by which women encountered literate modes and written texts. I conclude by suggesting that this context may also have been the reason women so rarely composed literary works in the fifteenth century. I am not suggesting that women were afraid to write, or felt that their families would not allow them to (although this may of course have been the case), but rather that it simply did not occur to them to do so. Perhaps they were not being "kept" from writing books, except of course in the very important sense that they never received the high-level academic training available to certain men, but were instead involved in practices that served familial (personal and spiritual) needs in ways that seemed more important to them. Even if they might have imagined that literary writing would be useful, they were already busy with literate activities that seemed, to them, more obviously beneficial. The fact that men continued to produce far more original texts than women did seems to me directly related to men's professional, especially clerical and administrative, training and, especially for highly sophisticated writing, to their familiarity with literary trends on the continent. The dominance of men in late medieval England, the inequality of access to education, and the expectation that women would be subordinate to men are facts about the past that will not go away. Yet this need not, as I hope this book has shown, keep us from noticing what medieval women were actually concerned with when they too began to depend on the written word.

Works Cited

Aers, David, and Lynn Staley. *The Powers of the Holy: Religion, Politics, and Gender in Late Medieval English Culture.* University Park, Pa.: Pennsylvania State University Press, 1996.

Alexander, Jonathan. "William Abell 'Lymnour' and Fifteenth-Century English Illumination." In *Kunsthistorische Forschungen: Otto Pächt zu seinem 70. Geburtstag,* edited by A. Rosenauer and G. Weber, 166–72. Salzburg: Residenz Verlag, 1972.

Allan, Alison. "Yorkist Propaganda: Pedigree, Prophecy and the 'British History' in the Reign of Edward IV." In *Patronage, Pedigree and Power in Later Medieval England,* edited by Charles Ross, 171–92. Gloucester: Sutton, 1979.

André, Bernard. "Vita Henrici Septimi." In *Memorials of King Henry VII,* edited by James Gairdner. Rolls series. London: Longman, Brown, Green, Longman, Roberts, 1858.

Archer, Rowena E. " 'How ladies . . . who live on their manors ought to manage their households and estates': Women as Landholders and Administrators in the Later Middle Ages." In *Woman is a Worthy Wight: Women in English Society c. 1200–1500,* edited by P. J. P. Goldberg, 149–81. Stroud, U.K.: Sutton, 1992.

——, ed. *Crown, Government, and People in the Fifteenth Century.* Stroud, U.K.: Sutton, 1995.

Armstrong, C. A. J. *England, France and Burgundy in the Fifteenth Century.* London: Hambledon, 1983.

Armstrong, Elizabeth Psakis. "Informing the Mind and Stirring up the Heart: Katherine of Siena at Syon." In *Studies in St. Birgitta and the Brigittine Order,* edited by James Hogg, 2:170–98. Salzburg: Institut für Anglistik und Amerikanistik, 1993.

Asad, Talal. *Genealogies of Religion: Discipline and Reasons of Power in Christianity and Islam.* Baltimore: Johns Hopkins University Press, 1993.

Aston, Margaret. *Lollards and Reformers: Images and Literacy in Late Medieval Religion.* London: Hambledon, 1984.

Aungier, G. J. *The History and Antiquities of Syon Monastery.* London: J. B. Nichols and Sons, 1840.

Austin, J. L. *How to Do Things with Words.* Cambridge: Harvard University Press, 1975.

Axon, W. E. "The Lady Margaret as a Lover of Literature." *The Library,* n.s., 8 (1907): 34–41.

Bainbridge, Virginia. "Women and the Transmission of Religious Culture: Benefactresses of Three Bridgettine Convents c. 1400–1600." *Birgittiana* 3 (1997): 55–76.

Ballard, George. *Memoirs of British Ladies, Who Have Been Celebrated for Their Writings or Skill in the Learned Languages, Arts and Sciences.* 1st ed. 1752. Reprint, Detroit, Mich.: Wayne State University Press, 1985.

Barakat, Robert A. *The Cistercian Sign Language: A Study in Non-Verbal Communication.* Kalamazoo, Mich.: Cistercian Publications, 1975.

Barratt, Alexandra. "Dame Eleanor Hull: A Fifteenth-Century Translator." In *The Medieval Translator: The Theory and Practice of Translation in the Middle Ages,* edited by Roger Ellis, 87–101. Cambridge: D. S. Brewer, 1989.

——, ed. *Women's Writing in Middle English.* London: Longman, 1992.

Barron, Caroline. "The Education and Training of Girls in Fifteenth-Century London." In *Courts, Counties and the Capital in the Later Middle Ages,* edited by Diana E. S. Dunn, 139–53. Stroud, U.K.: Sutton, 1996.

——. "The Expansion of Education in Fifteenth-Century London." In *The Cloister and the World: Essays in Honour of Barbara Harvey,* edited by John Blair and Brian Golding, 219–45. Oxford: Clarendon Press, 1996.

——. "Who Were the Pastons?" *Journal of the Society of Archivists* 4 (1972): 530–35.

Barron, Caroline M., and Anne F. Sutton, eds. *Medieval London Widows, 1300–1500.* London: Hambledon, 1994.

Bartlett, Anne Clark. *Male Authors, Female Readers: Representation and Subjectivity in Middle English Devotional Literature.* Ithaca, N.Y.: Cornell University Press, 1995.

Bartlett, Anne Clark, and Thomas H. Bestul, eds. *Cultures of Piety: Medieval English Devotional Literature in Translation.* Ithaca, N.Y.: Cornell University Press, 1999.

Bateson, Mary. *Catalogue of the Library of Syon Monastery Islesworth.* Cambridge: Cambridge University Press, 1898.

Beckett, Neil. "St. Bridget, Henry V and Syon Abbey." In *Studies in St. Birgitta and the Brigittine Order,* edited by James Hogg, 2:125–50. Salzburg: Institut für Anglistik und Amerikanistik, 1993.

Bell, David N. *What Nuns Read: Books and Libraries in Medieval English Nunneries.* Kalamazoo, Mich.: Cistercian Publications, 1995.

Bell, Susan Groag. "Medieval Women Book Owners: Arbiters of Lay Piety and Ambassadors of Culture." *Signs* 7 (1982): 742–68.

Bennett, H. S. *The Pastons and Their England: Studies in an Age of Transition.* 1922. Reprint, Cambridge: Cambridge University Press, 1991.

Bennett, Judith. "Medieval Women, Modern Women: Across the Great Divide." In *Culture and History, 1350–1600: Essays on English Communities, Identities, and Writing,* edited by David Aers, 147–75. Detroit, Mich.: Wayne State University Press, 1992.

Besnier, Niko. *Literacy, Emotion, and Authority: Reading and Writing on a Polynesian Atoll.* Cambridge: Cambridge University Press, 1995.

Betson, Thomas. *A Ryght Profytable Treatyse Compendiously Drawen Out of Many and Dyvers Wrytynges of Holy Men by Thomas Betson.* Cambridge: Cambridge University Press, 1905.

Bevington, David, ed. *Medieval Drama.* Boston: Houghton Mifflin, 1975.

Biblia Sacra Iuxta Vulgatam Versionem. Edited by Bonifatius Fischer, Robert Weber, et al. Stuttgart: Deutsche Bibelgesellschaft, 1983.

Blamires, Alcuin. *Woman Defamed and Woman Defended: An Anthology of Medieval Texts.* Oxford: Clarendon Press, 1992.

Boffey, Julia. "Women Authors and Women's Literacy." In *Women and Literature in Britain, 1150–1500,* edited by Carol M. Meale, 159–82. 1993. Reprint, Cambridge: Cambridge University Press, 1996.

The Book of the Knight of the Tower. Translated by William Caxton. Edited by Yvonne Offord. EETS, s.s., 2. Oxford: Oxford University Press, 1971.

Bornstein, Diane, ed. *Ideals for Women in the Works of Christine de Pizan.* Detroit, Mich.: Michigan Consortium for Medieval and Early Modern Studies, 1981.

Bourdieu, Pierre. *Language and Symbolic Power.* Translated by Gino Raymond and Matthew Adamson. Cambridge: Harvard University Press, 1991.

Boyarin, Jonathan, ed. *The Ethnography of Reading.* Berkeley: University of California Press, 1993.

Bradley, Ritamary. "The Speculum Image in Medieval Mystical Writers." In *The Medieval Mystical Tradition in England,* edited by Marion Glasscoe, 9–27. Cambridge: D. S. Brewer, 1984.

The Bridgettine Breviary of Syon Abbey. Edited by A. J. Collins. Worcester, U.K.: Boydell Press for the Henry Bradshaw Society, 1969.

Britnell, R. H., and A. J. Pollard, eds. *The McFarlane Legacy: Studies in Late Medieval Politics and Society.* Stroud, U.K.: Sutton, 1995.

Bruns, Gerald. *Inventions: Writing, Textuality, and Understanding in Literary History.* New Haven: Yale University Press, 1982.

Bynum, Caroline Walker. *Jesus as Mother: Studies in the Spirituality of the High Middle Ages.* Berkeley: University of California Press, 1982.

Calendar of Papal Registers 1364–1404. Edited by W. H. Bliss. Vol. 4. London: His Majesty's Stationery Office, 1902.

Camargo, Martin. *The Middle English Verse Love Epistle.* Tübingen: Max Niemeyer, 1991.

Carpenter, Christine. *Locality and Polity: A Study of Warwickshire Landed Society, 1401–1499.* Cambridge: Cambridge University Press, 1992.

Carruthers, Mary. *The Book of Memory: A Study of Memory in Medieval Culture.* Cambridge: Cambridge University Press, 1990.

——. "The Wife of Bath and the Painting of Lions." In *Feminist Readings in Middle English Literature: The Wife of Bath and All Her Sect,* edited by Ruth Evans and Lesley Johnson, 22–53. London: Routledge, 1994. First published in *PMLA* 94 (1979): 209–22.

Carthusian Spirituality: The Writings of Hugh of Balma and Guigo de Ponte. Translated by Dennis D. Martin. New York: Paulist, 1997.

Castor, Helen. "The Duchy of Lancaster and the Rule of East Anglia, 1399–1440: A Prologue to the Paston Letters." In *Crown, Government and People in the Fifteenth Century,* edited by Rowena Archer, 53–78. Stroud, U.K.: Sutton, 1995.

Cavanaugh, Susan H. "A Study of Books Privately Owned in England: 1300–1450." Ph.D. diss., University of Pennsylvania, 1980.

Caxton's Blanchardyn and Eglantine c. 1489. Edited by Leon Kellner. EETS, e.s., 58. London: Trübner, 1890.

The Cely Letters, 1472–1488. Edited by Alison Hanham. EETS, 273. London: Oxford University Press, 1975.

Chance, Jane, ed. *Gender and Text in the Later Middle Ages.* Gainesville: University Press of Florida, 1996.

The Chastising of God's Children. Edited by Joyce Bazire and Eric Colledge. Oxford: Blackwell, 1957.

Chaucer, Geoffrey. *The Riverside Chaucer.* Edited by Larry D. Benson. Boston: Houghton, 1987.

Christine de Pizan. *The Epistle of Othea.* Translated from the French text of Christine Pisan by Stephen Scrope. Edited by Curt F. Bühler. EETS, o.s., 264. London: Oxford University Press, 1970.

Clanchy, Michael T. *From Memory to Written Record, England 1066–1307.* Cambridge: Harvard University Press, 1979; 2d ed., Oxford: Blackwell, 1993.

The Cloud of Unknowing and the Book of Privy Counselling. Edited by Phyllis Hodgson. EETS, o.s., 218. Oxford: Oxford University Press, 1944.

Cohn, Samuel K., Jr., and Steven A. Epstein, eds. *Portraits of Medieval and Renaissance Living: Essays in Memory of David Herlihy.* Ann Arbor: University of Michigan Press, 1996.

Colish, Marcia. *Medieval Foundations of the Western Intellectual Tradition, 400–1400.* New Haven: Yale University Press, 1997.

——. *The Mirror of Language: A Study in the Medieval Theory of Knowledge.* New Haven: Yale University Press, 1968.

Constable, Giles. *Letters and Letter-Collections.* Turnhout, Belgium: Brepols, 1976.
——. *Three Studies in Medieval Religious and Social Thought.* 1995. Reprint, Cambridge: Cambridge University Press, 1998.
Cooper, Charles Henry. *Memoir of Margaret Countess of Richmond and Derby.* Cambridge: Bell, 1874.
Copeland, Rita. *Rhetoric, Hermeneutics, and Translation in the Middle Ages.* Cambridge: Cambridge University Press, 1991.
——. "Why Women Can't Read: Medieval Hermeneutics, Statutory Law, and the Lollard Heresy Trials." In *Representing Women: Law, Literature, and Feminism,* edited by Susan Sage Heinzelman and Zipporah Batshaw Wiseman, 253–86. Durham, N.C.: Duke University Press, 1994.
——, ed. *Criticism and Dissent in the Middle Ages.* Cambridge: Cambridge University Press, 1996.
Coss, P. R. "The Formation of the English Gentry." *Past and Present* 47 (1995): 38–64.
Craun, Edwin D. *Lies, Slander, and Obscenity in Middle English Literature: Pastoral Rhetoric and the Deviant Speaker.* Cambridge: Cambridge University Press, 1997.
Crawford, Anne. *Letters of the Queens of England.* Stroud, U.K.: Sutton, 1994.
Cressy, David. "Kinship and Kin Interaction in Early Modern England." *Past and Present* 113 (1986): 38–69.
Croft, P. J. *Lady Margaret Beaufort, Countess of Richmond: Descriptions of Two Unique Volumes Associated with One of the First Patrons of Printing in England.* London: Quaritch, 1958.
Cross, Claire. " 'Great reasoners in scripture': The Activities of Women Lollards, 1380–1530." In *Medieval Women,* edited by Derek Baker, 359–80. Oxford: Blackwell, 1978.
Davey, Samuel. " 'The Paston Letters,' with Special Reference to the Social Life of the Fourteenth and Fifteenth Centuries." In *Chaucer Memorial Lectures, 1900,* edited by Percy W. Ames. London: Asher and Company, 1900.
Davies, Richard G. "Lollardy and Locality." *Transactions of the Royal Historical Society,* 6th ser., 1 (1991): 191–212.
Davis, Norman. "The Language of the Pastons." Sir Israel Gollancz Memorial Lecture, Proceedings of the British Academy, vol. 40. London: Geoffrey Cumberlege, 1955.
——. "The Litera Troili and English Letters." *Review of English Studies* 16 (1965): 233–44.
Deanesly, Margaret. *The Incendium Amoris of Richard Rolle of Hampole.* Manchester: Longman, Green, 1915.
——. *The Lollard Bible and Other Medieval Biblical Versions.* Cambridge: Cambridge University Press, 1920.
De Hamel, Christopher. *Syon Abbey: The Library of the Bridgettine Nuns*

and Their Peregrinations after the Reformation. London: Roxburghe Club, 1991.

Desmond, Marilyn. *Reading Dido: Gender, Textuality, and the Medieval Aeneid.* Minneapolis: University of Minnesota Press, 1994.

Despres, Denise. "Ecstatic Reading and Missionary Mysticism: *The Orcherd of Syon.*" In *Prophets Abroad: The Reception of Continental Holy Women in Late-Medieval England,* edited by Rosalynn Voaden, 141–60. Cambridge: D. S. Brewer, 1996.

Dockray, Keith. "Why Did the Fifteenth-Century English Gentry Marry?" In *Gentry and Lesser Nobility in Late Medieval Europe,* edited by Michael Jones, 61–80. Gloucester: Sutton, 1986.

Dowling, Maria. *Fisher of Men: A Life of John Fisher, 1469–1535.* London: Macmillan, 1999.

Doyle, A. I. "Thomas Betson of Syon Abbey." *The Library,* 5th ser., 11 (1956): 115–18.

Driver, Martha. "Nuns as Patrons, Artists, Readers: Bridgettine Woodcuts in Printed Books Produced for the English Market." In *Art into Life: Collected Papers from the Kresge Art Museum Medieval Symposia,* edited by Carol Garrett Fisher and Kathleen L. Scott, 237–67. East Lansing, Mich.: Michigan State University Press, 1995.

Duffy, Eamon. *The Stripping of the Altars: Traditional Religion in England, 1400–1580.* New Haven: Yale University Press, 1992.

Dugdale, William. *William Dugdale's Monasticon Anglicanum: A History of the Abbies and Other Monasteries, Hospitals, Frieries.* Edited by John Caley, Henry Ellis, and Bulkeley Bandinel. Vol. 6. London: James Bohn, 1846.

Dunn, E. Catherine. "The *Myroure of Oure Ladye:* Syon Abbey's Role in the Continuity of English Prose." In *Diakonia. Studies in Honor of Robert T. Meyer,* edited by Thomas Halton and Joseph P Williman, 111–26. Washington, D.C.: Catholic University of America Press, 1986.

Dyer, Christopher. *Standards of Living in the Late Middle Ages: Social Change in England, c. 1200–1520.* Cambridge: Cambridge University Press, 1989.

Edwards, A. S. G., and Carol M. Meale. "The Marketing of Printed Books in Late Medieval England." *The Library,* 6th ser., 15 (1993): 95–124.

Ellis, Henry, ed. *Original Letters Illustrative of English History.* Vol. 1. London: Harding, Triphook and Lepard, 1824.

Ellis, Roger. *Viderunt eam filie Syon: The Spirituality of the English House of a Medieval Contemplative Order from Its Beginnings to the Present Day.* Analecta cartusiana 68. Salzburg: Institut für Anglistik und Amerikanistik, 1984.

——. "The Visionary and the Canon Lawyers: Papal and Other Revisions to the *Regula Salvatoris* of St. Bridget of Sweden." In *Prophets Abroad: The*

Reception of Continental Holy Women in Late Medieval England, edited by Rosalynn Voaden. Cambridge: D. S. Brewer, 1996.

An English Chronicle of the Reigns of Richard II, Henry IV, Henry V, and Henry VI. Edited by J. S. Davies. Camden Society, o.s., 64 (1856).

Erler, Mary. "The Books and Lives of Three Tudor Women." In *Privileging Gender in Early Modern England,* edited by Jean R. Brink, 5–17. Kirksville, Mo.: Sixteenth Century Journal Publishers, 1993.

——. "Syon Abbey's Care for Books: Its Sacristan's Account Rolls 1506/7–1535/6." *Scriptorium* 39 (1985): 293–307.

Evans, Ruth, and Lesley Johnson, eds. *Feminist Readings in Middle English Literature: The Wife of Bath and All Her Sect.* London: Routledge, 1994.

Fabian, Johannes. "Keep Listening: Ethnography and Reading." In *The Ethnography of Reading,* edited by Jonathan Boyarin, 80–97. Berkeley: University of California Press, 1993.

Ferguson, Arthur B. "Reginald Pecock and the Renaissance Sense of History." *Studies in the Renaissance* 13 (1966): 147–65.

Ferrante, Joan. *To the Glory of Her Sex: Women's Roles in the Composition of Medieval Texts.* Bloomington, Ind.: Indiana University Press, 1997.

The Fifteen Oes. STC 20195. 2d ed. 1491. Microfilm. Ann Arbor, Mich.: University Microfilms International, 1938.

Fines, John. "Heresy Trials in the Diocese of Coventry and Lichfield, 1511–12." *Journal of Ecclesiastical History* 14 (1963): 160–74.

Finke, Laurie. *Women's Writing in English: Medieval England.* London: Longman, 1999.

Fisher, Carol Garrett, and Kathleen L. Scott, eds. *Art into Life: Collected Papers from the Kresge Art Museum Medieval Symposia.* East Lansing, Mich.: Michigan State University Press, 1995.

Fisher, John. *The Works of John Fisher.* Edited by J. E. B. Mayor. EETS, e.s., 27. London: Trübner, 1876.

Foxe, John. *The Acts and Monuments of John Foxe.* Edited by George Townsend. 8 vols. New York: AMS, 1965.

French, Katherine. *The People of the Parish: Community Life in a Late Medieval Diocese.* Philadelphia: University of Pennsylvania Press, 2000.

Galbraith, V. H. *Literacy of the Medieval English Kings.* Raleigh Lecture on History, Proceedings of the British Academy, vol. 21. London: Humphrey Milord, 1935.

Galloway, Andrew. "Intellectual Pregnancy, Metaphysical Femininity, and the Social Doctrine of the Trinity in *Piers Plowman.*" *Yearbook of Langland Studies* 12 (1998): 117–52.

Ganz, David. " 'Mind in Character': Ancient and Medieval Ideas about the Status of the Autograph as an Expression of Personality." In *Of the Making of Books: Medieval Manuscripts, Their Scribes and Readers. Essays*

Presented to Malcolm B. Parkes, edited by P. R. Robinson and Rivkah Kim, 280–99. Aldershot, U.K.: Scolar, 1997.

Gardner, Elizabeth J. "The English Nobility and Monastic Education, c. 1100–1500." In *The Cloister and the World: Essays in Medieval History in Honour of Barbara Harvey,* edited by John Blair and Brian Golding, 80–94. Oxford: Clarendon Press, 1996.

Gardner, H. M. "The Text of the *Scale of Perfection.*" *Medium Aevum* 22 (1936): 11–30.

Gibson, Gail McMurray. *Theater of Devotion: East Anglian Drama and Society in the Late Middle Ages.* Chicago: University of Chicago Press, 1989.

Gies, Frances, and Joseph Gies. *A Medieval Family: The Pastons of Fifteenth-Century England.* New York: HarperCollins, 1998.

Gilchrist, Roberta. *Gender and Material Culture: The Archaeology of Religious Women.* London: Routledge, 1994.

Gillespie, Vincent. "Cura Pastoralis in Deserto." In *De Cella in Seculum: Religious and Secular Life and Devotion in Late Medieval England,* edited by Michael G. Sargent, 215–27. Cambridge: D. S. Brewer, 1989.

——. "Dial M for Mystic: Mystical Texts in the Library of Syon Abbey and the Spirituality of the Syon Brethren." In *The Medieval Mystical Tradition,* edited by Marion Glasscoe, 241–68. Cambridge: D. S. Brewer, 1999.

Glasscoe, Marion, ed. *The Medieval Mystical Tradition: England, Ireland, and Wales.* Exeter Symposium 6. Cambridge: D. S. Brewer, 1999.

——. *The Medieval Mystical Tradition in England: Papers Read at Dartington Hall, July 1984.* Exeter Symposium 3. Cambridge: D. S. Brewer, 1984.

——. *The Medieval Mystical Tradition in England: Papers Read at Dartington Hall, July 1987.* Exeter Symposium 4. Cambridge: D. S. Brewer, 1984.

Goldberg, P. J. P. *Women in England c. 1275–1525.* Manchester: Manchester University Press, 1995.

Green, Richard Firth. *A Crisis of Truth: Literature and Law in Ricardian England.* Philadelphia: University of Pennsylvania Press, 1999.

——. *Poets and Princepleasers: Literature and the English Court in the Late Middle Ages.* Toronto: University of Toronto Press, 1980.

Green, V. H. H. *Bishop Reginald Pecock: A Study in Ecclesiastical History and Thought.* Cambridge: Cambridge University Press, 1945.

Gribbin, Joseph A. *Aspects of Carthusian Liturgical Practice in Later Medieval England.* Analecta cartusiana 99:33. Salzburg: Institut für Anglistik und Amerikanistik, 1995.

——. " 'Ex Oblatione Fidelium'—The Liturgy of the London Charterhouse and the Laity." In *The Mystical Tradition and the Carthusians,* edited by James Hogg, 83–104. Analecta cartusiana 130:5. Salzburg: Institut für Anglistik und Amerikanistik, 1996.

Griffiths, R. A., ed. *Patronage, Crown and Provinces in Later Medieval England.* Gloucester: Sutton, 1981.

Halsted, Caroline. *Life of Margaret Beaufort, Countess of Richmond and Derby.* London: London, Smith, Elder, 1839.

Hamburger, Jeffrey. *Nuns as Artists: The Visual Culture of a Medieval Convent.* Berkeley: University of California Press, 1997.

——. *The Visual and the Visionary: Art and Female Spirituality in Late Medieval Germany.* New York: Zone Books, 1998.

Hanna, Ralph, III. "The Difficulty of Ricardian Prose Translation: The Case of the Lollards." *MLQ* 50 (1990): 319–40.

——. "Some Norfolk Women and Their Books, ca. 1390–1440." In *The Cultural Patronage of Medieval Women,* edited by June Hall McCash, 288–305. Athens: University of Georgia Press, 1996.

——. " 'Vae octuplex,' Lollard Socio-Textual Ideology, and Ricardian-Lancastrian Prose Translation." In *Criticism and Dissent in the Middle Ages,* edited by Rita Copeland, 244–63. Cambridge: Cambridge University Press, 1996.

Hannay, Margaret Patterson, ed. *Silent but for the Word: Tudor Women as Patrons, Translators, and Writers of Religious Works.* Kent, Ohio: Kent State University Press, 1985.

Hansen, Elaine Tuttle. *Chaucer and the Fictions of Gender.* Berkeley: University of California Press, 1992.

Harding, Wendy. "Medieval Women's Unwritten Discourse on Motherhood." *Women's Studies* 21 (1992): 197–209.

Harvey, E. Ruth. "*The Ymage of Love.*" In *A Dialogue Concerning Heresies,* edited by Thomas M. C. Lawler, Germain Marchadour, and Richard C. Marius. Vol. 6, pt. 2. New Haven: Yale University Press, 1981.

Harvey, I. M. W. "Was There Popular Politics in Fifteenth-Century England?" In *The McFarlane Legacy: Studies in Late Medieval Politics and Society,* edited by R. H. Britnell and A. J. Pollard, 155–74. Stroud, U.K.: Sutton, 1995.

Havely, Nick, and Helen Phillips, eds. *Chaucer's Dream Poetry.* London: Longman, 1997.

Heresy Trials in the Diocese of Norwich, 1428–1431. Edited by Norman P. Tanner. Camden Society, ser. 4, vol. 20. London: Office of the Royal Historical Society, 1977.

Hilton, Walter. *The Scale of Perfection by Walter Hilton . . . Modernised from the First Printed Edition of Wynkyn de Worde.* London: London, Burns, Oates, and Washbourne, 1927.

Hoccleve, Thomas. *Hoccleve's Works. The Minor Poems.* Edited by F. J. Furnivall. EETS, e.s., 61. London: Kegan Paul, Trench, Trübner, 1892.

——. *Regement of Princes.* Edited by Frederick J. Furnivall. EETS, e.s., 72. Millwood, N.Y.: Kraus Reprint, 1978.

Hodgson, Phyllis. "The Orcherd of Syon and the English Mystical Tradition." *Proceedings of the British Academy* 50 (1964): 229–49.

Hogg, James. "Richard Whytford." In *Studies in St. Birgitta and the Brigittine Order,* edited by James Hogg, 2:254–66. Analecta cartusiana 35:19. Salzburg: Institut für Anglistik und Amerikanistik, 1993.

——, ed. *Studies in St. Birgitta and the Brigittine Order.* 2 vols. Analecta cartusiana 35:19. Salzburg: Institut für Anglistik und Amerikanistik, 1993.

Holloway, Julia Bolton. "Bride, Margery, Julian, and Alice: Bridget of Sweden's Textual Community in Medieval England." In *Margery Kempe: A Book of Essays,* edited by Sandra J. McEntire, 203–22. New York: Garland, 1992.

The Holy Bible . . . Made from the Latin Vulgate by John Wycliffe and His Followers. Edited by Josiah Forshall and Frederic Madden. Oxford: Oxford University Press, 1850.

Horae Eboracenses: The Prymer or Hours of the Blessed Virgin Mary According to the Use of the Illustrious Church of York. Edited by C. Wordsworth. Durham, U.K.: Andrews and Company for the Surtees Society, 1920.

Hudson, Anne. *Lollards and Their Books.* London: Hambledon, 1985.

——. *The Premature Reformation: Wycliffite Texts and Lollard History.* Oxford: Clarendon Press, 1988.

Hughes, Jonathan. *Pastors and Visionaries: Religion and Secular Life in Late Medieval Yorkshire.* Woodbridge, Suffolk: Boydell, 1988.

Hutchison, Ann M. "Devotional Reading in the Monastery and in the Late Medieval Household." In *De Cella in Seculum: Religious and Secular Life and Devotion in Late Medieval England,* edited by Michael G. Sargent, 215–27. Cambridge: D. S. Brewer, 1989.

——. "What the Nuns Read: Literary Evidence from the English Bridgettine House, Syon Abbey." *Medieval Studies* 57 (1995): 205–22.

The Imitation of Christ. Edited by John K. Ingram. EETS, e.s., 63. London: Kegan Paul, Trench, Trübner, 1893.

Innes, Matthew. "Memory, Orality and Literacy in an Early Medieval Society." *Past and Present* 158 (1998): 3–36.

Ives, E. W. *The Common Lawyers of Pre-Reformation England. Thomas Kebell: A Case Study.* Cambridge: Cambridge University Press, 1983.

Jacob, Ernest F. "The Judgment of Reason: Bishop Pecock's Contentions." *Times Literary Supplement,* 29 September 1945, 462.

——. "Reynold Pecock, Bishop of Chicester." *Proceedings of the British Academy* 37 (1951): 121–54.

Jambeck, Karen. "Patterns of Women's Literary Patronage: England, 1200–ca. 1475." In *The Cultural Patronage of Medieval Women,* edited by June Hall McCash, 228–65. Athens: University of Georgia Press, 1996.

James, M. R. *A Descriptive Catalogue of the Fifty Manuscripts from the Collection of Henry Yates Thompson.* Cambridge: Cambridge University Press, 1898.

Johnston, F. R. "English Defenders of St. Bridget." In *Studies in St. Birgitta and the Brigittine Order,* edited by James Hogg, 1:263–75. Analecta cartusiana 35:19. Salzburg: Institut für Anglistik und Amerikanistik, 1993.

——. "Joan North, First Abbess of Syon, 1420–33, 'Qui Celestia Simul et Terrena Moderaris.' " *Birgittiana* 1 (1996): 47–65.

Jones, Michael, and Malcolm Underwood. *The King's Mother: Lady Margaret Beaufort, Countess of Richmond and Derby.* Cambridge: Cambridge University Press, 1992.

Justice, Steven. "Inquisition, Speech, and Writing: A Case from Late-Medieval Norwich." *Representations* 48 (1994): 1–29.

——. *Writing and Rebellion: England in 1381.* Berkeley: University of California Press, 1994.

Keiser, George. "The Mystics and the Early English Printers: The Economics of Devotionalism." In *The Medieval Mystical Tradition,* edited by Marion Glasscoe, 9–26. Cambridge: D. S. Brewer, 1987.

Kemp, Theresa D. "The Knight of the Tower and the Queen in Sanctuary: Elizabeth Woodville's Use of Meaningful Silence and Absence." *New Medieval Literatures* 4 (2001): 171–88.

Kempe, Margery. *The Book of Margery Kempe.* Edited by Sanford Brown Meech and Hope Emily Allen. EETS, o.s., 212. Oxford University Press, 1940.

Ker, N. R. *Medieval Manuscripts in British Libraries.* London: Oxford University Press, 1969.

Kingsford's Stonor Letters and Papers, 1290–1483. Edited by Christine Carpenter. Cambridge: Cambridge University Press, 1996.

Kleinberg, Aviad M. *Prophets in Their Own Country: Living Saints and the Making of Sainthood in the Later Middle Ages.* Chicago: University of Chicago Press, 1992.

Knowles, David. *The Religious Orders in England.* Cambridge: Cambridge University Press, 1955.

Krug, Rebecca. "The Fifteen Oes." In *Cultures of Piety: Medieval English Devotional Literature in Translation,* edited by Anne Clark Bartlett and Thomas H. Bestul, 107–17 and 212–16. Ithaca, N.Y.: Cornell University Press, 1999.

Kümin, Beat. *The Shaping of a Community: The Rise and Reformation of an English Parish, c. 1400–1560.* Brookfield, Vt.: Scolar Press, 1996.

Lamb, Mary Ellen. "The Cooke Sisters: Attitudes toward Learned Women in the Renaissance." In *Silent but for the Word: Tudor Women as Patrons, Translators, and Writers of Religious Works,* edited by Margaret Patterson Hannay, 107–25. Kent, Ohio: Kent State University Press, 1985.

The Lanterne of Light. Edited by Lilian M. Swinburn. EETS, o.s., 151. Oxford: Kegan Paul, Trench, Trübner, 1917.

Lawrence, Veronica. "The Role of the Monasteries of Syon and Sheen in the

Production, Ownership and Circulation of Mystical Literature in the Late Middle Ages." In *The Mystical Tradition and the Carthusians,* edited by James Hogg, 101–15. Analecta cartusiana 130:10. Salzburg: Institut für Anglistik und Amerikanistik, 1996.

Lawton, David. "Dullness and the Fifteenth Century." *ELH* 54 (1987): 761–99.

——. "Voice, Authority, and Blasphemy in the *Book of Margery Kempe.*" In *Margery Kempe: A Book of Essays,* edited by Sandra J. McEntire, 93–115. New York: Garland, 1992.

Leclerq, Jacques. *The Love of Learning and the Desire for God: A Study of Monastic Culture.* 2d ed. New York: Fordham University Press, 1977.

Lipking, Lawrence. "Aristotle's Sister: A Poetics of Abandonment." *Critical Inquiry* 19 (1983): 61–81.

Lochrie, Karma. *Margery Kempe and Translations of the Flesh.* Philadelphia: University of Pennsylvania Press, 1991.

Lochrie, Karma, Peggy McCracken, and James A. Schultz, eds. *Constructing Medieval Sexuality.* Minneapolis: University of Minnesota Press, 1997.

Lollard Sermons. Edited by Gloria Cigman. EETS, 294. Oxford: Oxford University Press, 1989.

Lovatt, Roger. "The *Imitation of Christ* in Late Medieval England." *Transactions of the Royal Historical Society* 18 (1968): 97–121.

——. "The Library of John Blacman and Contemporary Carthusian Spirituality." *Journal of Ecclesiastical History* 43 (1992): 195–230.

Lydgate's Minor Poems: The Two Nightingale Poems. Edited by Otto Glauning. EETS, e.s., 80. London: Kegan Paul, Trench, Trübner, 1900.

Madden, Frederick. "Genealogical and Historical Notes from Ancient Calendars, and c." In *Collectanea Topographica et Genealogica,* edited by Frederic Madden, Bulkeley Bandinel, et al., 1:277–80. London: John Bowyer Nichols and Son, 1834.

Margherita, Gayle. *The Romance of Origins: Language and Sexual Difference in Middle English Literature.* Philadelphia: University of Pennsylvania Press, 1994.

Mate, Mavis. *Daughters, Wives, and Widows after the Black Death: Women in Sussex, 1350–1535.* Woodbridge, Suffolk: Boydell, 1998.

Mauss, Marcel. *The Gift.* Translated by W. D. Halls. New York: W. W. Norton, 1990.

McCash, June Hall, ed. *The Cultural Patronage of Medieval Women.* Athens: University of Georgia Press, 1996.

McEntire, Sandra J., ed. *Margery Kempe: A Book of Essays.* New York: Garland, 1992.

McSheffrey, Shannon. *Gender and Heresy: Women, Men, and the Lollard Movement, 1420–1530.* Philadelphia: University of Pennsylvania Press, 1996.

——. "Literacy and the Gender Gap in the Late Middle Ages: Women and Reading in Lollard Communities." In *Women, the Book, and the Godly,* edited by Lesley Smith and Jane H. M. Taylor, 157–70. Cambridge: D. S. Brewer, 1995.

Meale, Carol M. " 'Alle the bokes that I haue of latyn, englisch, and frensch': Laywomen and Their Books in Late Medieval England." In *Women and Literature in Britain, 1150–1500,* edited by Carol M. Meale, 128–58. 1993. Reprint, Cambridge: Cambridge University Press, 1996.

——, ed. *Women and Literature in Britain, 1150–1500.* 1993. Reprint, Cambridge: Cambridge University Press, 1996.

Michalove, Sharon D. "The Education of Aristocratic Women in Fifteenth-Century England." In *Estrangement, Enterprise and Education in Fifteenth-Century England,* edited by Sharon D. Michalove and A. Compton Reeves, 117–39. Stroud, U.K.: Sutton, 1998.

Michalove, Sharon D., and A. Compton Reeves, eds. *Estrangement, Enterprise and Education in Fifteenth-Century England.* Stroud, U.K.: Sutton, 1998.

Mirroure of Golde for the Synfull Soule. STC 6894.5. 1506[?]. Microfilm. Ann Arbor, Mich.: University Microfilms International, 1938.

Moi, Toril. "Appropriating Bourdieu: Feminist Theory and Pierre Bourdieu's Sociology of Culture." *New Literary History* 22 (1991): 1017–49.

Moran, Jo Ann Hoeppner. *The Growth of English Schooling, 1340–1548: Learning, Literacy, and Laicization in Pre-Reformation York Diocese.* Princeton: Princeton University Press, 1985.

More, Thomas. *A Dialogue Concerning Heresies.* In *The Complete Works of St. Thomas More,* edited by Thomas M. C. Lawler, Germain Marchadour, and Richard C. Marius. Vol. 6, pt. 2. New Haven: Yale University Press, 1981.

Morris, Bridget. *St. Birgitta of Sweden.* Woodbridge, Suffolk: Boydell, 1999.

Mueller, Janel. *The Native Tongue and the Word: Developments in English Prose Style, 1380–1580.* Chicago: University of Chicago Press, 1984.

Muir, Bernard J. "The Early Insular Prayer Book Tradition and the Development of the Book of Hours." In *The Art of the Book: Its Place in Medieval Worship,* edited by Margaret M. Manion, 9–19. Exeter: University of Exeter Press, 1998.

Murphy, James J. *Rhetoric in the Middle Ages.* Berkeley: University of California Press, 1974.

The Myroure of Oure Ladye. Edited by John Henry Blunt. EETS, e.s., 19. London: Trübner, 1873.

Netter, Thomas. *Doctrinale antiquitatum fidei Catholicae ecclesiae.* Edited by Bonavenura Blanciotti. 3 vols. Farnborough, U. K.: Gregg Press, 1967.

Newman, Barbara. *From Virile Woman to WomanChrist.* Philadelphia: University of Pennsylvania Press, 1995.

Nichols, John Gough, and John Bruce, eds. *Wills from Doctors' Commons.* Westminster: Nichols for the Camden Society, 1863.

Nowakowski, Denise Baker. *Julian of Norwich's Showings: From Vision to Book.* Princeton: Princeton University Press, 1994.

Ong, Walter J. "Latin Language Study as a Renaissance Puberty Rite." *Studies in Philology* 56 (1959): 103–24.

Orcherd of Syon. Edited by Phyllis Hodgson and Gabriel Liegey. EETS, 258. London: Oxford University Press, 1966.

Orme, Nicholas. *Education and Society in Medieval and Renaissance England.* London: Hambledon, 1989.

——. *From Childhood to Chivalry: The Education of the English Kings and Aristocracy, 1066–1530.* New York: Methuen, 1984.

Ortner, Sherry B. *Making Gender: The Politics and Erotics of Culture.* Boston: Beacon, 1996.

Painter, George D. *William Caxton: A Biography.* New York: Putnam, 1977.

The Paston Letters and Papers of the Fifteenth Century. Edited by Norman Davis. 2 vols. Oxford: Clarendon Press, 1971.

Payling, Simon. "The Politics of Family: Late Medieval Marriage Contracts." In *The McFarlane Legacy: Studies in Late Medieval Politics and Society,* edited by R. H. Britnell and A. J. Pollard, 21–48. Stroud, U.K.: Sutton, 1995.

Pearsall, Derek. "Hoccleve's *Regement of Princes:* The Poetics of Royal Self-Representation." *Speculum* 69 (1994): 386–410.

——. *John Lydgate.* Charlottesville: University of Virginia Press, 1970.

Pecock, Reginald. *The Repressor of Overmuch Blaming of the Clergy.* Edited by Churchill Babington. Rolls series 19. 2 vols. London: Green, Longman and Roberts, 1860.

——. *The Reule of Crysten Religioun.* Edited by William Cabell Greet. EETS, o.s., 171. Millwood, N.Y.: Kraus Reprint, 1987.

Phillips, Susan E. "Gossips' Work: The Problems and Pleasures of Not-So-Idle Talk in Late Medieval England." Ph.D. diss., Harvard University, 1999.

Plumb, Derek. "A Gathered Church? Lollards and Their Society." In *The World of Rural Dissenters, 1520–1725,* edited by Margaret Spufford, 132–63. Cambridge: Cambridge University Press, 1995.

The Plumpton Letters and Papers. Edited by Joan Kirby. Camden 5th ser., vol. 8. Cambridge: Cambridge University Press, 1996.

The Poems of the Pearl Manuscript. Edited by Malcolm Andrew and Ronald Waldron. Exeter: University of Exeter Press, 1996.

Pollard, A. F., ed. *The Reign of Henry VII from Contemporary Sources.* Vol. 1. London: Longmans, Green and Company, 1913.

Powell, Susan. "Lady Margaret Beaufort and Her Books." *The Library,* 6th ser., 20 (1998): 197–240.

——. "Syon, Caxton, and the *Festial.*" *Birgittiana* 2 (1996): 187–208.

Power, Eileen. *Medieval English Nunneries.* Cambridge Studies in Medieval Life and Thought. Cambridge: Cambridge University Press, 1922.

Rawcliffe, Carole. *The Staffords, Earls of Stafford and Dukes of Buckingham, 1394–1521.* Cambridge: Cambridge University Press, 1978.

Razi, Zvi. "The Myth of the Immutable English Family." *Past and Present* 140 (1993): 3–44.

Reed, A. W. "The Regulation of the Book Trade before the Proclamation of 1538." *Transactions of the Bibliographical Society* 15 (1918): 163–66.

Renevey, Denis. " 'The Name Poured Out': Margins, Illuminations, and Miniatures as Evidence for the Practice of Devotions to the Name of Jesus in Late Medieval England." In *The Mystical Tradition and the Carthusians,* edited by James Hogg, 127–47. Analecta cartusiana 130:9. Salzburg: Institut für Anglistik und Amerikanistik, 1996.

The Revelations of St. Birgitta. Edited from the Fifteenth-Century Ms. in the Garrett Collection in the Library of Princeton University. Edited by William Patterson Cumming. EETS, o.s., 178. London: Oxford University Press, 1929.

The Rewyll of Seynt Sauioure. Edited by James Hogg. Vol. 2, *The Rewyll of Seynt Sauiore and Other Middle English Brigittine Legislative Texts.* Salzburg: Institut für Englische Sprache und Literatur, 1978. Vol. 3, *The Syon Additions for the Brethren and The Boke of Sygnes;* and vol. 4, *The Syon Additions for the Sisters from the British Library MS Arundel 146.* Salzburg: Institut für Anglistik und Amerikanistik, 1980.

Rhodes, J. T. "Syon Abbey and Its Religious Publications in the Sixteenth Century." *Journal of Ecclesiastical History* 44 (1993): 11–25.

Richmond, Colin. "Hand and Mouth: Information Gathering and Use in England in the Late Middle Ages." *Journal of Historical Sociology* 1 (1988): 233–52.

——. *The Paston Family: Fastolf's Will.* Cambridge: Cambridge University Press, 1996.

——. *The Paston Family in the Fifteenth Century: The First Phase.* Cambridge: Cambridge University Press, 1990.

Rickert, Edith. "The So-Called Beaufort Hours and York Psalter." *Burlington Magazine* 104 (1962): 238–46.

——. "Some English Personal Letters of 1402." *Review of English Studies* 8 (1932): 257–63.

Riddy, Felicity. "Engendering Pity in 'The Franklin's Tale.' " In *Feminist Readings in Middle English Literature: The Wife of Bath and All Her Sect,* edited by Ruth Evans and Lesley Johnson, 54–71. London: Routledge, 1994.

——. " 'Women talking about the things of God': A Late Medieval Sub-Culture." In *Women and Literature in Britain, 1150–1500,* edited by Carol

M. Meale, 104–27. 1993. Reprint, Cambridge: Cambridge University Press, 1996.
Rosenthal, Joel T. *Patriarchy and Families of Privilege in Fifteenth-Century England.* Philadelphia: University of Pennsylvania Press, 1991.
Ross, Charles. "Rumour, Propaganda and Popular Opinion During the Wars of the Roses." In *Patronage, Crown and Provinces in Later Medieval England,* edited by R. A. Griffiths, 15–32. Gloucester: Sutton, 1981.
Rossignol: An Edition and Translation. Edited by J. L. Baird and John R. Kane. Kent, Ohio: Kent State University Press, 1978.
Rotuli Parliamentorum 1278–1503. Edited by John Strachey. Vol. 3. London: n.p., 1832.
Routh, E. M. G. *A Memoir of Lady of Lady Margaret Beaufort, Countess of Richmond and Derby, Mother of Henry VII.* London: Oxford University Press, 1924.
Ryckes, John. *The Ymage of Love. STC* 21471.5. 1525. Microfilm. Ann Arbor, Mich.: University Microfilms International, 1938.
Sargent, Michael G. *James Grenehalgh as Textual Critic.* 2 vols. Analecta cartusiana 85. Salzburg: Institut für Anglistik und Amerikanistik, 1984.
——. "The Transmission by the English Carthusians of Some Late Medieval Spiritual Writings." *Journal of Ecclesiastical History* 27 (1976): 225–40.
——. "Walter Hilton's *Scale of Perfection:* The London Manuscript Group Reconsidered." *Medium Aevum* 52 (1983): 189–216.
——, ed. *De Cella in Seculum: Religious and Secular Life and Devotion in Late Medieval England.* Cambridge: D. S. Brewer, 1989.
Scase, Wendy. "Reginald Pecock." In *Authors of the Middle Ages: English Writers of the Late Middle Ages,* edited by M. C. Seymour, 69–146. Aldershot, U.K.: Variorum, 1996.
Schreiner, Klaus. "Konnte Maria Lesen? Von der Magd des Herrn zur Symbolgestalt mittelalterlicher Frauenbildung." *Merkur* 44 (1990): 82–88.
Schulenberg, Jane Tibbets. *Forgetful of Their Sex: Female Sanctity and Society, ca. 500–1100.* Chicago: University of Chicago Press, 1998.
Scott, Kathleen. *Later Gothic Manuscripts, 1390–1490. A Survey of Manuscripts Illuminated in the British Isles.* 2 vols. London: Harvey Miller, 1996.
Searle, John R. *Speech Acts: An Essay in the Philosophy of Language.* Cambridge: Cambridge University Press, 1969.
Shklar, Ruth. "Cobham's Daughter: *The Book of Margery Kempe* and the Power of Heterodox Thinking." *MLQ* 56 (1995): 277–304.
Smith, Lesley, and Jane H. M. Taylor, eds. *Women, the Book, and the Godly.* Cambridge: D. S. Brewer, 1995.
Spacks, Patricia Meyer. *Gossip.* New York: Knopf, 1985.
Spencer, H. Leith. *English Preaching in the Late Middle Ages.* Oxford: Oxford University Press, 1993.

Spufford, Margaret, ed. *The World of Rural Dissenters, 1520–1725*. Cambridge: Cambridge University Press, 1995.
Staley, Lynn. *Margery Kempe's Dissenting Fictions.* University Park, Pa.: Pennsylvania State University Press, 1994.
Stanbury, Sarah. "Women's Letters and Private Space in Chaucer." *Exemplaria* 6 (1994): 271–85.
Steuer, Susan Marie Burns. "Widows and Religious Vocation: Options and Decisions in the Medieval Province of York." Ph.D. diss., University of Minnesota, 2001.
Stock, Brian. *Augustine the Reader: Meditation, Self-Knowledge, and the Ethics of Interpretation.* Cambridge: Harvard University Press, 1996.
——. *The Implications of Literacy: Written Language and Models of Interpretation in the Eleventh and Twelfth Centuries.* Princeton: Princeton University Press, 1983.
——. "The Self and Literary Experience." *New Literary History* 25 (1994): 839–52.
Strohm, Paul. *Hochon's Arrow: The Social Imagination of Fourteenth-Century Texts.* Princeton: Princeton University Press, 1992.
Sutton, Anne F., and Livia Visser-Fuchs. *The Hours of Richard III.* Stroud, U.K.: Sutton, 1996.
——. *Richard III's Books: Ideals and Reality in the Life and Library of a Medieval Prince.* Stroud, U.K.: Sutton, 1997.
Swanson, R. N. *Church and Society in Late Medieval England.* Oxford: Blackwell, 1989.
Thomas, Keith. *Religion and the Decline of Magic.* New York: Charles Scribner's Sons, 1971.
Thomson, J. A. F. *The Later Lollards, 1414–1520.* London: Oxford University Press, 1965.
Twelve Conclusions of the Lollards, Rogeri Dymmok: Liber Contra XII Errores et Hereses Lollardorum. Edited by Rev. H. S. Cronin. London: Kegan Paul, Trench, Trübner, 1921.
Underwood, Malcolm G. "Politics and Piety in the Household of Lady Margaret Beaufort." *Journal of Ecclesiastical History* 38 (1987): 39–52.
Vance, Eugene. *Mervelous Signals: Poetics and Sign Theory in the Middle Ages.* Lincoln: University of Nebraska Press, 1986.
Verbrugge, Rita. "Margaret More Roper's Personal Expression in the *Devout Treatise upon the Pater Noster.*" In *Silent but for the Word: Tudor Women as Patrons, Translators, and Writers of Religious Works,* edited by Margaret Patterson Hannay, 30–42. Kent, Ohio: Kent State University Press, 1985.
Voaden, Rosalynn, ed. *Prophets Abroad: The Reception of Continental Holy Women in Late Medieval England.* Cambridge: D. S. Brewer, 1996.
Ward, Jennifer. *Women of the English Nobility and Gentry, 1066–1500.* Manchester: Manchester University Press, 1995.

Warnicke, Retha. "The Lady Margaret, Countess of Richmond: A Noblewoman of Independent Wealth and Status." *Fifteenth-Century Studies* 9 (1984): 215–48.

Watson, Nicholas. "Censorship and Cultural Change in Late-Medieval England: Vernacular Theology, the Oxford Translation Debate, and Arundel's Constitutions of 1409." *Speculum* 70 (1995): 822–64.

Weinstein, Donald, and Rudolph M. Bell. *Saints and Society: The Two Worlds of Western Christendom, 1000–1700.* Chicago: University of Chicago Press, 1982.

Whytford, Richard. *A Werke for Housholders. A Dayly Exercyse and Experyence of Dethe.* Edited by James Hogg. Salzburg: Institut für Anglistik und Amerikanistik, 1979.

Wickham, Chris. "Gossip and Resistance among the Medieval Peasantry." *Past and Present* 16 (1998): 3–24.

Wieck, Roger S. *Painted Prayers: The Book of Hours in Medieval and Renaissance Art.* New York: George Braziller, 1997.

William of Palerne: An Alliterative Romance. Edited by G. H. V. Bunt. Groningen: Bouma Boekhuis, 1985.

Wogan-Browne, Jocelyn, Nicholas Watson, Andrew Taylor, and Ruth Evans, eds. *The Idea of the Vernacular: An Anthology of Middle English Literary Theory, 1280–1520.* University Park, Pa.: Pennsylvania State University Press, 1999.

Wormald, Francis, and Phyllis M. Giles. *A Descriptive Catalogue of the Additional Illuminated Manuscripts in the Fitzwilliam Museum.* Vol. 1. Cambridge: Cambridge University Press, 1982.

Wyclif, John. *The English Works of Wyclif.* Edited by F. D. Matthew. EETS, 74. 2d rev. ed. London: N. Trübner, 1902.

Wylie, J. H. *The Reign of Henry the Fifth.* Cambridge: Cambridge University Press, 1914.

Žižek, Slavoj. *The Sublime Object of Ideology.* London: Verso, 1989.

Index